CATCH-UP MATH

Get your child back on track!

Counting ◎ Comparing Numbers
Addition ◎ Subtraction ◎ Shapes
Measurement ◎ Patterns ◎ Time
Position ◎ Graphs ◎ Money

Author
Chandra Prough, M.S.Ed., NBCT

Consultant

Angela Gallo, M.A.Ed
Richardson Independent School District

Publishing Credits

Corinne Burton, M.A.Ed., *President* and *Publisher*
Gabe Thibodeau, *Content Director*
Véronique Bos, *VP of Creative*
Lynette Ordoñez, *Content Manager*
Melissa Laughlin, *Editor*
Kevin Pham, *Graphic Designer*

Image Credits: all images from iStock/or Shutterstock.

Standards

A division of Teacher Created Materials

5482 Argosy Avenue
Huntington Beach, CA 92649
www.tcmpub.com/shell-education
ISBN 979-8-7659-8213-6

Printed by: 590835
Printed in: China

Contents

Contents

8. MEASUREMENT

9. PATTERNS

10. TIME

11. DATA

12. SPATIAL REASONING

13. MONEY

ANSWERS

About Catch-Up Math

The **Catch-Up Math** series enables children to start from scratch when they are struggling with grade-level math. Each book takes math back to the foundation and ensures that all basic concepts are consolidated before moving forward. Lots of revisions and opportunities to practice and build confidence are provided before moving on to new topics.

Each new topic is introduced clearly with simple explanations, examples, and trial questions (with answers) before children move to the Practice section. To help students understand difficult topics, instructional videos are included throughout the book.

A QR code on a topic page provides access to the video.

This book has 13 chapters that cover a variety of mathematical concepts. The chapters are:

1. Counting
2. Number Sense
3. Compare Numbers
4. Addition
5. Subtraction
6. 2D Shapes
7. 3D Shapes
8. Measurement
9. Patterns
10. Time
11. Data
12. Spatial Reasoning
13. Money

★ A review section that can be used as an assessment and to check children's progress is included at the end of each chapter.

★ Answers are at the back of the book.

Each **Your Turn** section contains a **SELF CHECK** for students to reflect and give self-assessment on their understanding.

How to Use This Book

Children can work through the pages from front to back or choose individual topics to reinforce areas where they are struggling.

The topics are introduced with:

- clear instructions, using simple language
- completed examples and incomplete examples for students to tackle before moving on to the **Your Turn** sections
- videos linked by QR codes to provide additional instruction and clarify difficult concepts

How to Use the QR Codes in Catch-Up Math

A unique aspect of the **Catch-Up Math** series is the instructional videos.

The videos further explain and clarify various mathematical concepts. The videos are simply accessed via QR codes and can be watched on a phone or tablet. Or, view all the videos by following this link: tcmpub.digital/cumathk.

Access the video by scanning the QR code with your device.

Each video shows the page from the book. An instructor talks through the concepts and examples and demonstrates what children need to do. The solutions to the examples are presented before children tackle the **Your Turn** sections. This careful instruction ensures that children can confidently move on to the following Practice questions. Children should be encouraged to check their **Your Turn** answers before moving on.

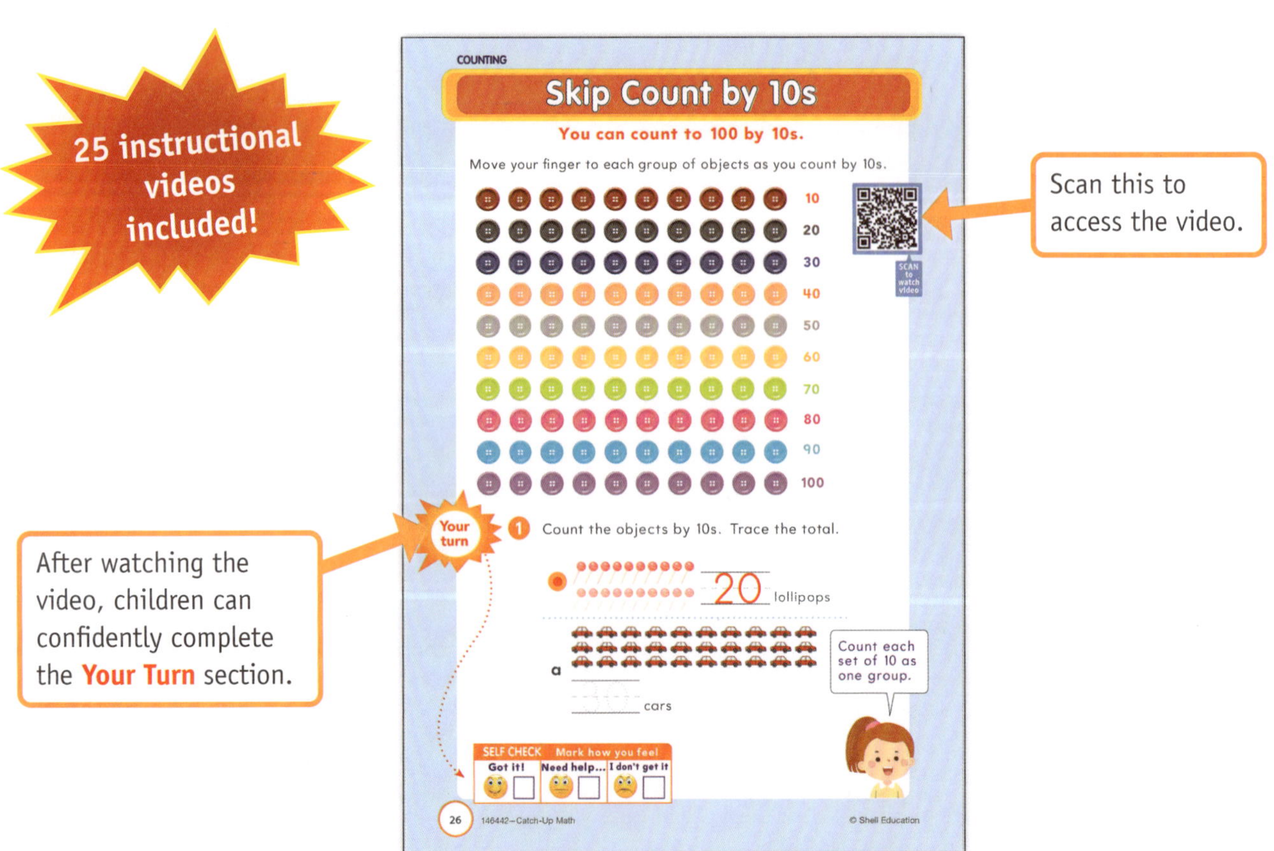

Math Skills

This book contains key math skills from both pre-K and kindergarten to help your child catch up to grade level.

Prekindergarten Math Skills	Pages
Recite numbers to 20 in order.	9–25
Count up to 10 objects using one-to-one correspondence.	9–25
Understand that the last number said tells the number of objects counted.	9–25
Identify and name ordinal numbers.	35–37
Recognize and know some written numerals.	9–14
Recognize instantly the quantity of a small group of objects (up to 4) in organized arrangements.	42–44
Begin to understand the concept of *part* and *whole* using real objects.	48–50
Compare two groups of up to 5 objects, and communicate whether one group has more, an equal number, or less than the other group.	56–67
Understand that adding 1 or taking away 1 changes the number by exactly 1.	70–72, 88–90
Understand that putting two groups of objects together will make a bigger group and that a group of objects can be taken apart into smaller groups.	70–84, 88–102
Solve simple addition and subtraction problems within 10.	73–81, 91–99
Use strategies to solve problems.	82–84, 100–102
Identify, describe, and construct a variety of shapes.	106–126, 129–146
Sort and classify objects by one or more attributes, into two or more groups.	121–123, 144–146
Combine different shapes.	124–126
Compare two objects by length, weight, or capacity.	149–162
Order objects by size.	149–162
Measure length using concrete units laid end-to-end.	149–156
Measure the passage of time using non-standard or standard measures.	180–190
Identify positions of objects in space.	208–222

Math Skills

Kindergarten Math Skills	Pages
Accurately count objects in the standard order.	9–25
Count to answer "how many?" questions with up to 20 objects arranged in various ways.	9–25
Count to 100 by ones and by tens.	23–28
Count forward from a given number.	29–31
Understand that the last number said tells the number of objects counted.	15–34
Write numbers from 0 to 20. Represent a number of objects with a written numeral 0–20.	9–22
Compose and decompose numbers from 11 to 19.	51–53
Identify whether the number of objects in one group is greater than, less than, or equal to the number of objects in another group.	56–64
Recognize instantly the quantity of a small group of objects in organized arrangements.	42–44
Draw pictures to represent a number up to 20.	45–47, 51–53
Compare two numbers between 1 and 10.	56–67
Represent addition and subtraction with objects and drawings.	70–84, 88–102
For any number from 1 to 9, find the number that makes 10 when added to it.	76–78
Fluently add and subtract within 5.	79–81, 97–99
Correctly name shapes regardless of their orientations or size.	106–120, 129–143
Compare two- and three-dimensional shapes, in different sizes and orientations.	106–120, 129–143
Compose simple shapes to form larger shapes.	124–126
Describe measurable attributes of objects, such as length or weight.	149–162
Compare two objects with a measurable attribute in common.	149–162
Create, extend, and describe repeating patterns, and explain the pattern.	165–176
Collect, sort, and organize data into two or three categories.	194–196
Use data to create picture graphs, and draw conclusions from picture graphs.	197–204
Describe objects using names of shapes, and describe the relative positions of these objects.	208–222
Identify pennies, nickels, dimes, and quarters. Know their names and values.	226–233

Number Names 1 to 10

You can write numbers from 1 to 10.

Numbers tell how many.

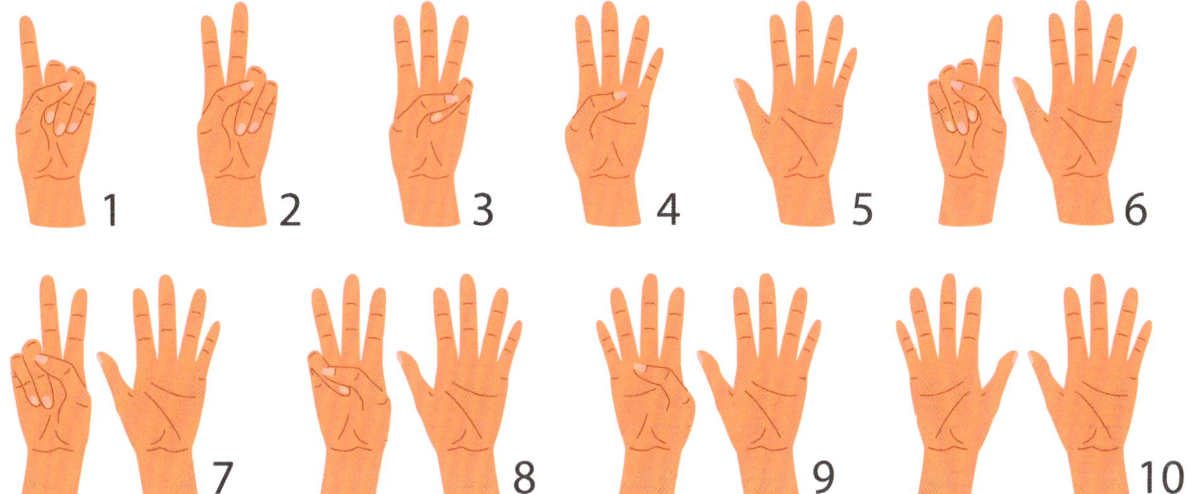

1 Trace each row of numbers with the colors of the rainbow.

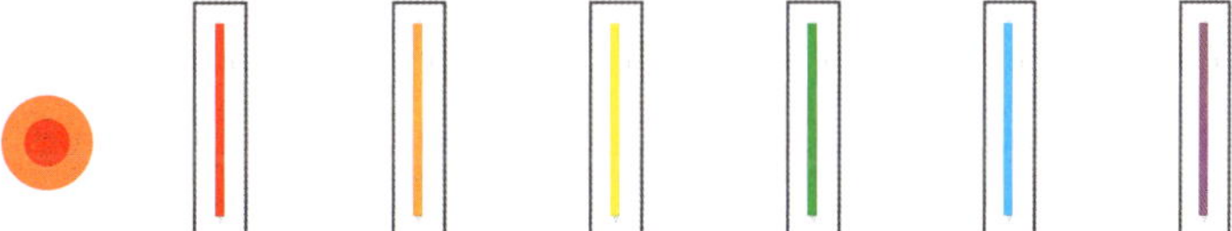

a 2 2 2 2 2 2

b 3 3 3 3 3 3

Practice

 Trace each row of numbers with the colors of the rainbow.

a 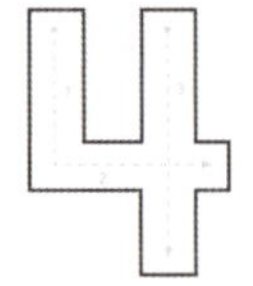 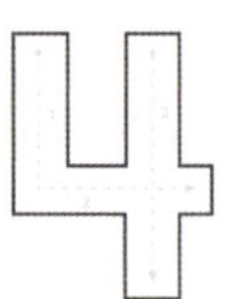 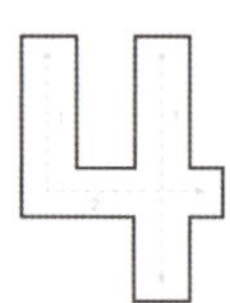 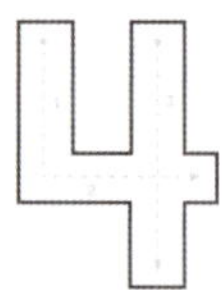

b     

c      

d     

e 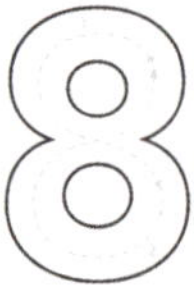     

f    

g      

2 Trace each row of numbers.

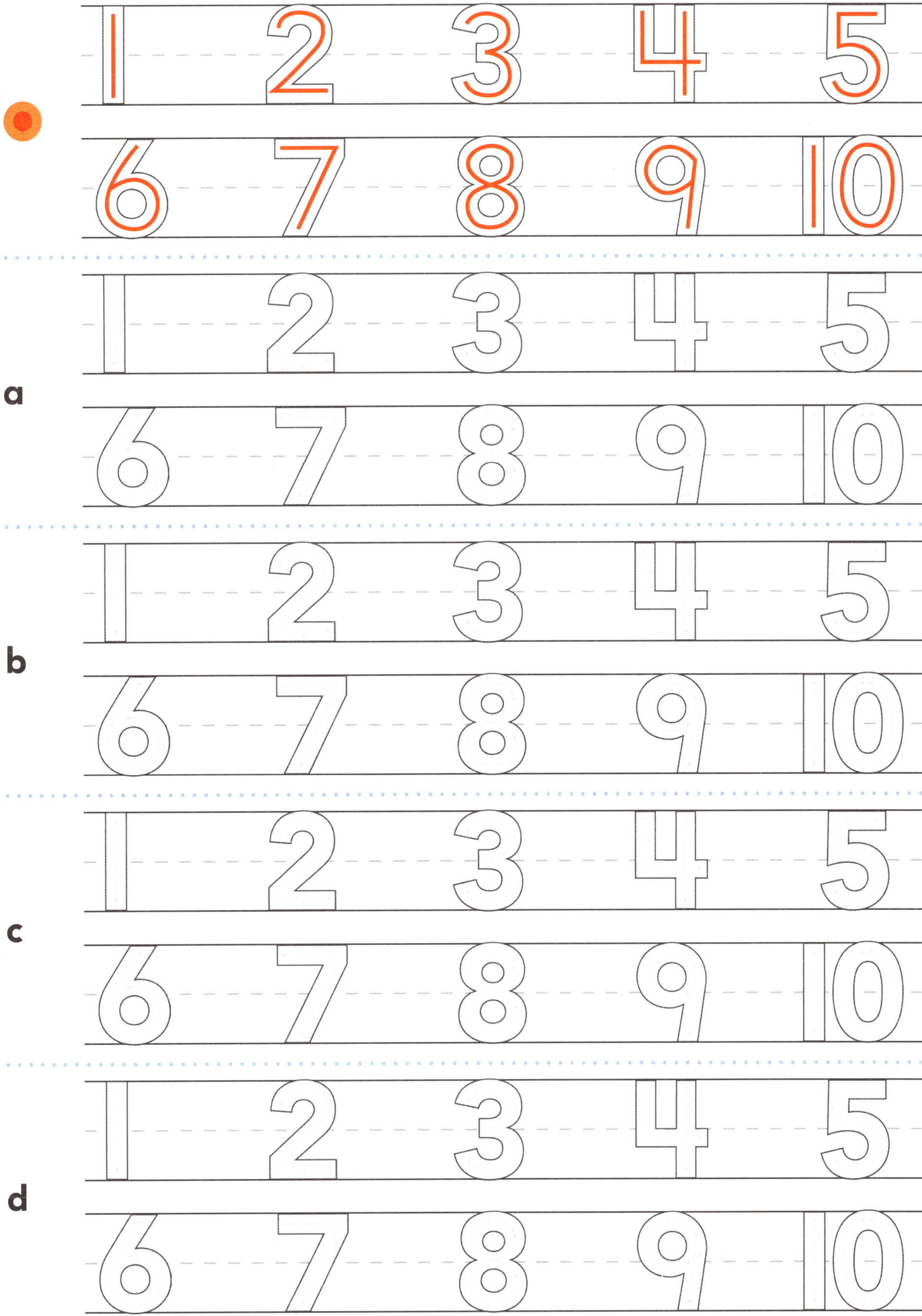

Number Names 11 to 20

You can write numbers 11 to 20.

A bundle shows 10. A stick shows 1.

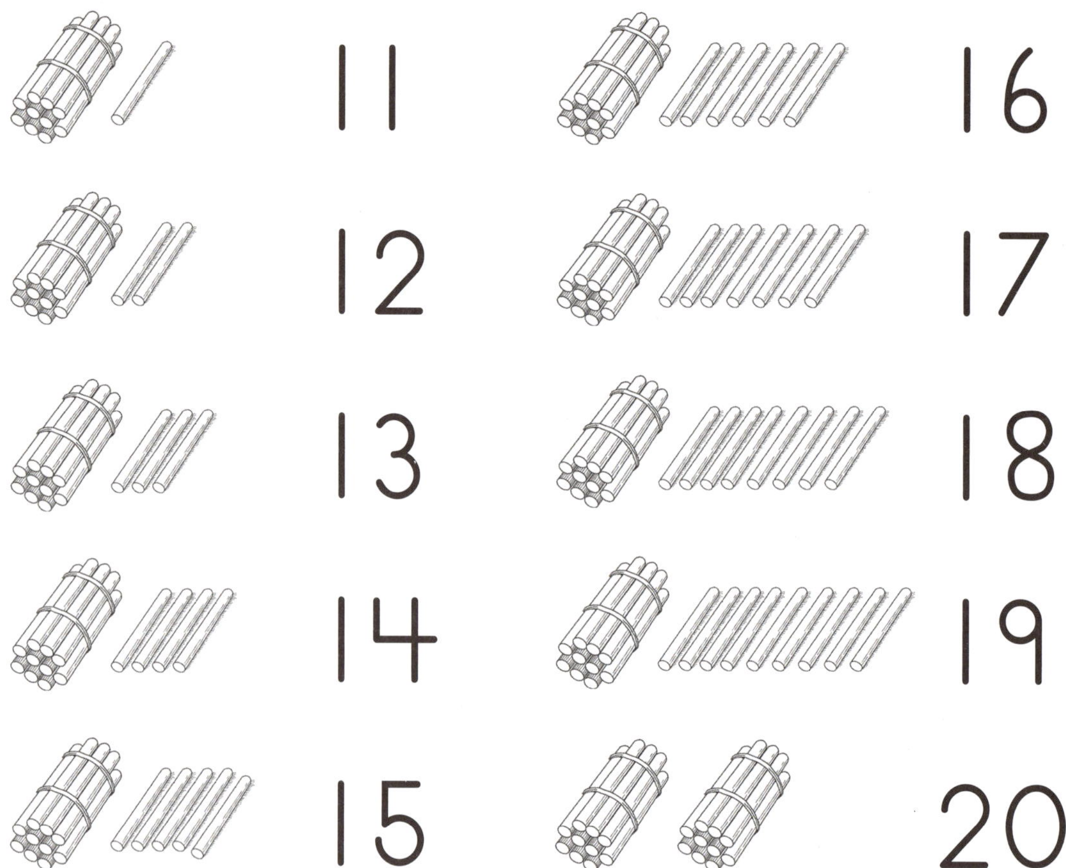

1 Trace each row of numbers with the colors of the rainbow.

SELF CHECK	Mark how you feel	
Got it! ☐	Need help... ☐	I don't get it ☐

Practice

1 Trace each row of numbers with the colors of the rainbow.

13 13 13 13 13 13

a 14 14 14 14 14 14

b 15 15 15 15 15 15

c 16 16 16 16 16 16

d 17 17 17 17 17 17

e 18 18 18 18 18 18

f 19 19 19 19 19 19

g 20 20 20 20 20

2 Trace each row of numbers.

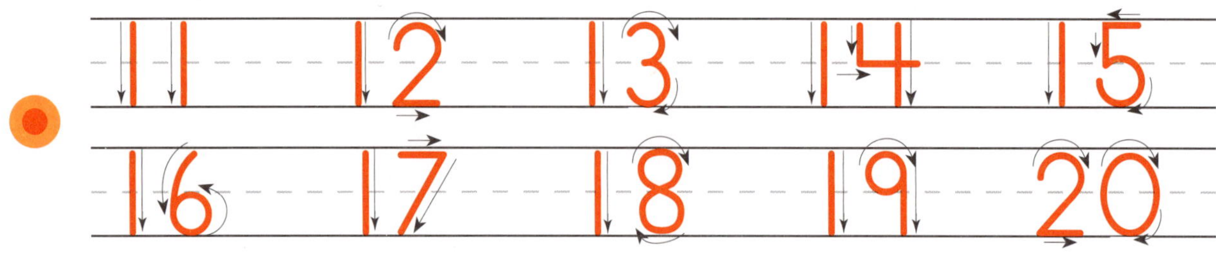

a

11 12 13 14 15
16 17 18 19 20

b

11 12 13 14 15
16 17 18 19 20

c

11 12 13 14 15
16 17 18 19 20

d

11 12 13 14 15
16 17 18 19 20

Count to 5

You can count to 5. Point to each object. Say the number as you point.

Touch and count each object.

There are 5 apples.

Your turn

1 Touch and count the objects. Write each total.

4 bugs

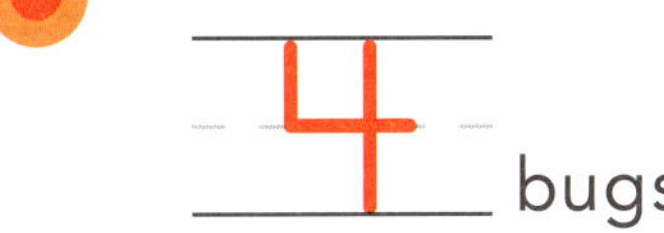

a

_____ coins

b

_____ frogs

SELF CHECK Mark how you feel		
Got it! ☐	Need help... ☐	I don't get it ☐

Practice

1 Touch and count the objects. Write each total.

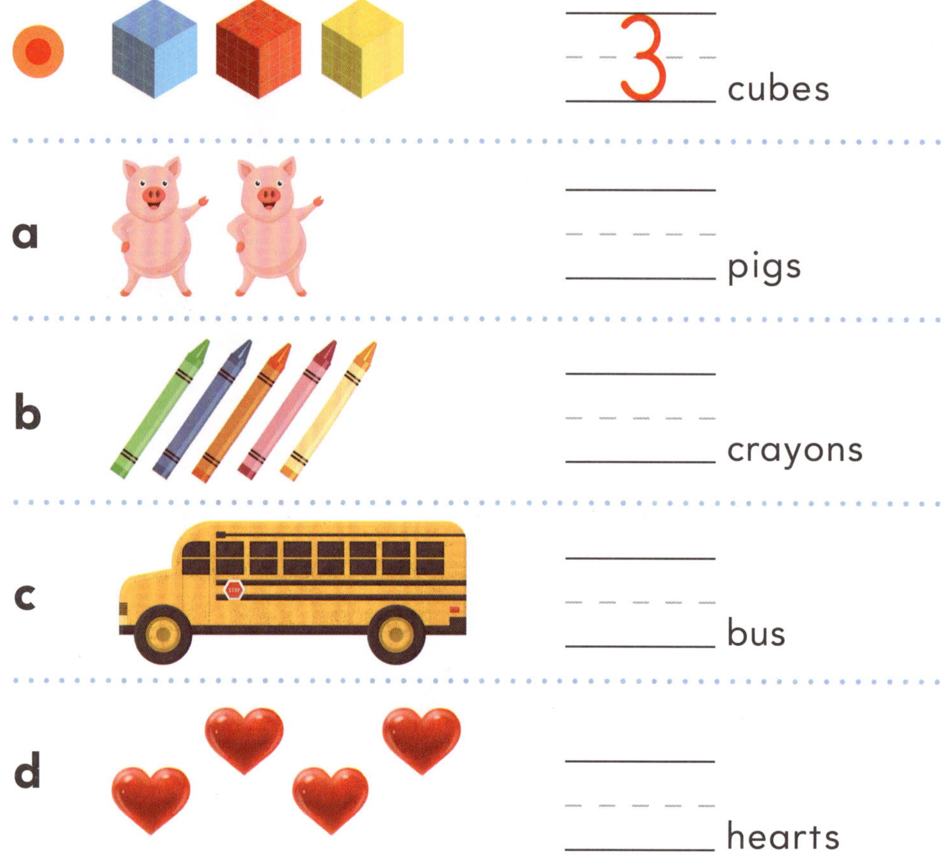

● 3 cubes

a ____ pigs

b ____ crayons

c ____ bus

d ____ hearts

2 Touch and count the objects. Draw a line to the total.

● 4

a 5

b 3

c 2

Count to 10

You can count to 10. Say the number as you point to each item.

Touch and count each one.

There are 10 drops.

1 Touch and count the objects. Write each total.

8 muffins

a

_____ balls

b

_____ hats

SELF CHECK	Mark how you feel	
Got it! ☐	Need help... ☐	I don't get it ☐

1 Touch and count the objects. Write each total.

2 Touch and count the objects. Draw a line to the total.

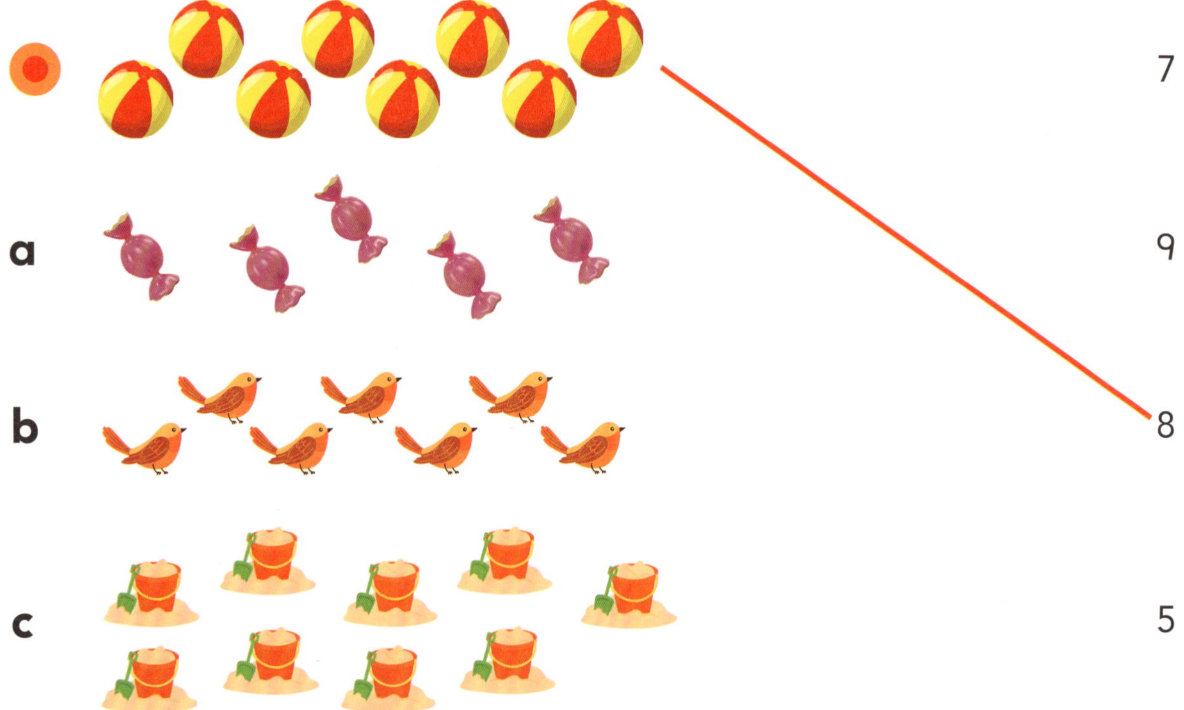

3 Draw a line from each set of objects to the number.

- ● 1
- a 2
- b 3
- c 4
- d 5
- e 6
- f 7
- g 8
- h 9
- i 10

Count to 20

You can count to 20. You can write the total.

Touch and count each object.

There are 20 stars.

1 Touch and count the objects. Write the total.

Count up by 1 when you touch a new object.

16 snowflakes

a ________ hats

SELF CHECK Mark how you feel

Got it!	Need help...	I don't get it
☐	☐	☐

Practice

1 Touch and count the objects. Write each total.

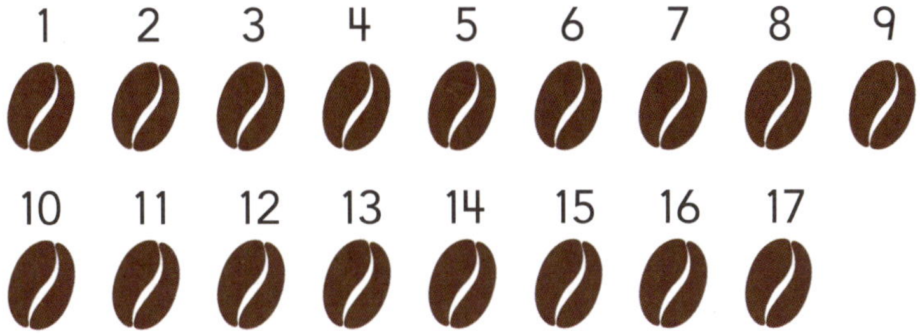

1 2 3 4 5 6 7 8 9

10 11 12 13 14 15 16 17

17 beans

a ______ pumpkins

b ______ bugs

c ______ suns

2 Touch and count the objects. Draw a line to the total.

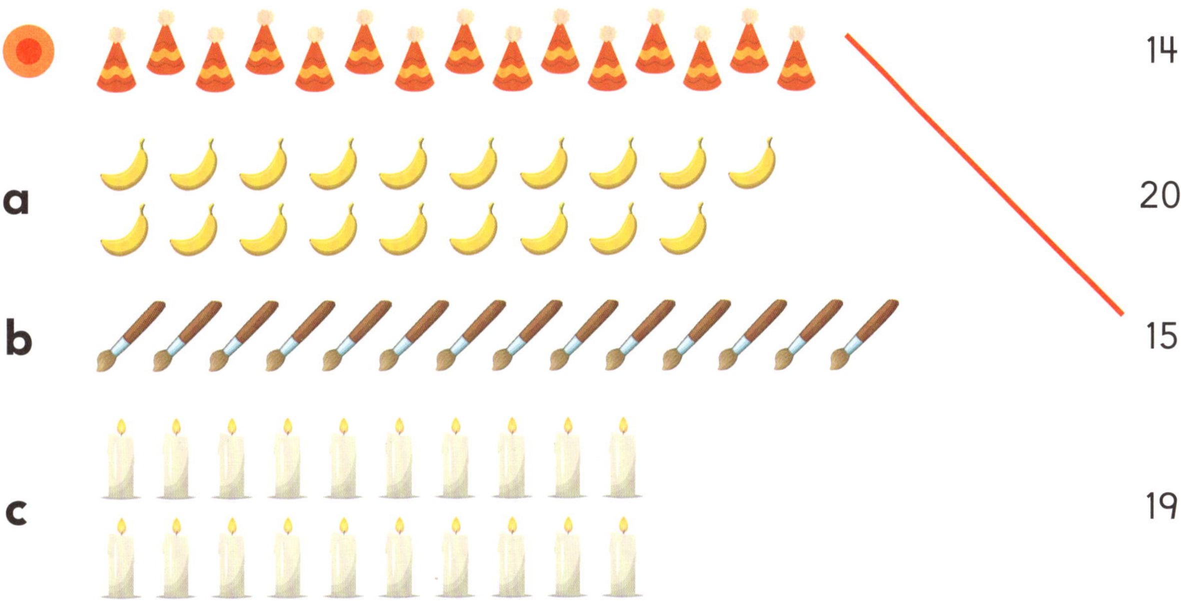

a

b

c

14

20

15

19

3 Draw a line from each number to the matching set of objects.

- ● 11
- **a** 12
- **b** 13
- **c** 14
- **d** 15
- **e** 16
- **f** 17
- **g** 18
- **h** 19
- **i** 20

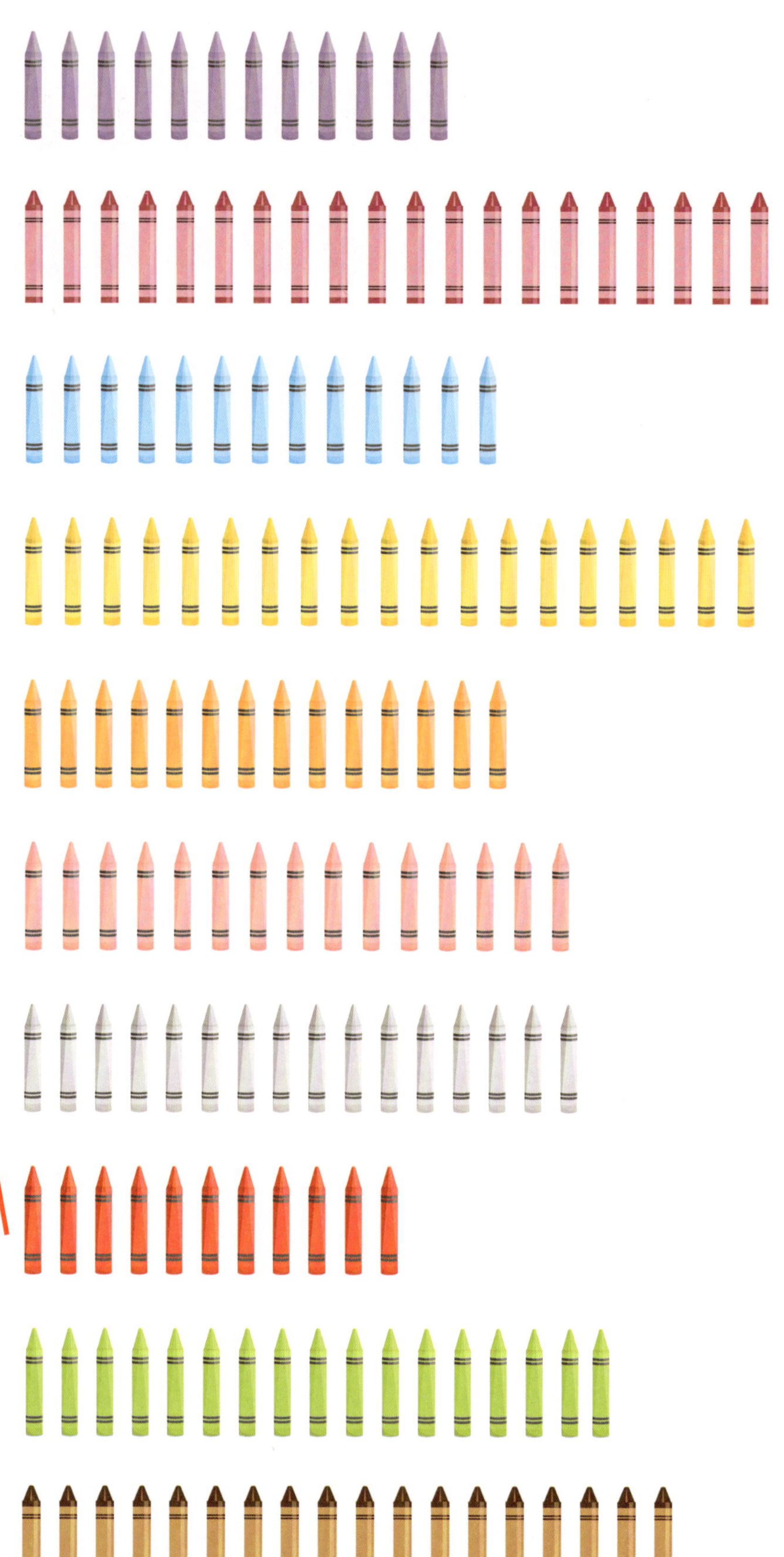

Count to 100

You can count to 100 by ones.

Touch each object as you count by ones.

You can also touch each object with a pencil.

There are  100 hearts.

Your turn

1 Touch each object as you count. Trace the total.

20 cars

---

a

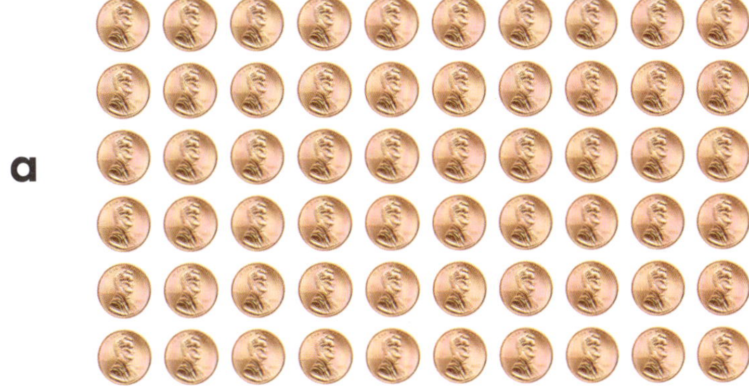

60 pennies

SELF CHECK Mark how you feel

Got it!	Need help...	I don't get it
☐	☐	☐

Practice

1 Touch and count the objects. Trace each total.

a

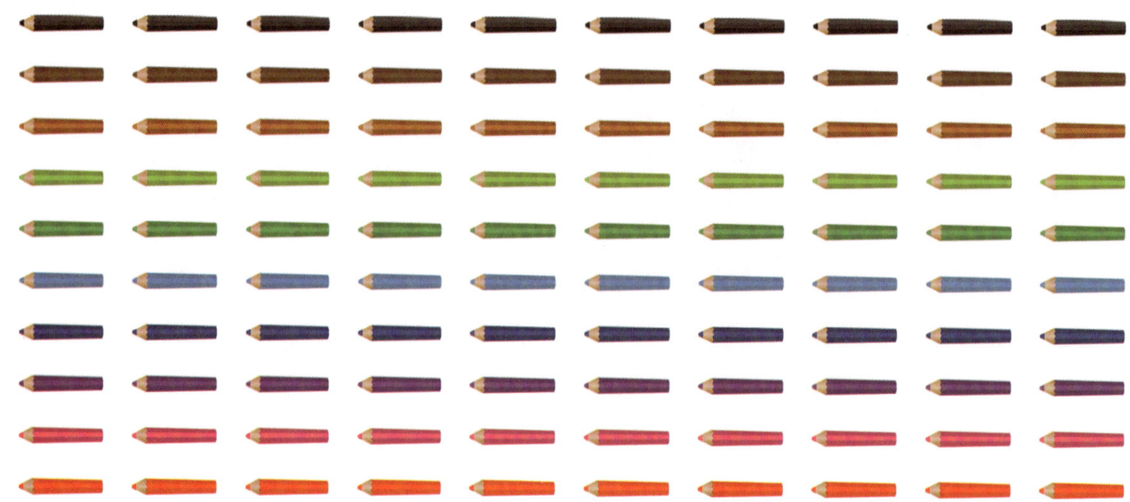

100 crayons

80 bees

2 Touch and count the objects. Trace each total.

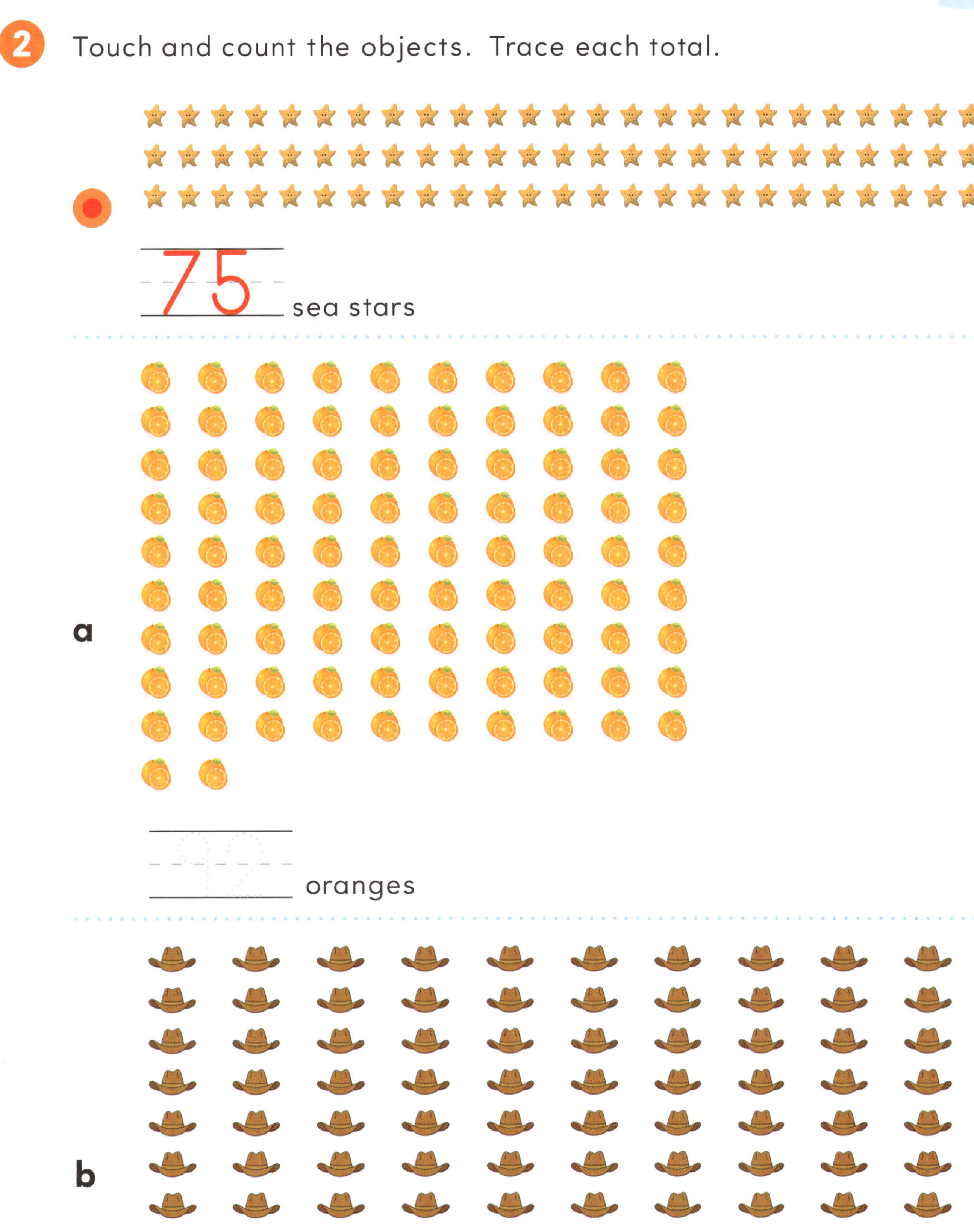

75 sea stars

a

92 oranges

b

86 hats

Skip Count by 10s

You can count to 100 by 10s.

Move your finger to each group of objects as you count by 10s.

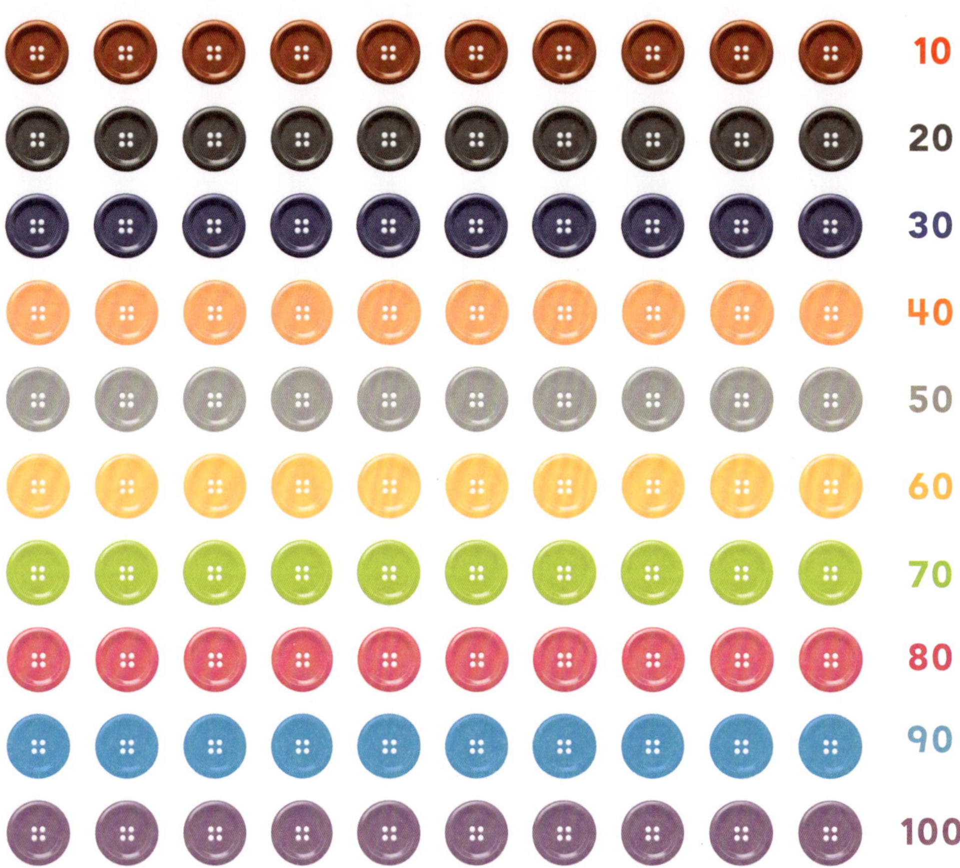

SCAN to watch video

Your turn

1 Count the objects by 10s. Trace the total.

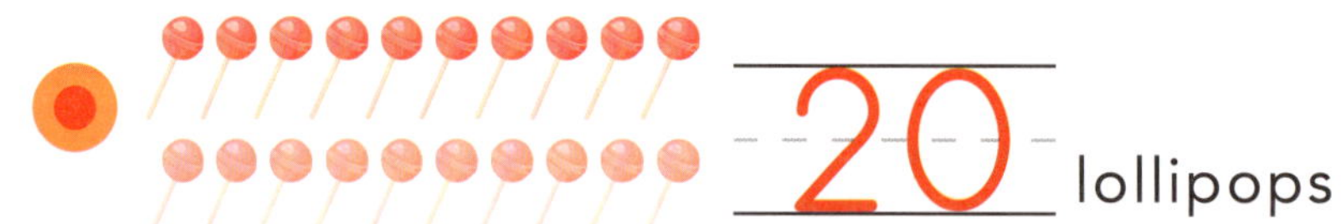

20 lollipops

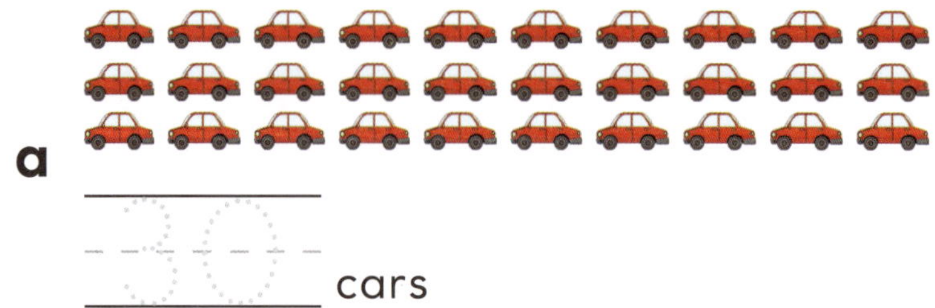

a 30 cars

Count each set of 10 as one group.

SELF CHECK Mark how you feel

Got it! | Need help... | I don't get it

Practice

1 Count the objects by 10s. Trace each total.

40 balloons

a ____ jellybeans

b ____ basketballs

c ____ spoons

d ____ tractors

2 Count the objects by 10s. Draw a line to the total.

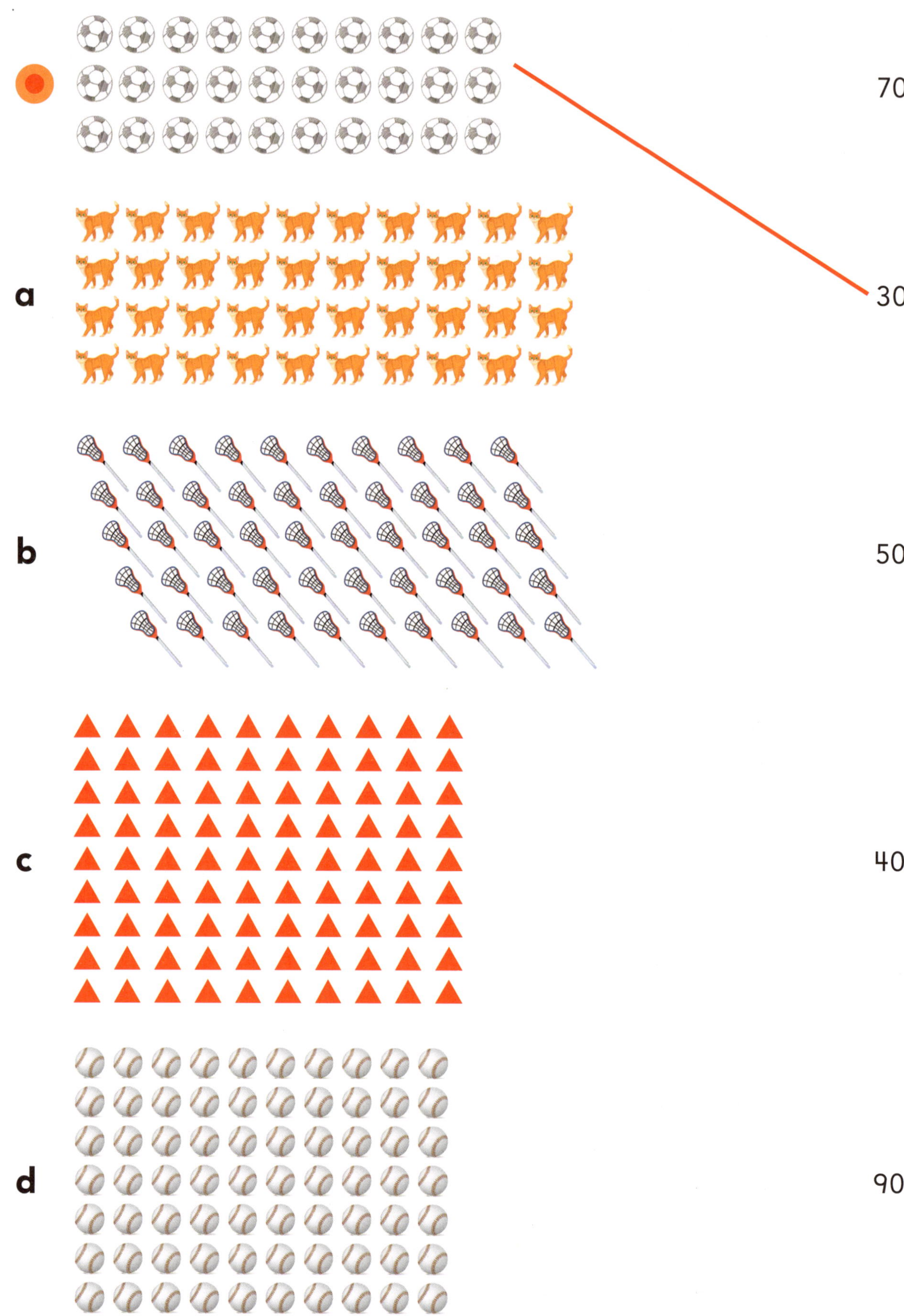

Counting On

You can count forward starting at any number.

Start with the group, and continue counting.

10

11 12 13 14 15 16

It does not matter what number you start with. You can still count up!

Your turn

1 Start with the labeled group. Count up. Write the total.

3

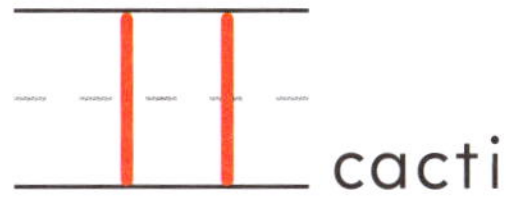

11 cacti

a

9

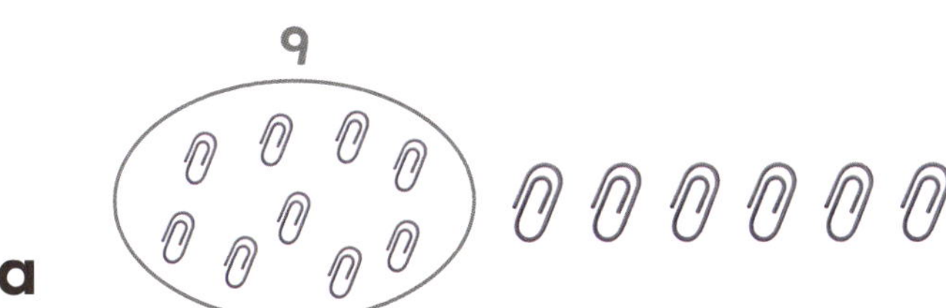

_____ paper clips

b

2

_____ rocks

SELF CHECK Mark how you feel

Got it!	Need help...	I don't get it
 ☐	 ☐	 ☐

Practice

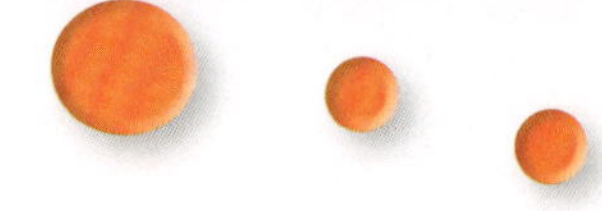

1 Start with the labeled group. Count up. Trace or write the total.

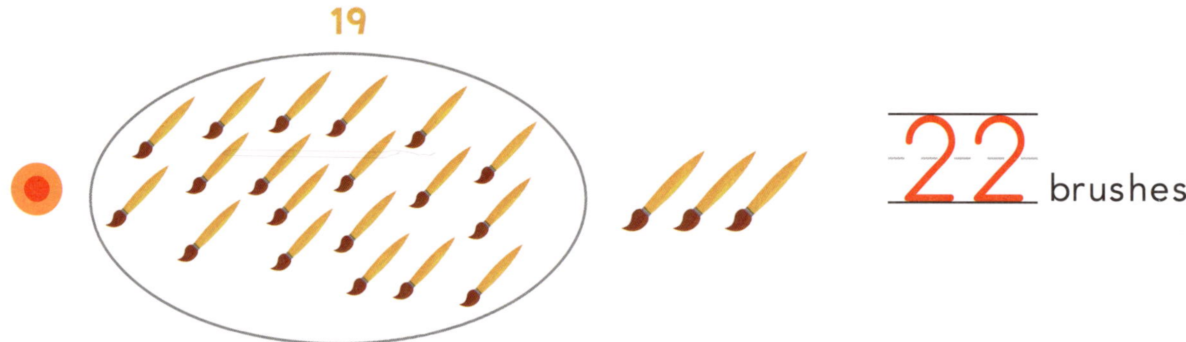

22 brushes

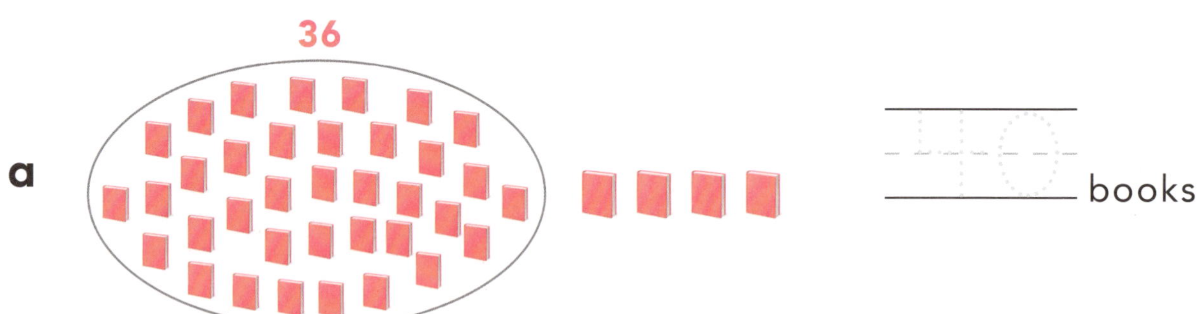

a 40 books

b 27 hearts

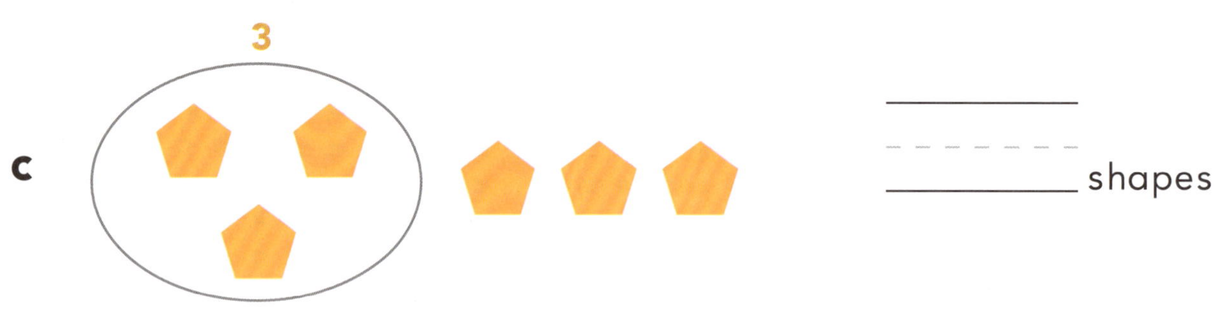

c ______ shapes

d ______ bows

2 Start with the labeled group. Count up. Draw a line to the total.

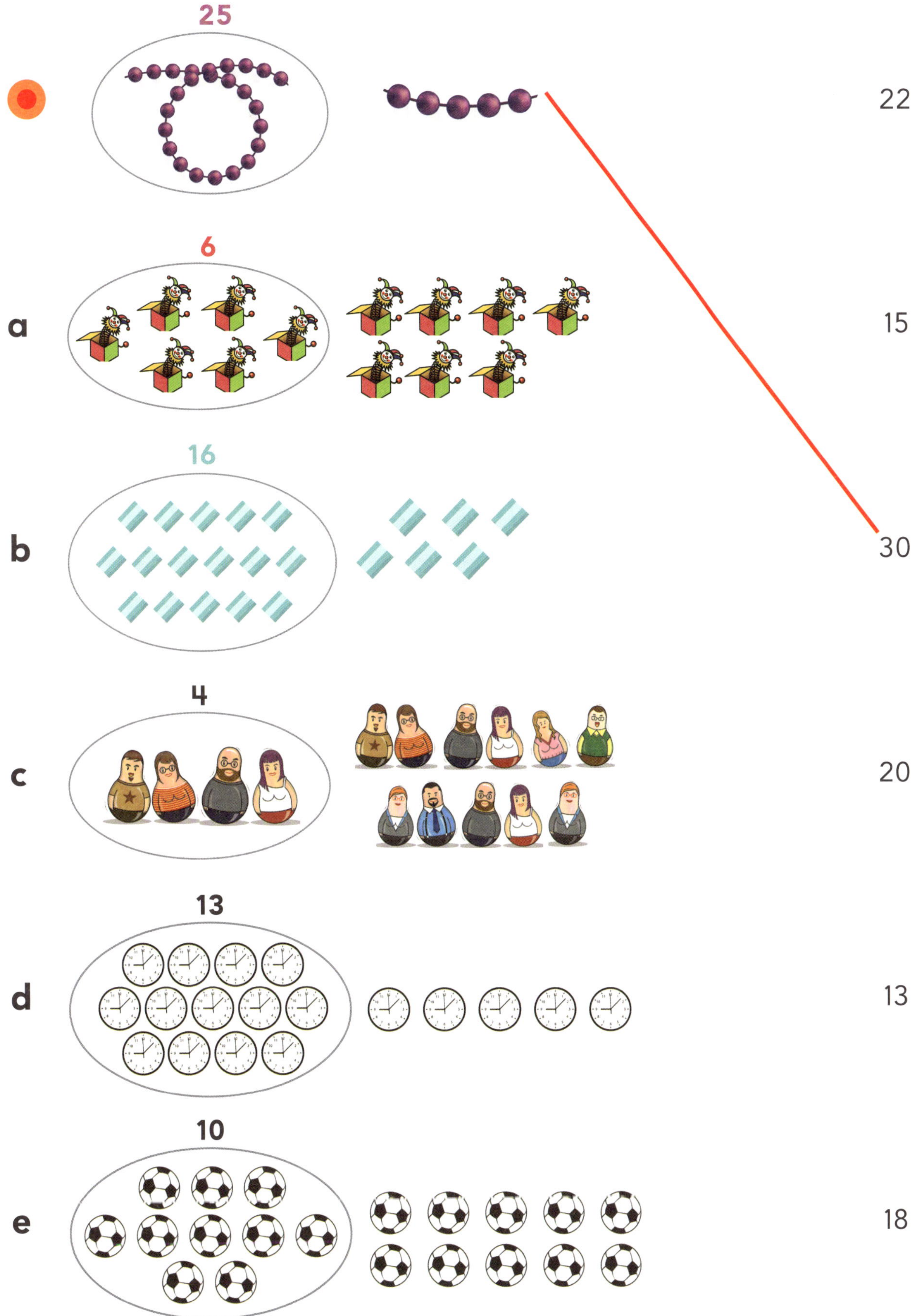

Counting Backward

You can count backward.

When you count backward, you start with the highest number.

5
4
3
2
1
Blastoff!

5 seconds until blastoff!

1 Count backward. Trace the numbers as you count.

a

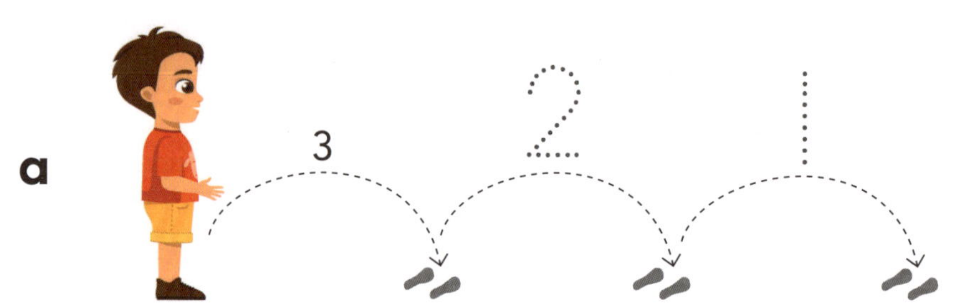

b

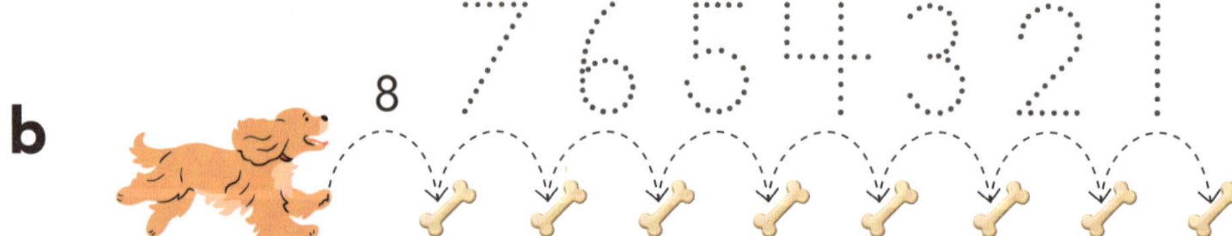

SELF CHECK Mark how you feel

Got it!	Need help...	I don't get it

Practice

1 Count backward. Trace the numbers as you count.

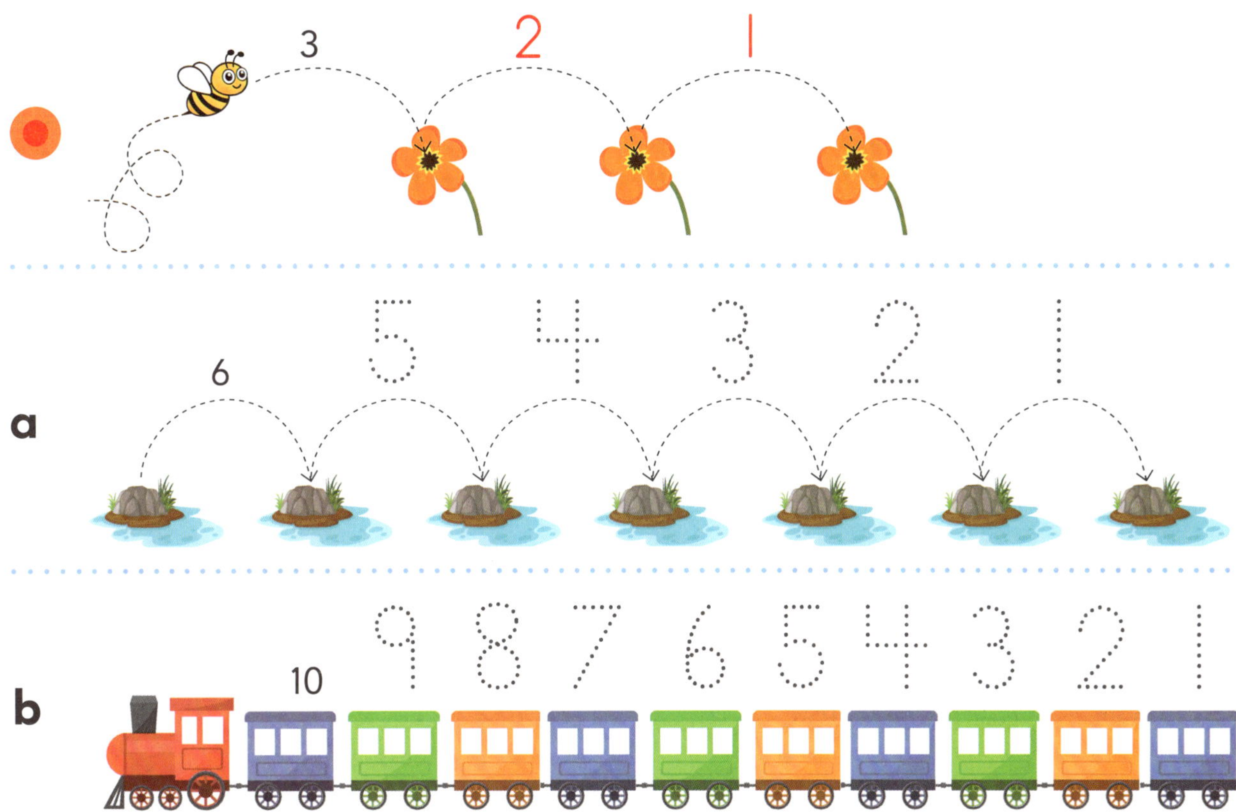

2 Count backward. Write the numbers as you count.

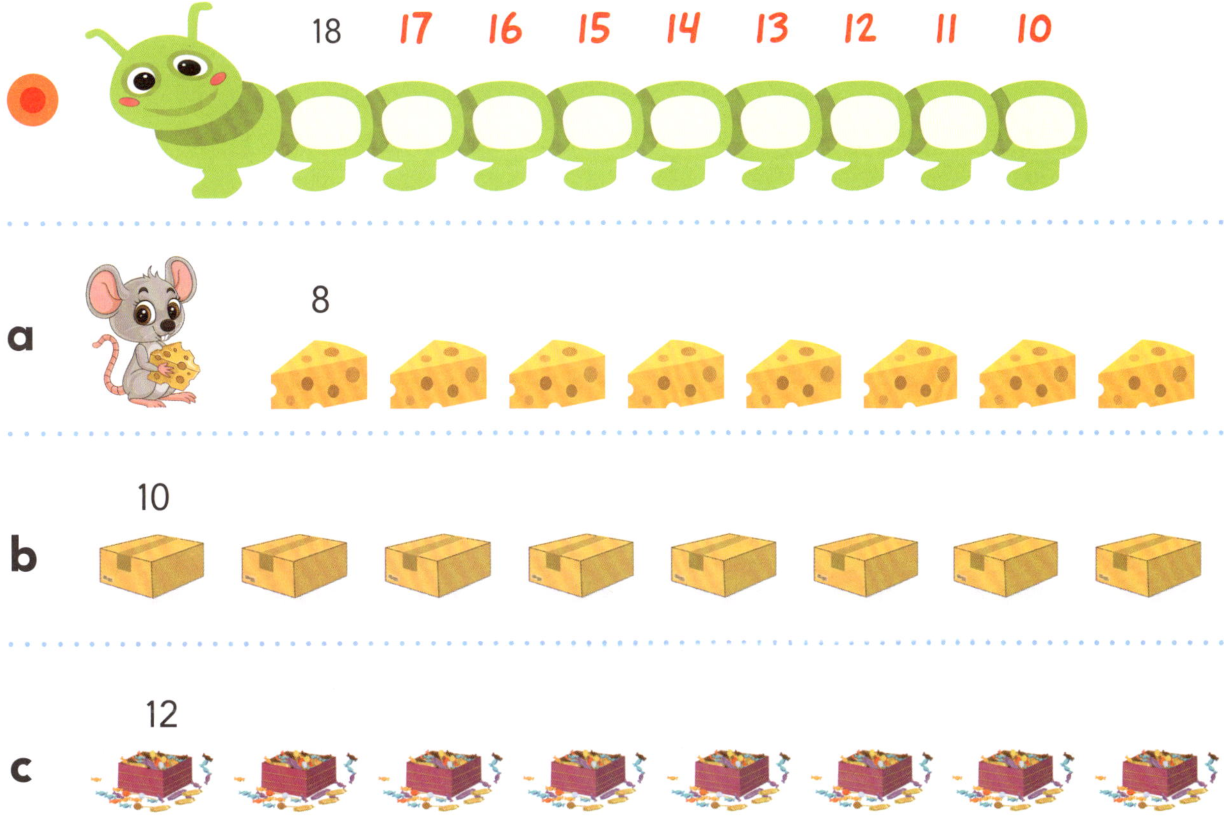

3 Count backward. Write the numbers as you count.

- 12 11 10 9 8 7 6

a 10 ___ ___ ___ ___ ___ ___

b 20 ___ ___ ___ ___ ___

c 7 ___ ___ ___ ___ ___ ___

d 18 ___ ___ ___ ___ ___

4 Count backward from 20.

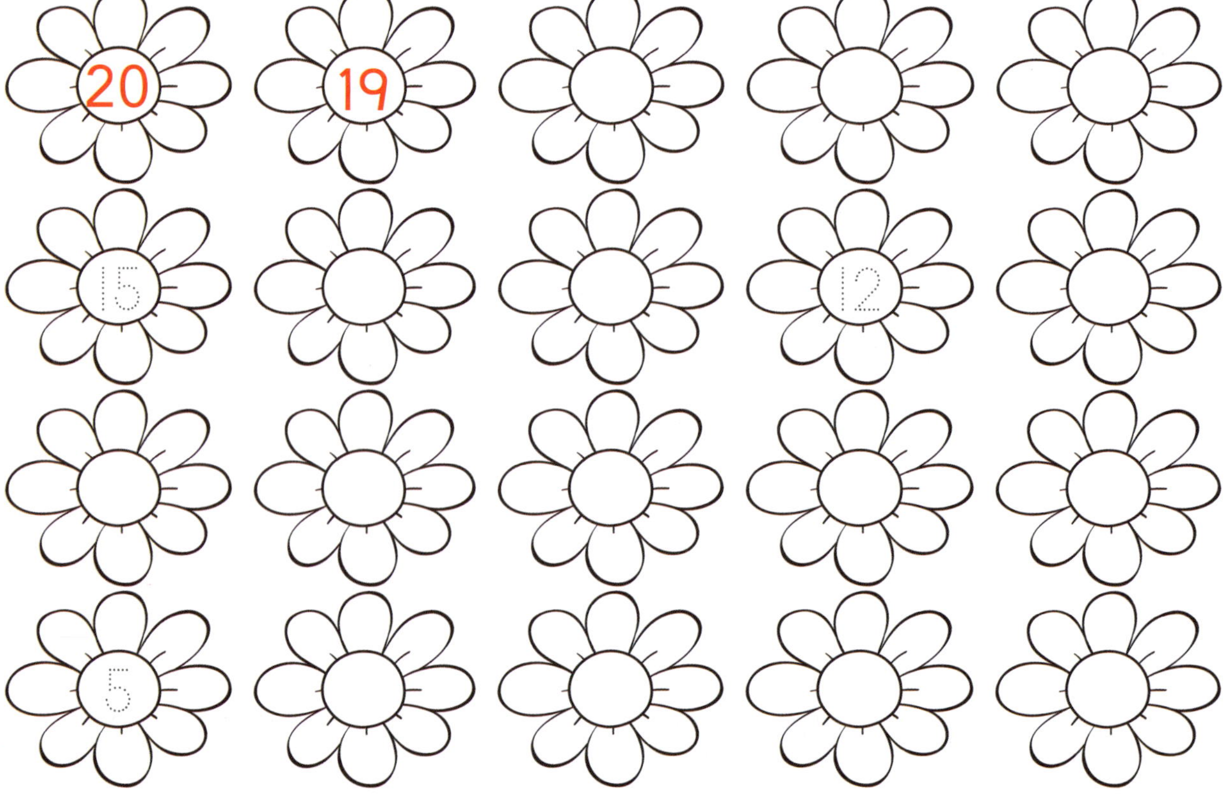

Ordinal Numbers

You can count using ordinal numbers.

Ordinal numbers tell the position of something in a group or a line. The winner is first. The next person is second. The next person is third, and so on.

Ordinal numbers tell us the order of things.

1 Circle the **third** item in each set.

a     

b   

c      

SELF CHECK	Mark how you feel	
Got it! ☐	Need help... ☐	I don't get it ☐

1 Underline the **second** item in each set.

a 

b 

c 

2 Color each set of objects. Color the first object red. Color the second object orange. Color the third object yellow. Color the fourth object green. Color the fifth object blue.

a

b 

c 

d

3 Circle the **first** item in each set.

4 Draw lines to show what place each runner is in.

second first fourth fifth third

Counting Review

1 Touch and count the objects in each set. Write the total.

a

______ cats

b

______ snakes

c

______ cookies

2 Count the objects by 1s. Draw a line to the total.

a

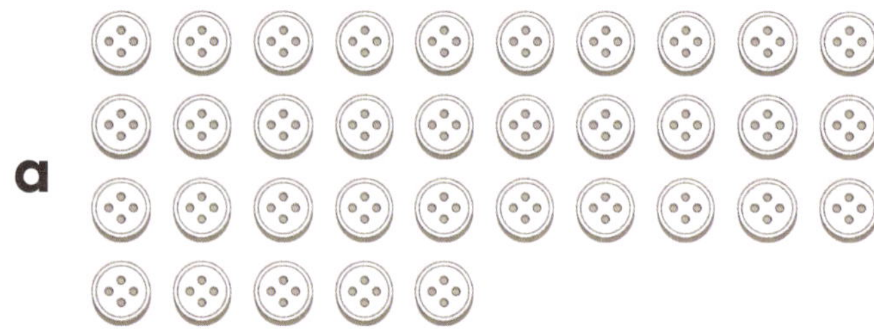

55

b

23

c

35

Review

3 Count the objects by 10s. Write each total.

a 10 10 10 10 10 10 10 10 10 10

______ crayons

b 

______ marbles

c 

______ cookies

4 Start with the labeled group. Count up. Write the total.

a 

______ ducks

b 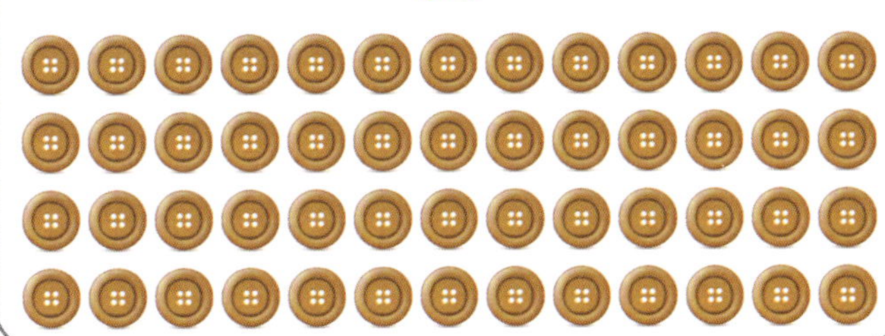

______ buttons

c 18

______ stars

Review

5 Count the objects in each set. Write the total.

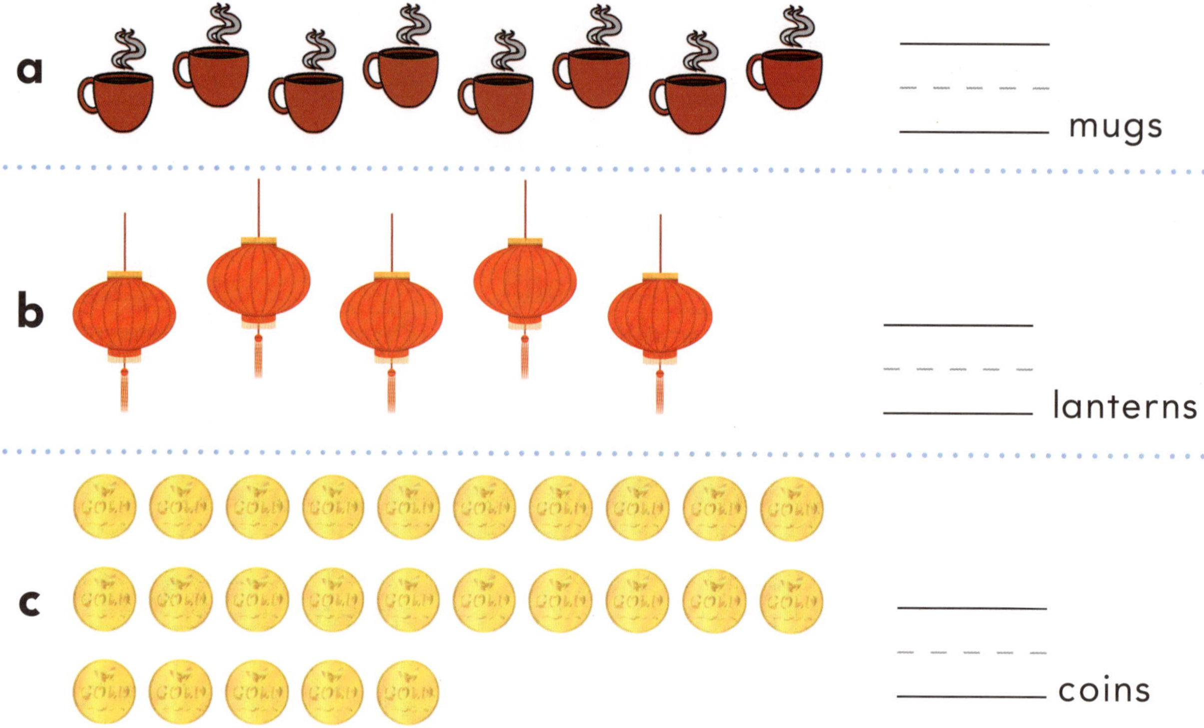

a ________ mugs

b ________ lanterns

c ________ coins

6 Count backward. Write the numbers as you count.

a 8

b 6

c 17

Review

7 Circle the **second** object in each set.

a     

b    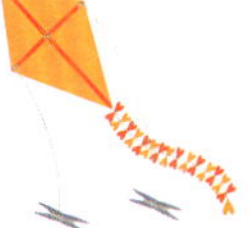

c  

d   

8 Color each set of objects. Color the first object red. Color the second object blue. Color the third object green. Color the fourth object yellow. Color the fifth object pink.

a     

b   

c 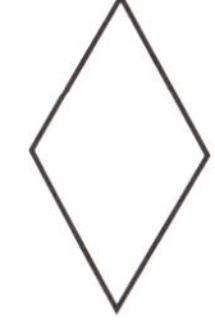   

d 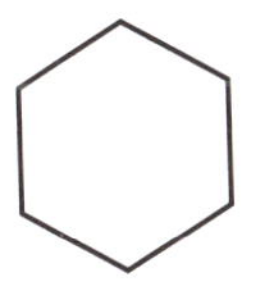 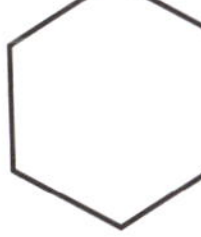

Subitize

You can quickly name small sets without counting.

Subitizing is seeing how many objects are in a set without needing to count.

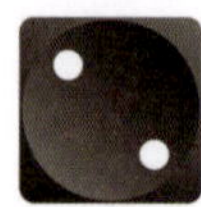

2

We can quickly see sets on number cubes or fingers.

1 Tell how many without counting. Write each number.

 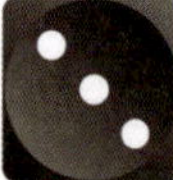 

a 

b 

c 

d 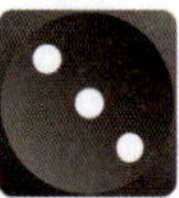

Subitizing will help you add and subtract.

SELF CHECK Mark how you feel

Got it!	Need help...	I don't get it

Practice

1 Tell how many fingers without counting. Write each number.

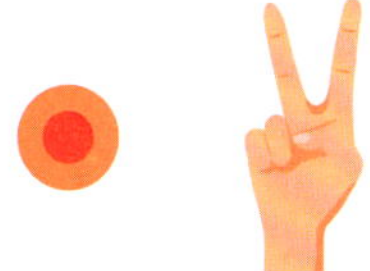

a  ______

c  ______

b 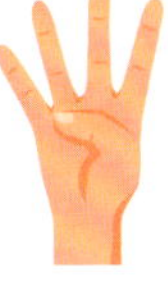 ______

d  ______

2 Look at the dots on each ladybug. Write the number.

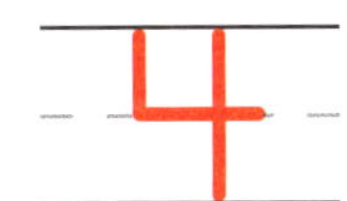

a  ______

c  ______

b  ______

d  ______

3 Look at each five frame. Tell how many without counting. Write the number.

●	●					1
a	●	●	●	●		
b	●	●				
c	●					
d	●	●	●			
e	●	●				
f	●	●	●	●	●	

Generate Numbers

You can look at a number and draw a set.

Drawing pictures can help you learn the numbers, too.

Your turn

1 Draw each number using circles.

a 4

b 3

c 8

d 6

Practice

1 Draw each number using dots.

● 8 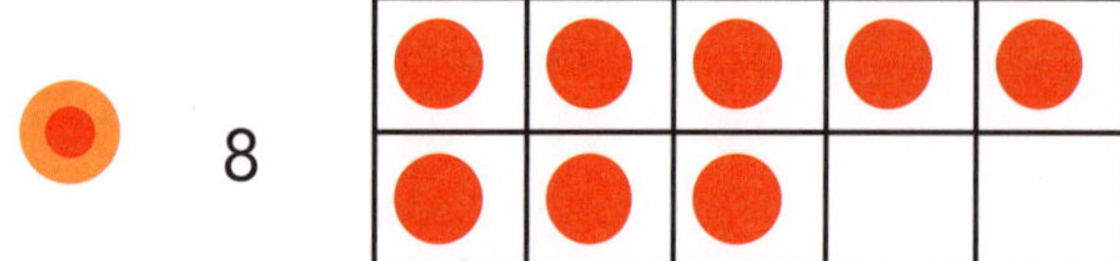

a 10 

c 2 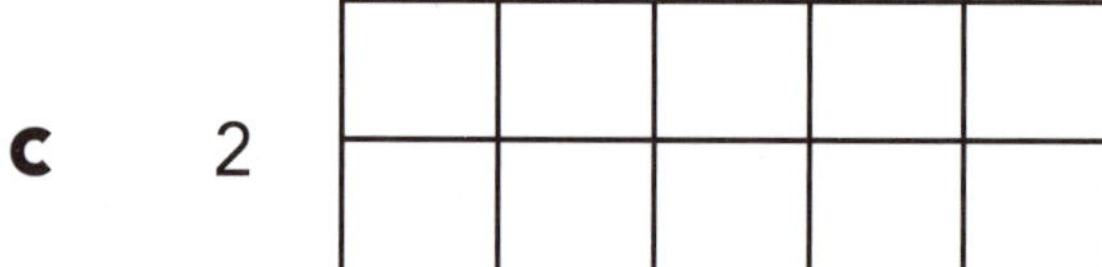

b 9 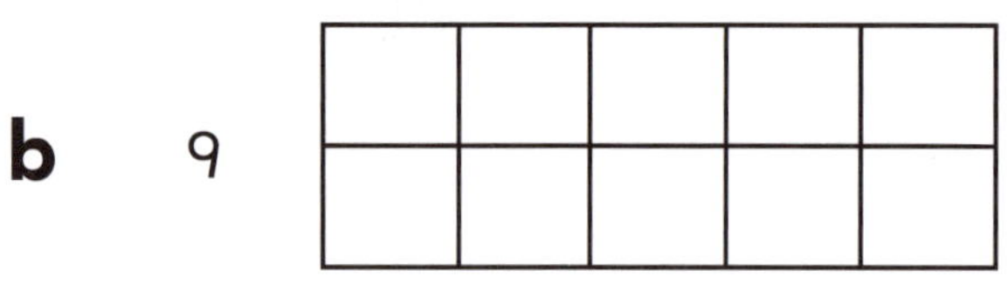

d 7 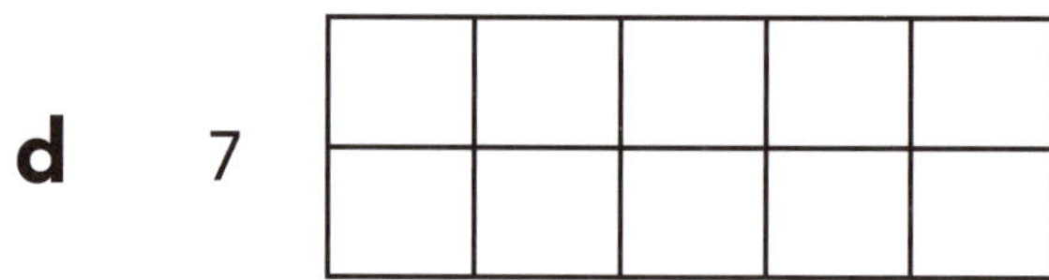

2 Draw each set of objects.

● 5 butterflies      

a 4 flowers

b 6 circles

c 9 happy faces

d 7 snakes

3 Draw each number using dots.

 15

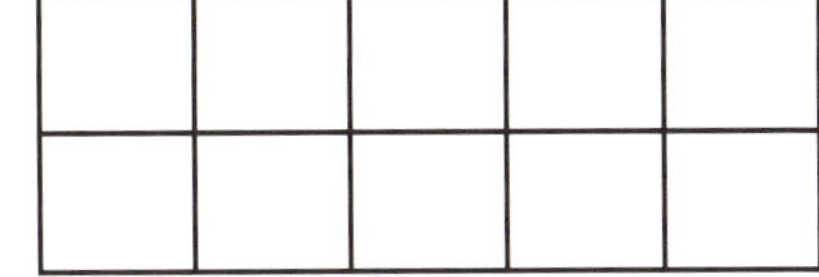

a 18

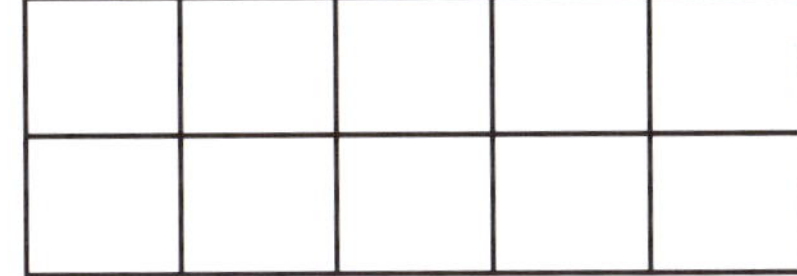

b 14

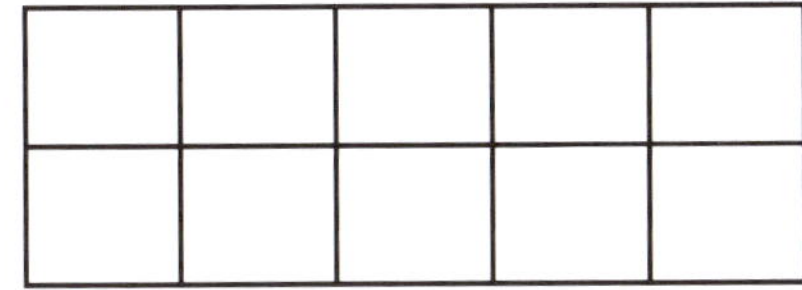
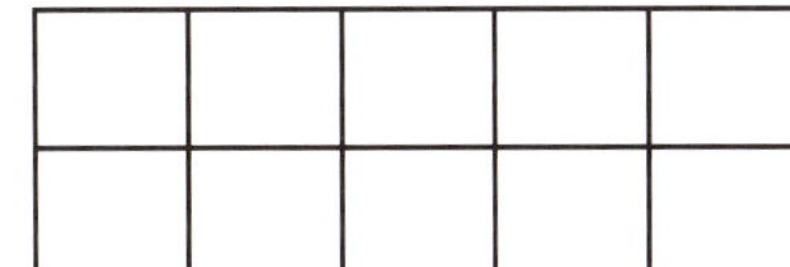

c 12

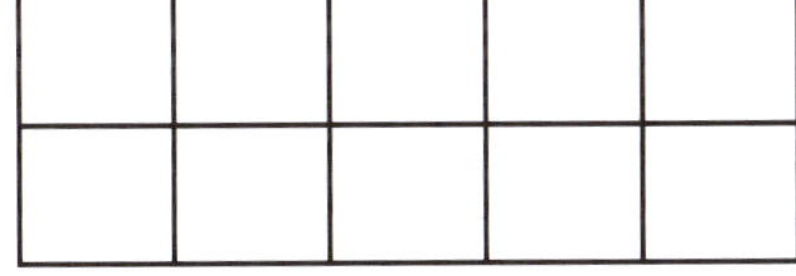
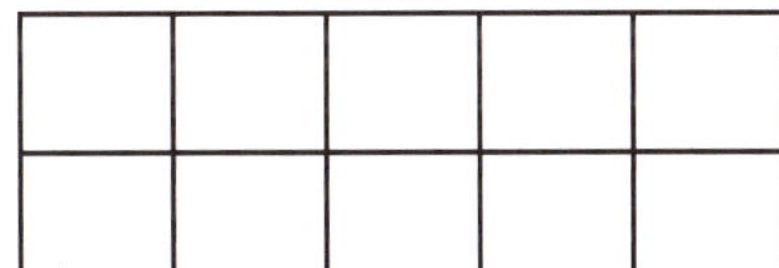

d 4

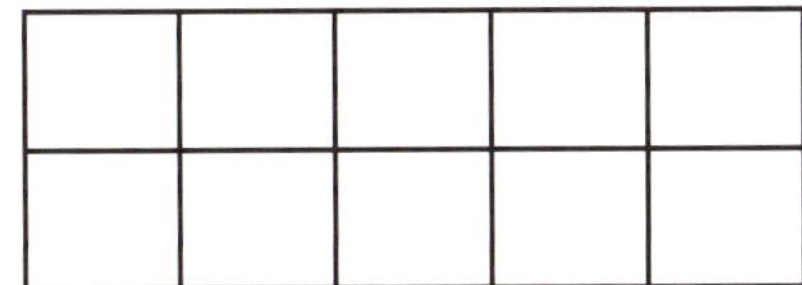

e 6

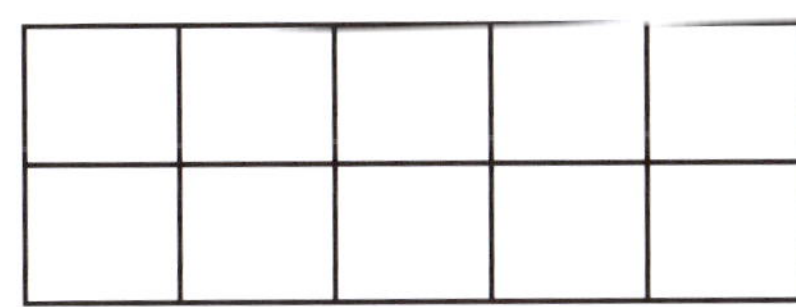

f 17

Whole and Part

You can tell a whole from a part.

An entire pizza is a **whole** pizza.

A slice is **part** of the whole pizza.

Parts can be big.

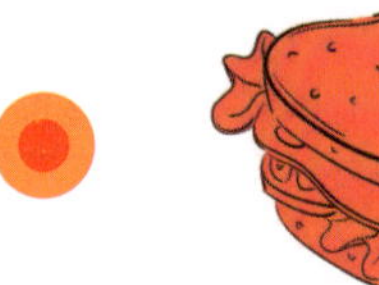

Or, parts can be small.

1 Look at the objects. If it is whole, color it blue. If it is a part, color it red.

a 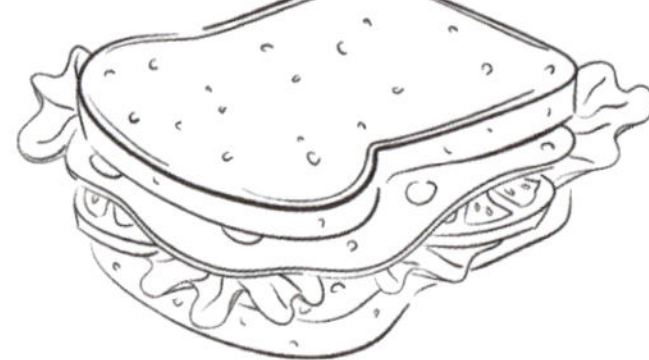

c

b 

d 

SELF CHECK Mark how you feel

Got it!	Need help...	I don't get it
  ☐	  ☐	 ☐

Practice

1 Color the whole.

a 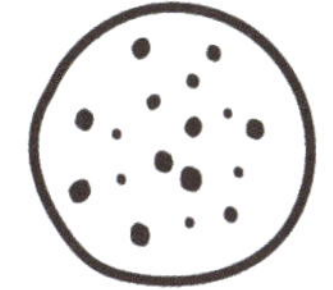 

c  

b 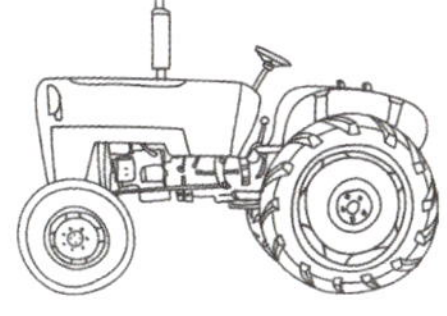 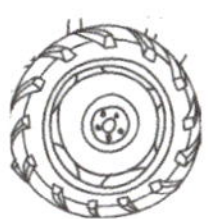

d  

2 Circle the part.

a 

c  

b  

d 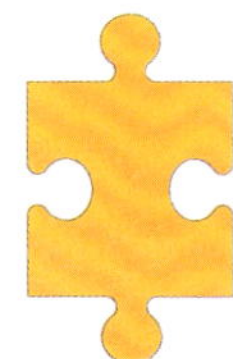 

3 Color the part.

a 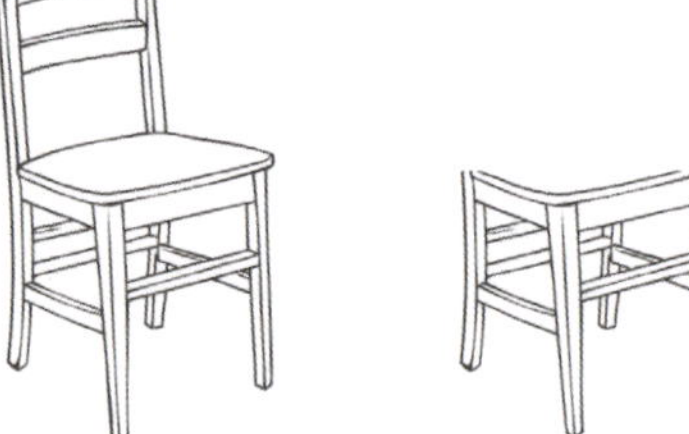

c 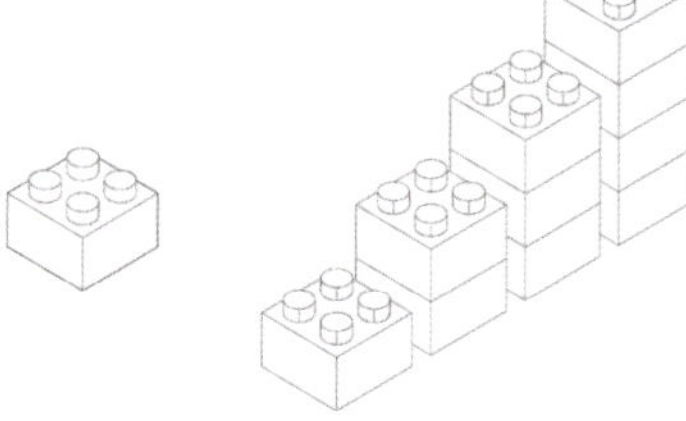

b  

d  

4 Circle the whole.

a  

c  

b  

d  

Foundations in Place Value

You can draw and label a group of 10 and some more.

Teen numbers are a group of 10 and some more ones.
The number 13 is 1 ten and 3 more ones.

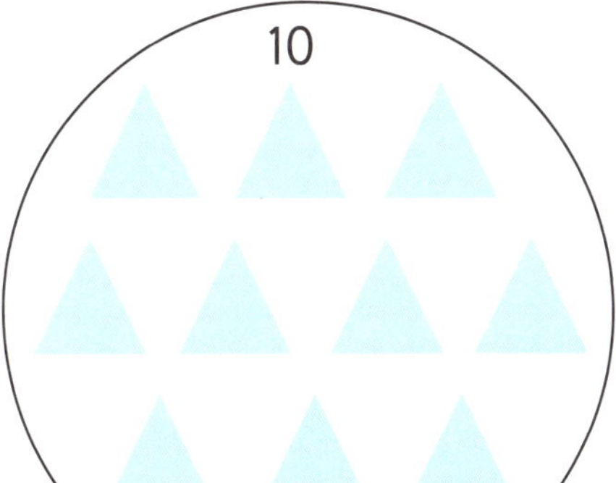

3 more ones

The number 24 has 2 tens and 4 more ones!

1 Draw more circles to build each number. Write numbers to count what you added.

  12 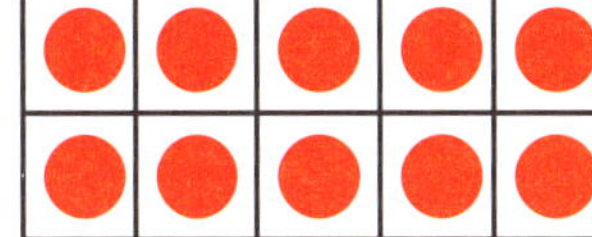  

a 15 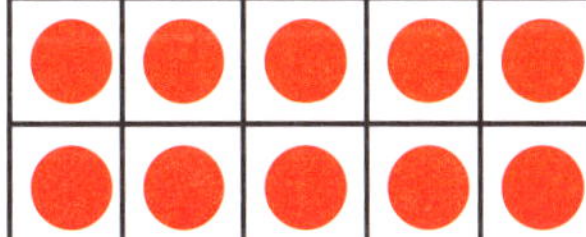

b 11 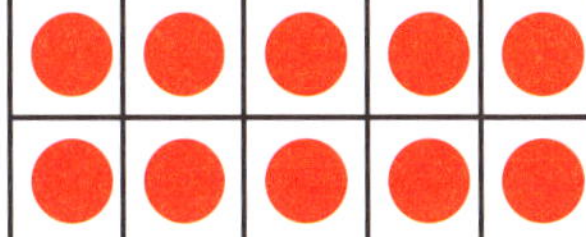

c 19 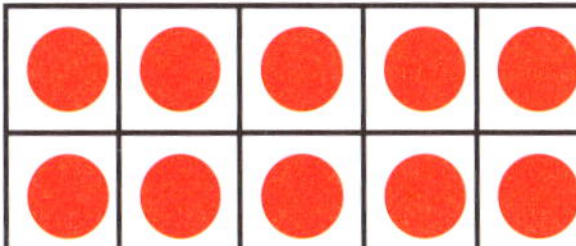

d 16 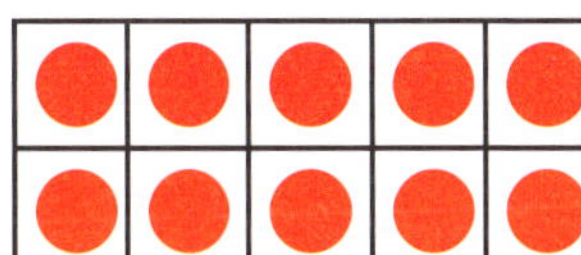

SELF CHECK Mark how you feel

Got it!	Need help...	I don't get it

Practice

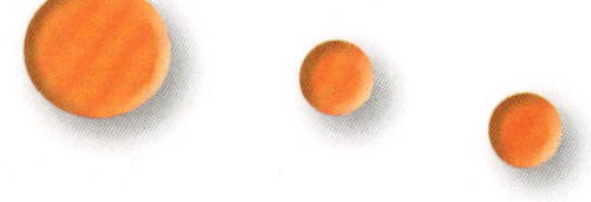

1 Draw the teen number with circles. Then, circle your group of 10.

● 14 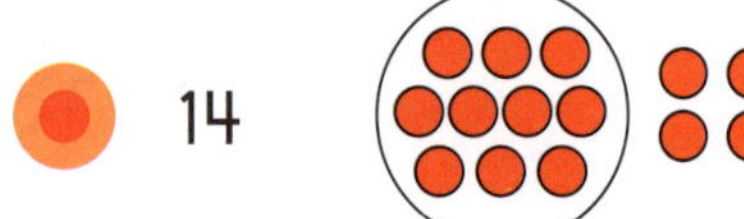

b 18

a 12

c 13

2 Write how many more ones there are. Then, write the whole number.

● 16 10 and

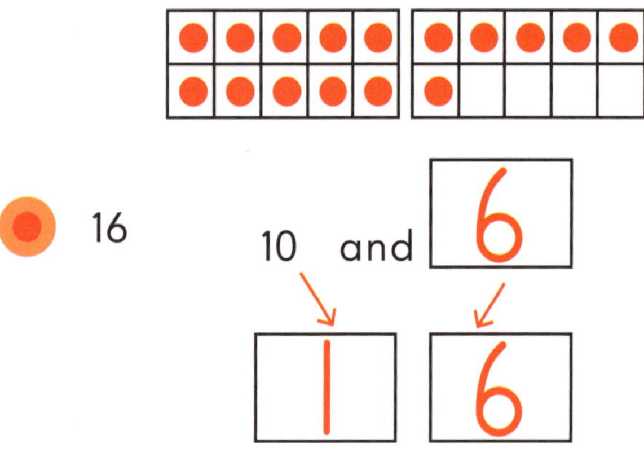

b 17 10 and

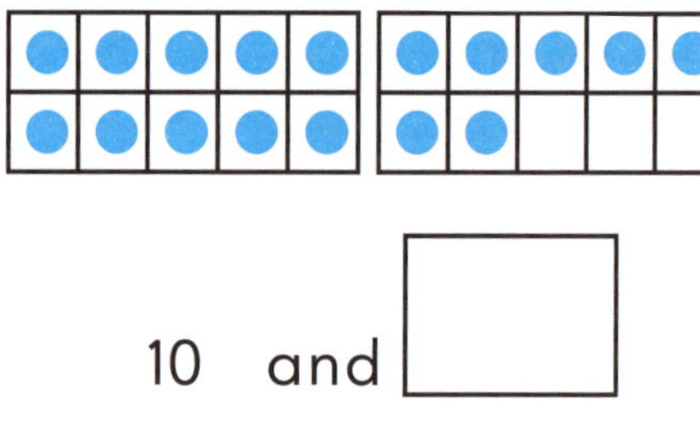

a 11 10 and

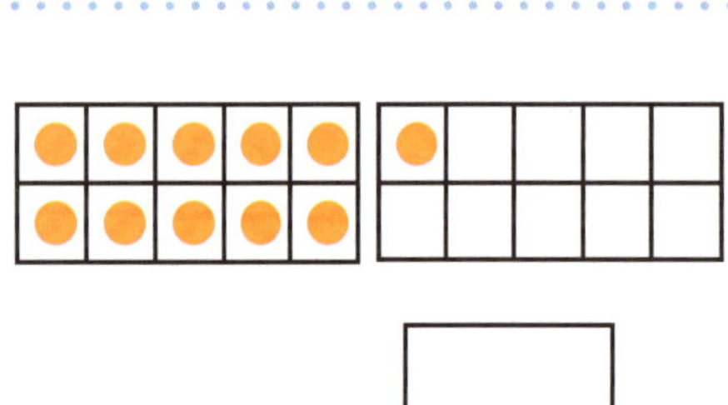

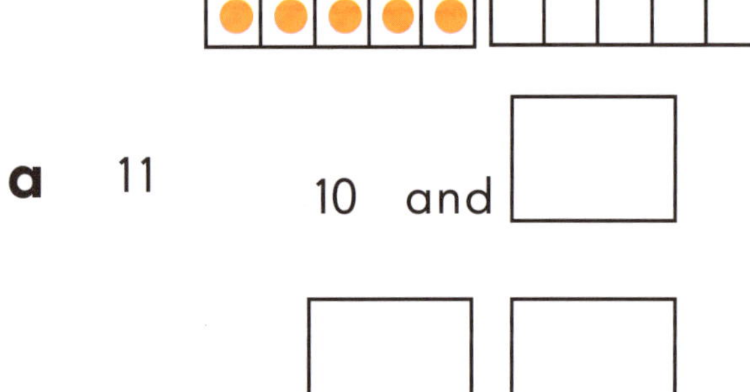

c 15 10 and

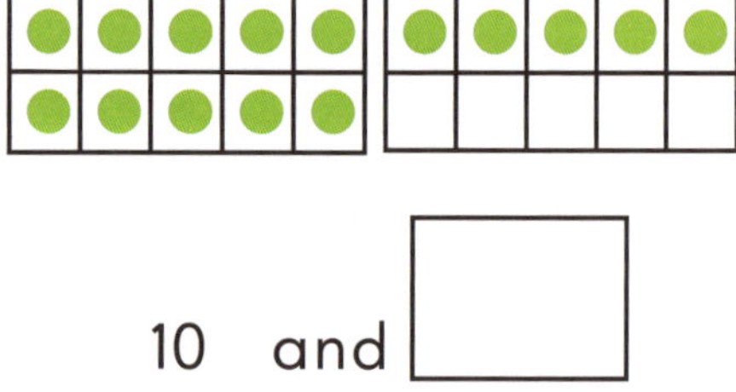

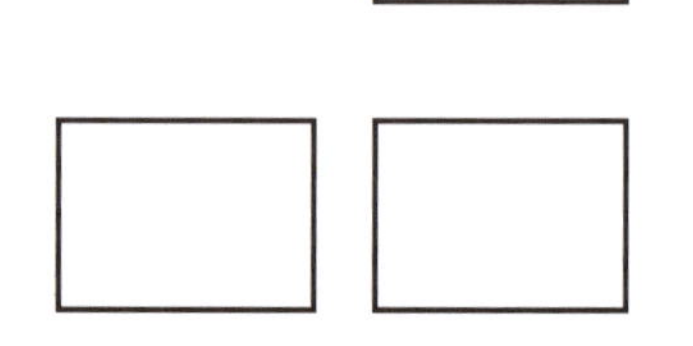

3 Write the matching number.

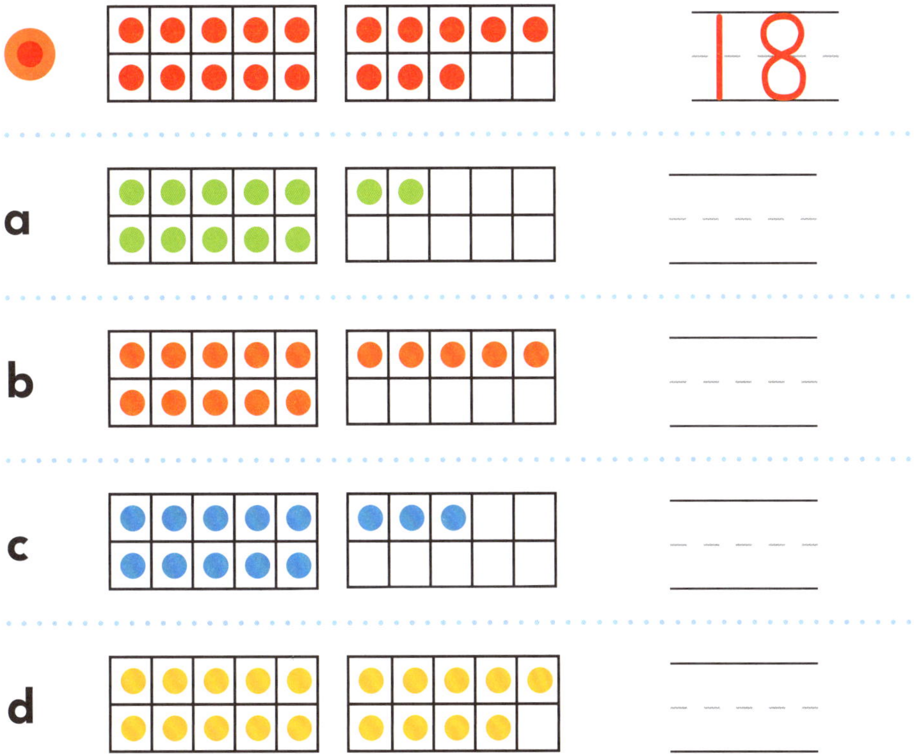

4 Count each set. Draw a line from the set to the matching number.

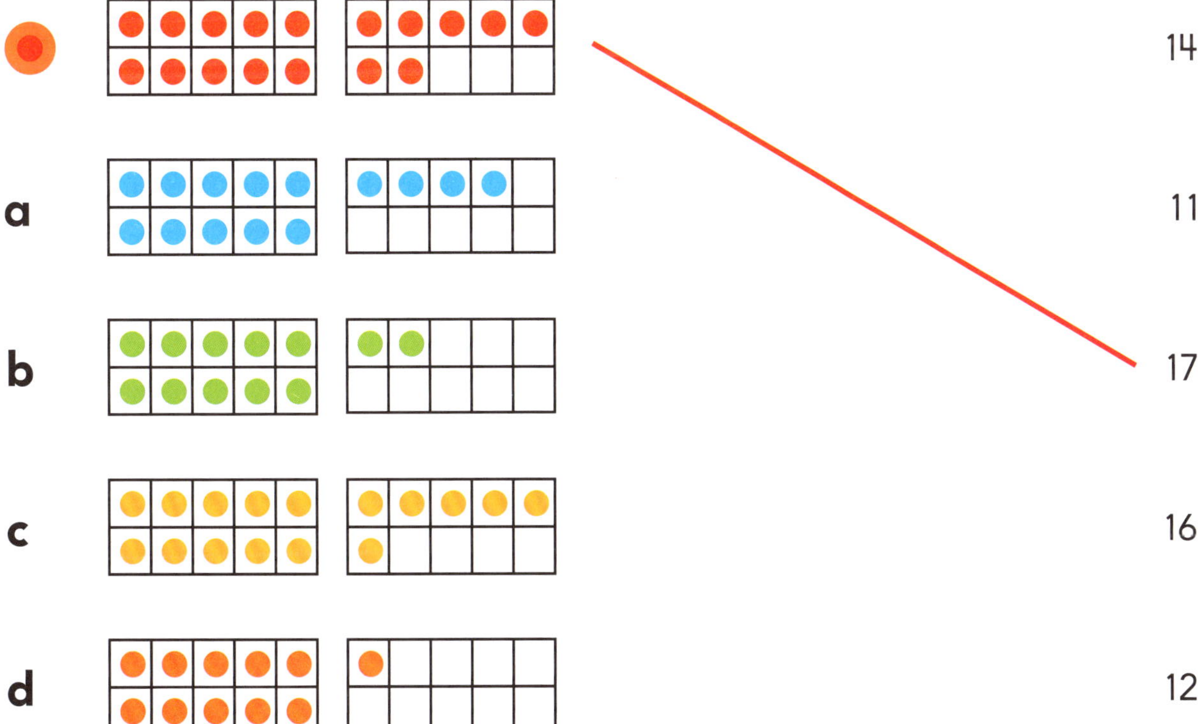

Number Sense Review

1 Draw each number using dots.

a 6

b 15

c 20

2 Circle the part.

a  

b 

c  

d  

3 Write each number without counting.

a  ______

b  ______

c  ______

d  ______

Review

4 Draw each number using dots. Then, circle the group of 10.

a 12

b 18

c 11

5 Draw each set of objects.

a 13 leaves

b 4 houses

c 15 flags

6 Count and write each total.

a 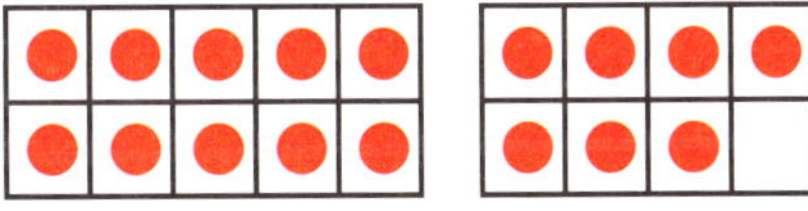 ______

b  ______

c   ______

d 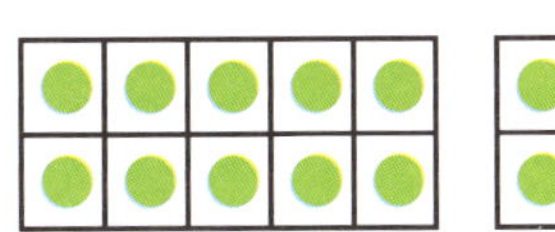 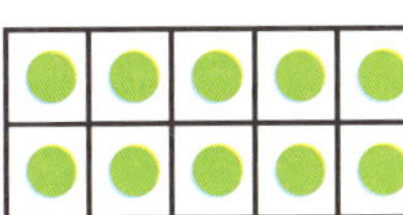 ______

Greater Than

You can tell when a set is greater than another.

This nest has more eggs than the other nest.

The number of eggs is **greater than** the other.

SCAN to watch video

Your turn

1 Circle the set that is greater than the other.

a

b

c

You can check which set is greater by counting.

SELF CHECK Mark how you feel

Got it!	Need help...	I don't get it
 ☐	 ☐	 ☐

Practice

1 Circle the set that is greater than the other.

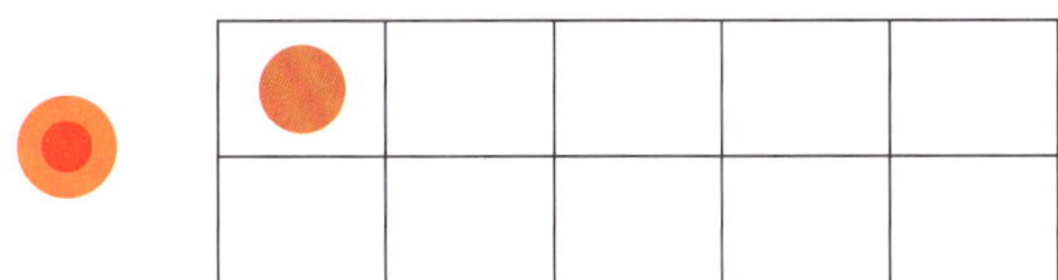

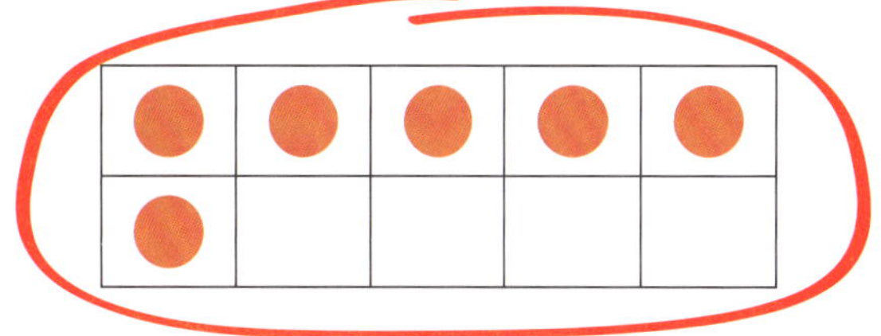

a

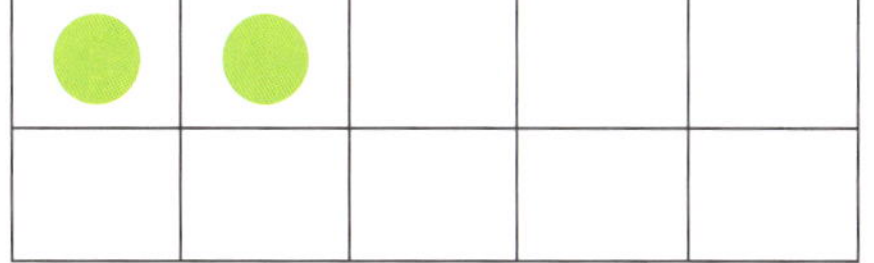

b

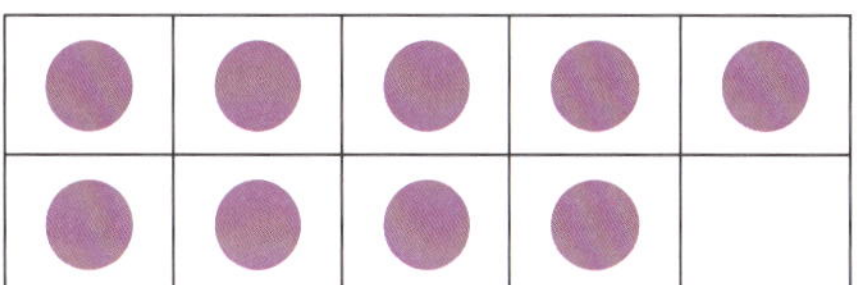

c

d

e

f

2 Draw a set that is greater than the set shown.

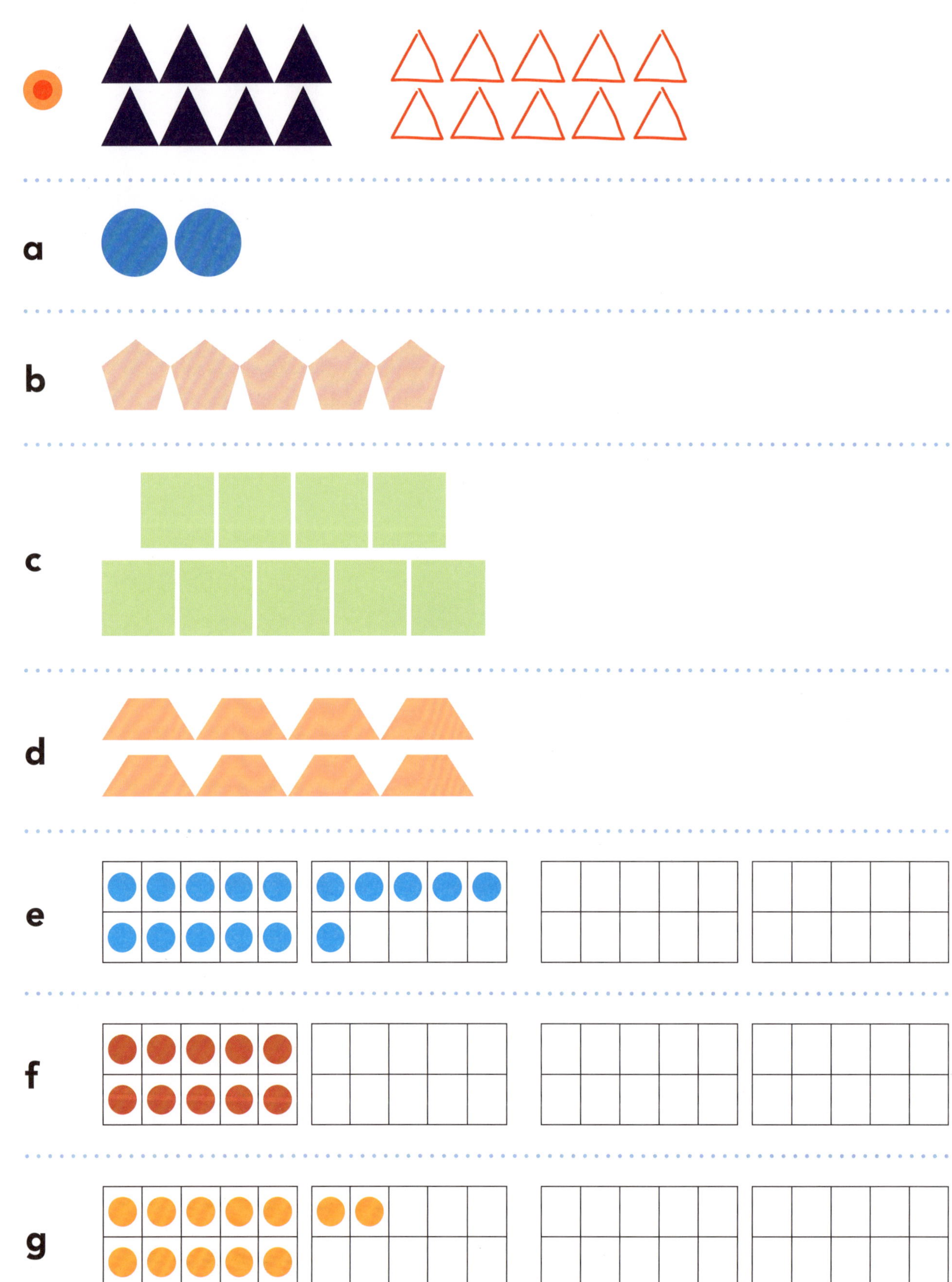

Less Than

You can tell when a set is less than another.

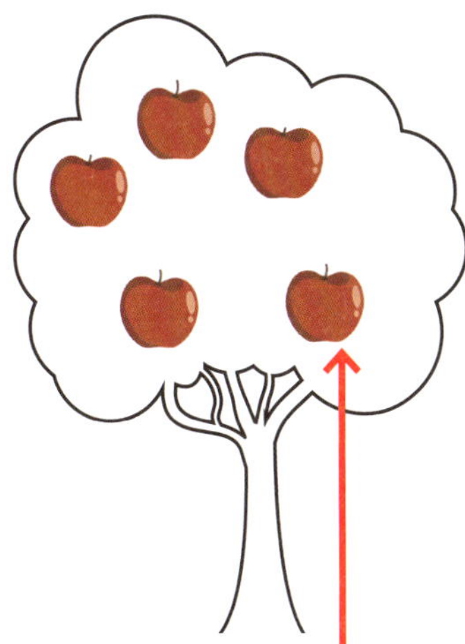

This tree has fewer apples than the other tree. The number of apples is **less than** the other tree.

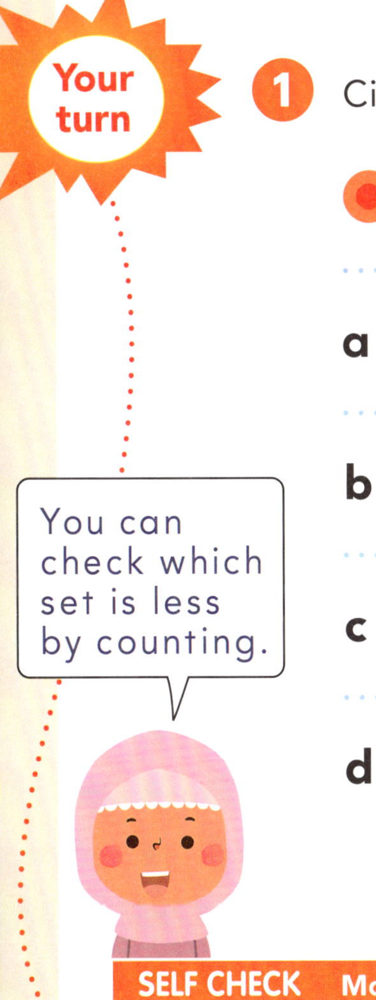

1 Circle the set that is less than the other.

a

b

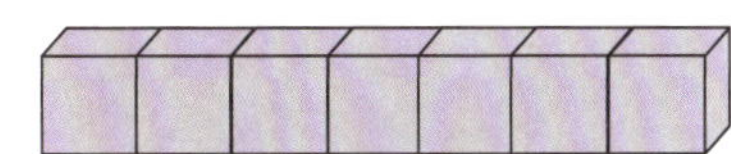

c

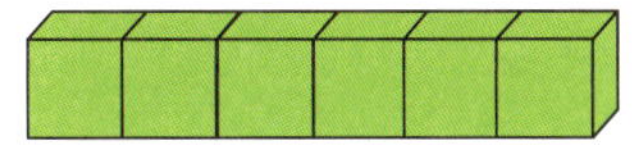

d

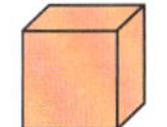

SELF CHECK Mark how you feel

Got it!	Need help...	I don't get it

Practice

1 Circle the set that is less than the other.

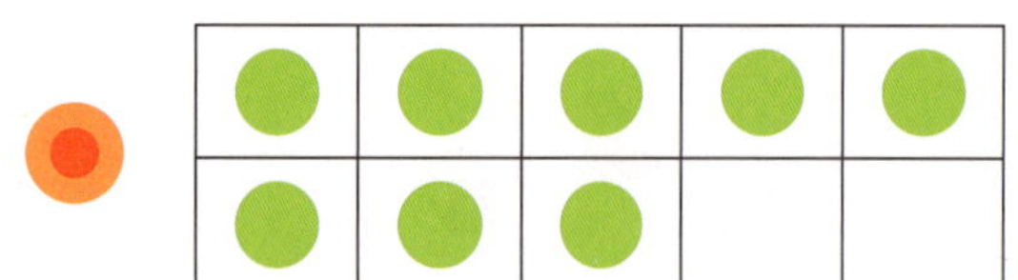

a

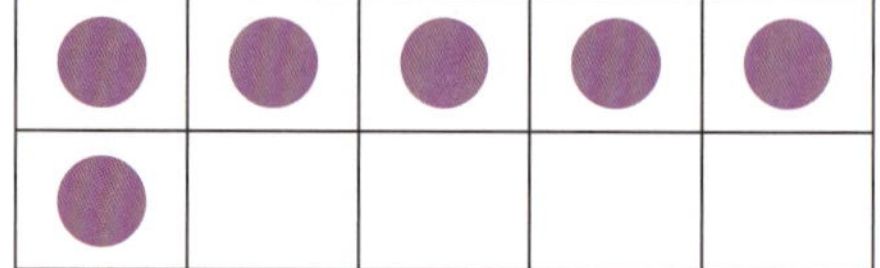

b

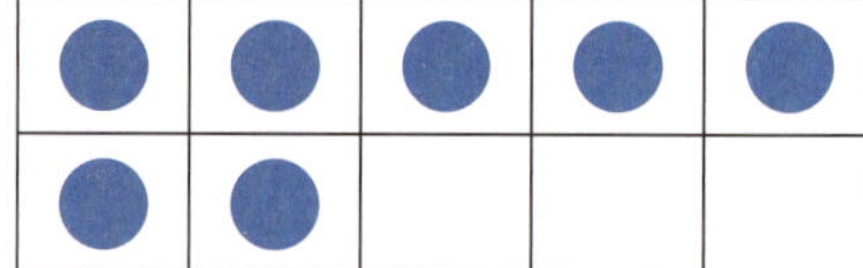

c

d

e

f

2 Draw a set that is less than the set shown.

a

b

c

d

e

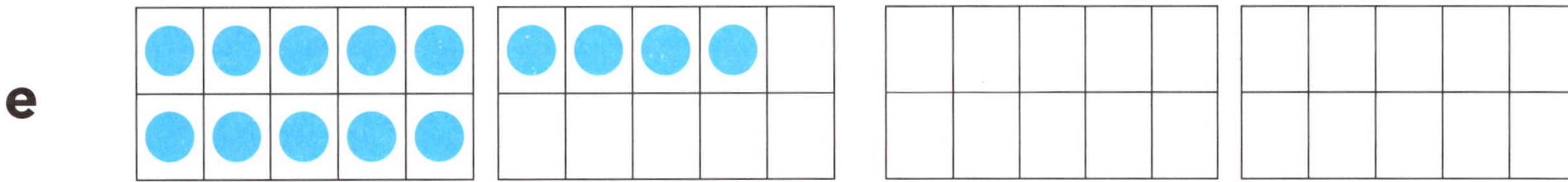

f

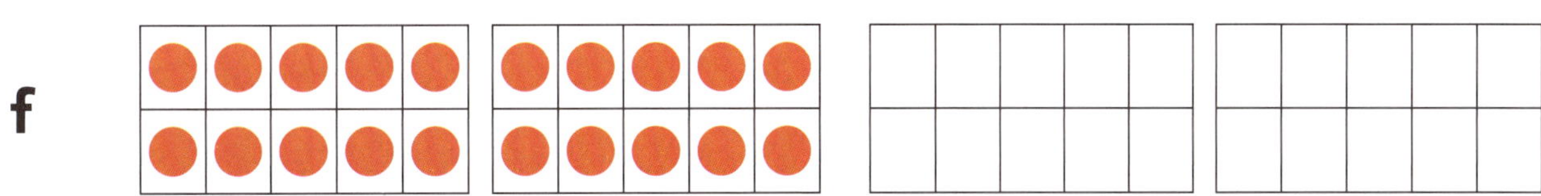

g

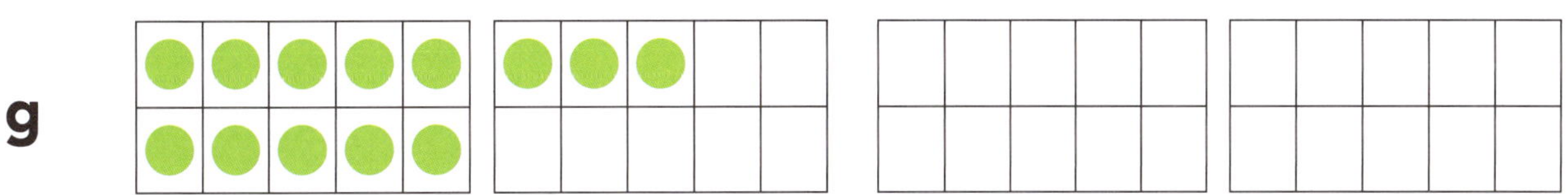

Equal To

You can tell when a set is equal to another.

Sets that are the same size are equal to each other.
Each of these sets has 3 pumpkins.

1 Connect the sets that are the same size.

Equal to means there is the same number in both groups.

SELF CHECK Mark how you feel

Got it!	Need help...	I don't get it
 ☐	 ☐	☐

Practice

1 Draw dots to show an equal set.

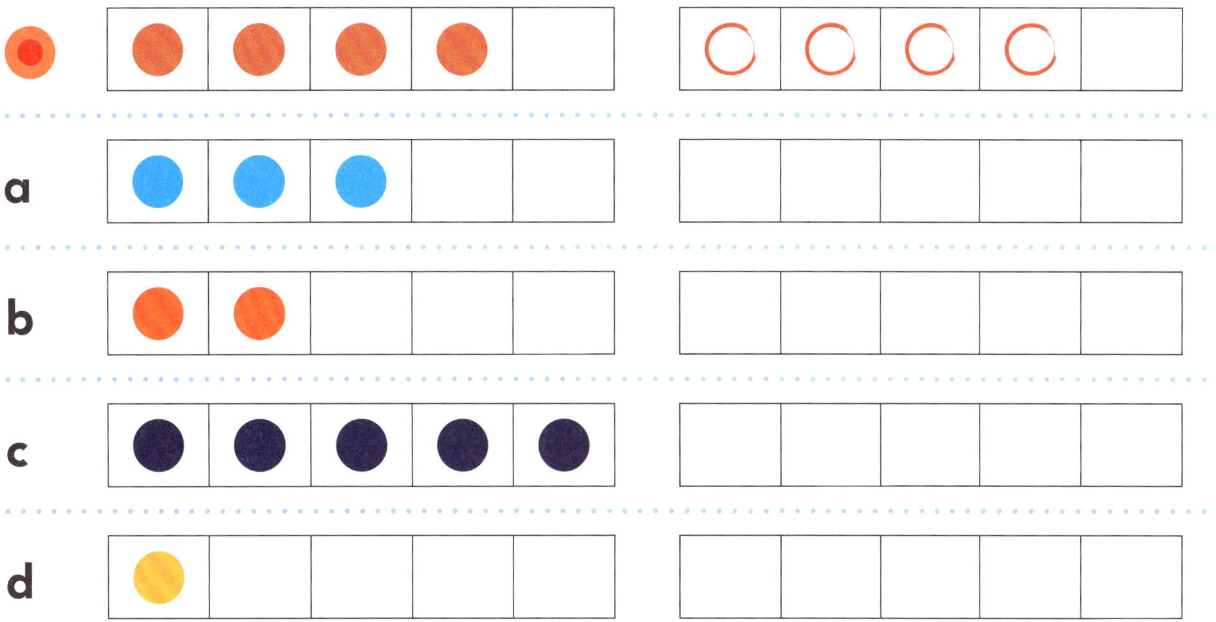

2 Circle the set that is equal to the first set.

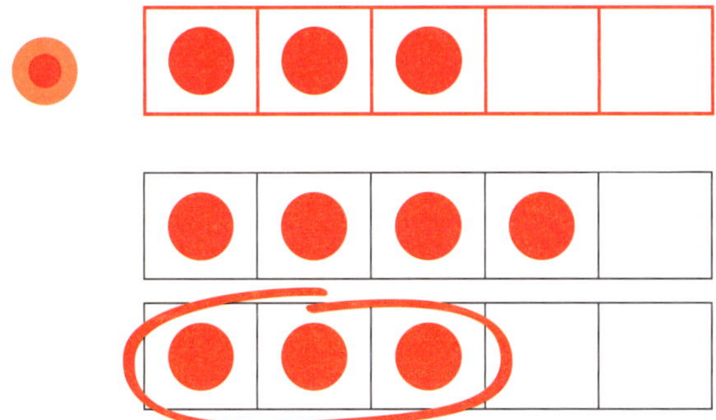

a

c

b

d

3 Draw a set that is equal to the set shown.

a

b

c

4 Draw dots to show an equal set.

a

b

c

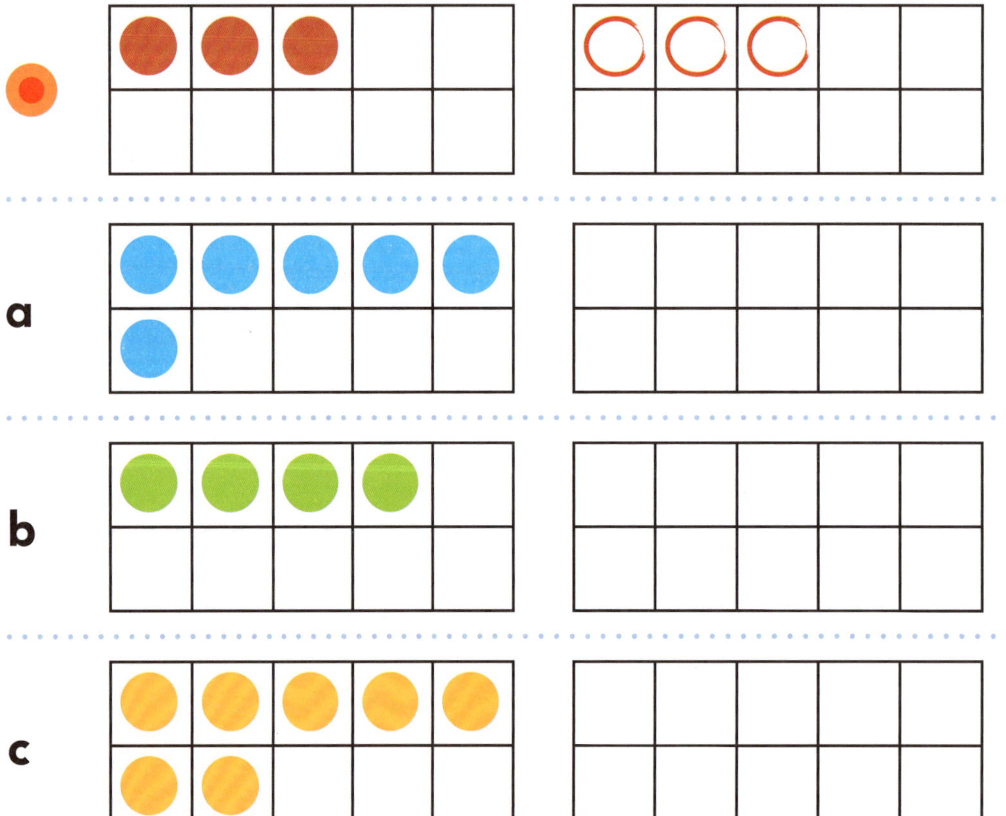

Written Numerals

You can compare numbers.

You can use the words *more than*, *equal to*, and *less than* to compare numbers.

1 Write the number of objects in each set. Circle the number that is less.

a

b

c

The bigger one is *more than*. The smaller one is *less than*. The one with the same is *equal to*.

SELF CHECK Mark how you feel

Got it! | Need help... | I don't get it

Practice

1 Write the number of objects in each set. Circle the number that is more.

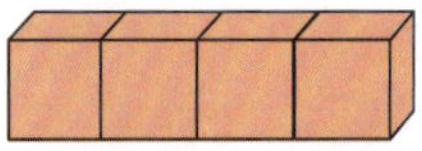

- 4
- (11) 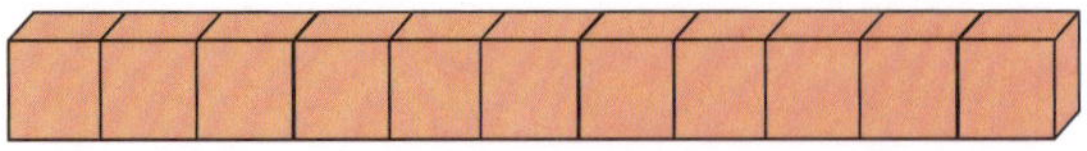

a

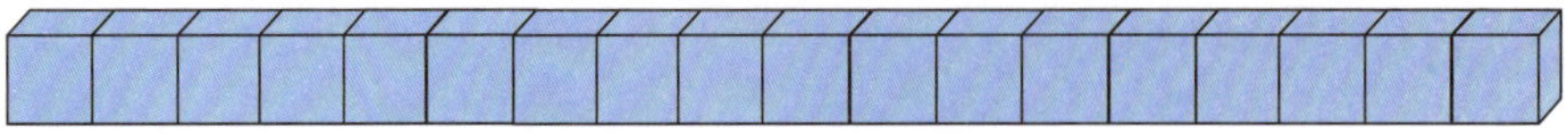

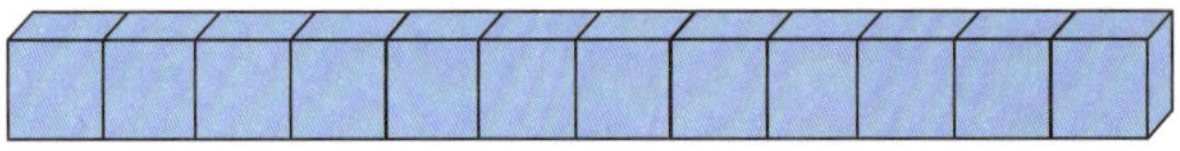

b

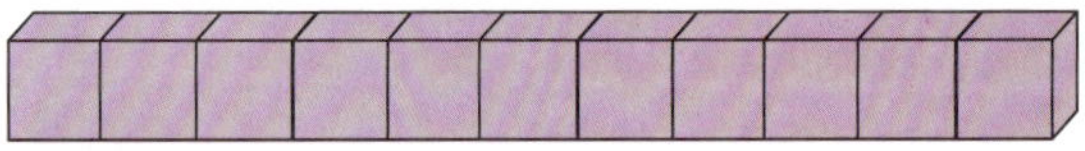

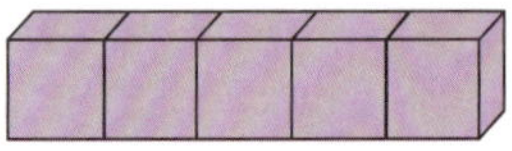

c

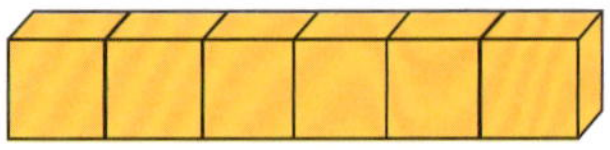

2 Compare each set of numbers. Circle the one that is less.

- 6 and (5)

a 8 and 9

b 5 and 1

c 7 and 4

d 9 and 2

3 Compare each set of numbers. Underline the one that is more.

- 14 and <u>19</u>

a 15 and 18

b 12 and 17

c 4 and 15

d 19 and 14

4 Compare each set of numbers. Circle them if they are equal. Cross them out if they are not equal.

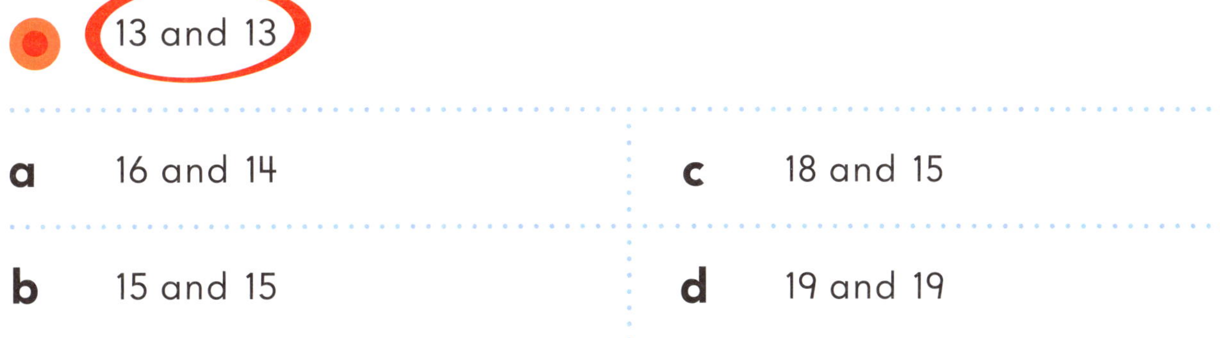

- 13 and 13

a 16 and 14

b 15 and 15

c 18 and 15

d 19 and 19

5 Compare each set of numbers. Circle the words that complete each sentence.

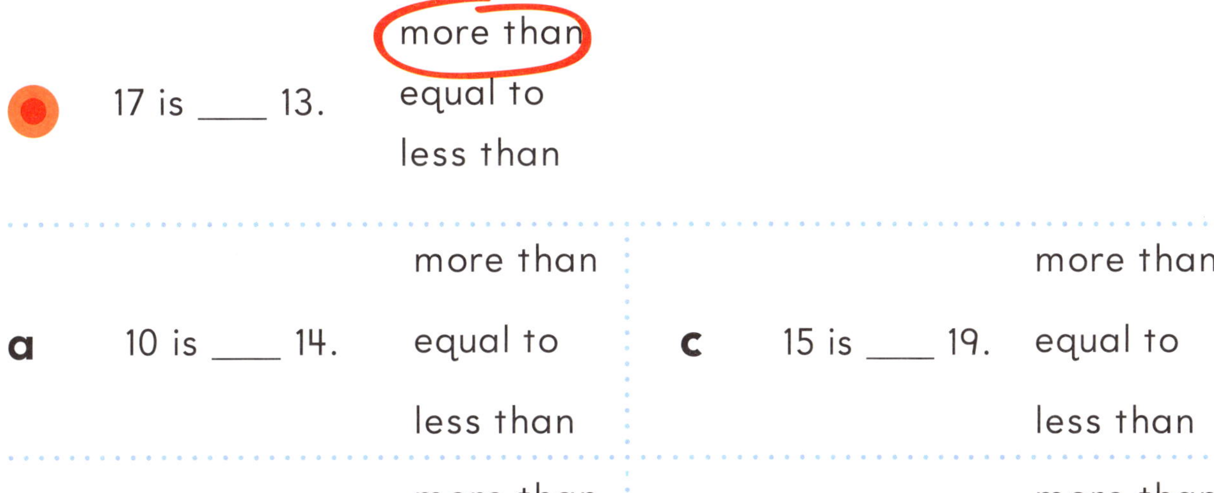

- 17 is ____ 13. more than / equal to / less than

a 10 is ____ 14. more than / equal to / less than

b 16 is ____ 16. more than / equal to / less than

c 15 is ____ 19. more than / equal to / less than

d 13 is ____ 12. more than / equal to / less than

Compare Numbers Review

1 Draw a set that is more than the set shown.

a

b

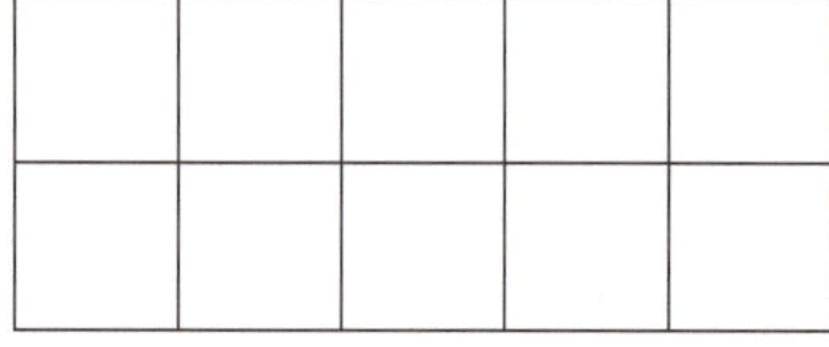

c

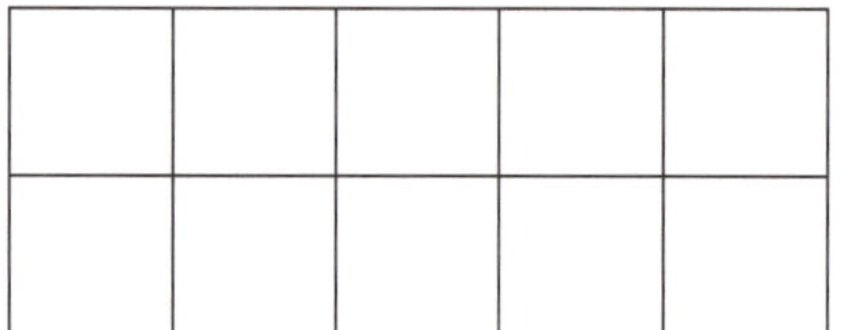

2 Circle the set that is equal to the first set.

a

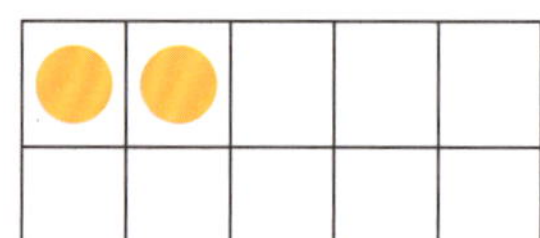

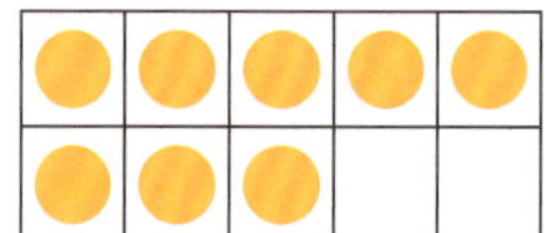

b

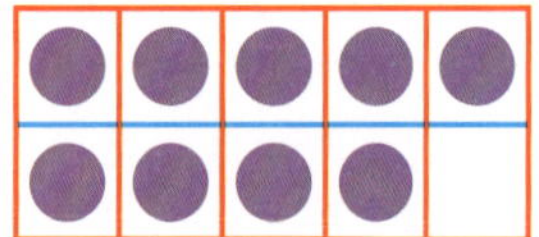

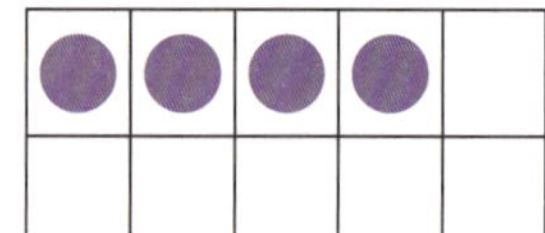

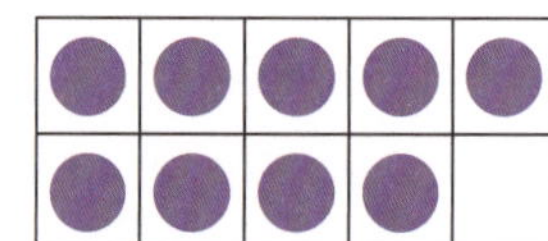

c

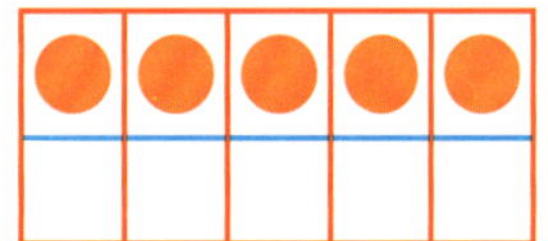

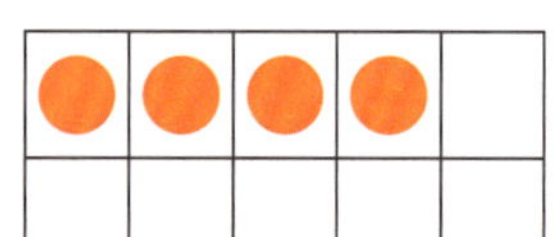

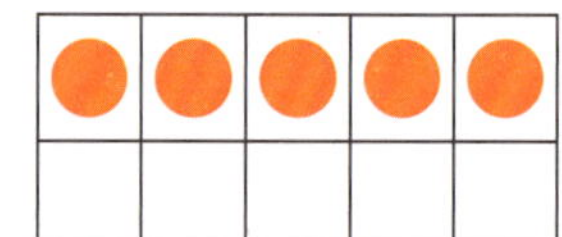

3 Circle the set that is less than the other set.

a

b

Review

4 Compare each set of numbers. Circle the words that complete the sentence.

a 20 is ____ 16. more than / equal to / less than

c 19 is ____ 19. more than / equal to / less than

b 12 is ____ 18. more than / equal to / less than

d 15 is ____ 10. more than / equal to / less than

5 Draw a set that is less than the set shown.

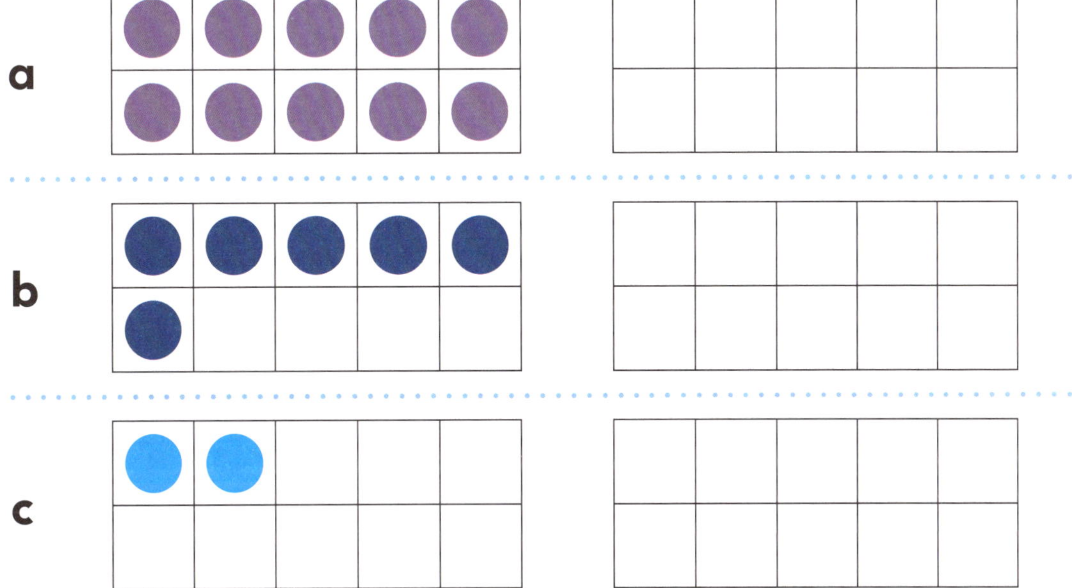

a

b

c

6 Write each number. Circle the number that is more.

a

b

c

Add 1

You can add 1 to a number by counting on.

There are 3 flowers.

If you add 1 more flower, there will be 4.

This is also called **adding** 1.

1 Count the items. Draw 1 more and count on. Write the new number.

      6

a   ____

b    ____

c  ____

d  ____

SELF CHECK	Mark how you feel	
Got it!  ☐	Need help...  ☐	I don't get it  ☐

Practice

1 Add 1 more to each ten frame. Write the new number.

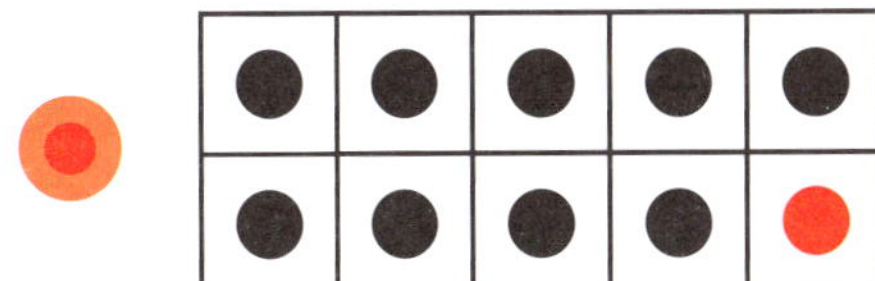
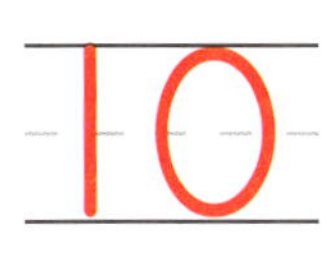

a 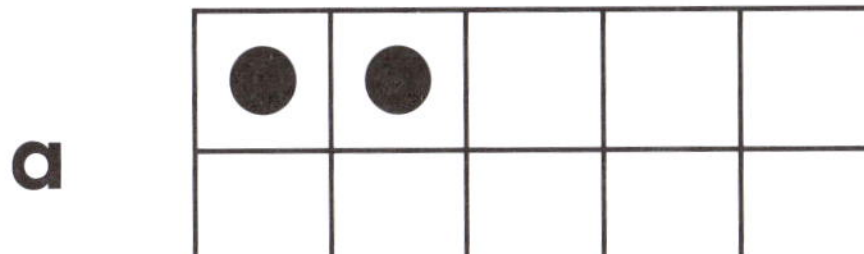

b 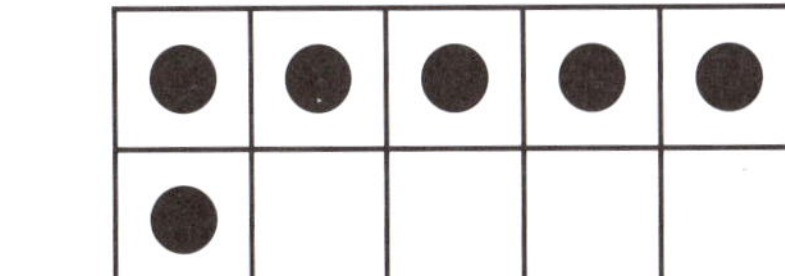

c 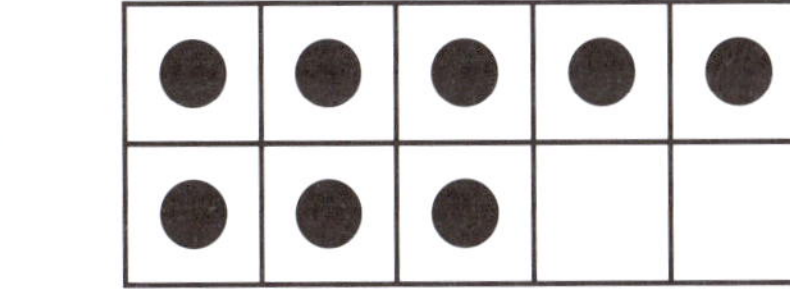

d

2 Draw a picture to show each number. Then, draw 1 more. Write the new number.

 5  

a 12

b 15

c 18

3 Trace each frog's jumps. Add 1 more jump. Write the new number.

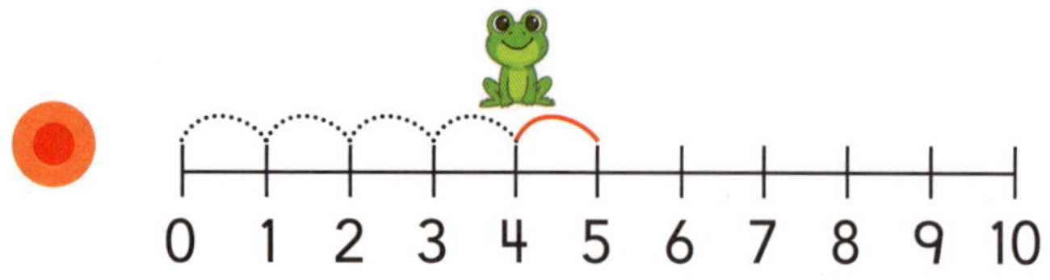

a 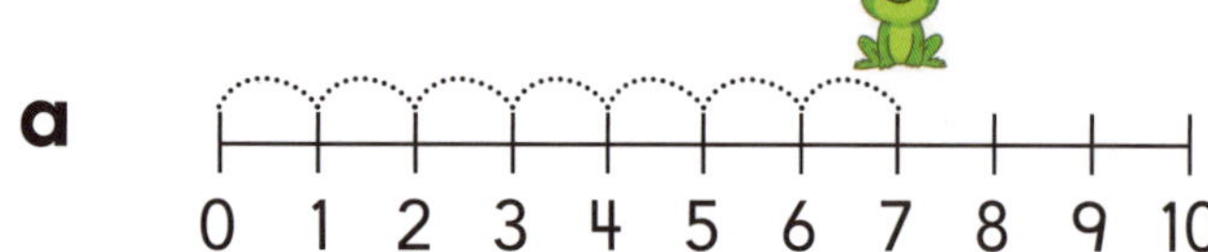

b 

c 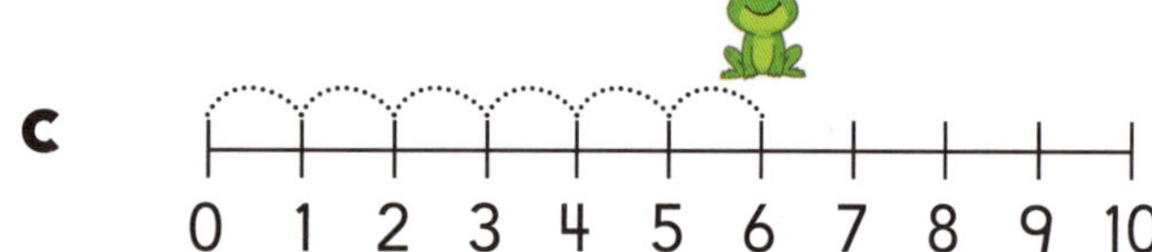

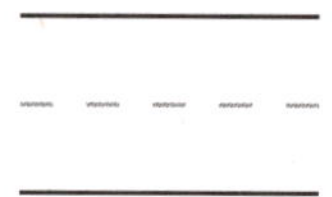

4 Count the dots. Draw 1 more. Write the new number.

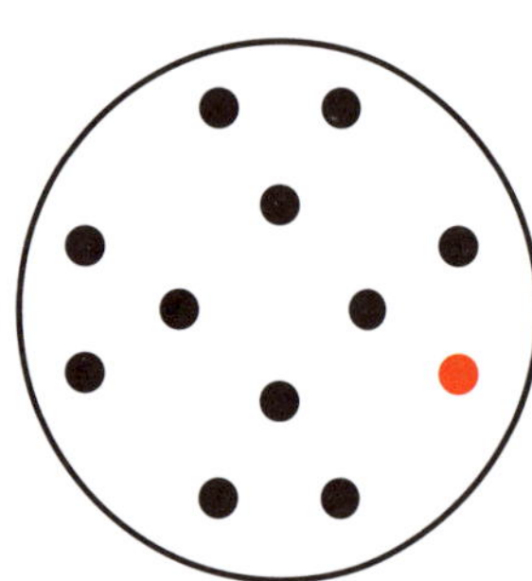

b 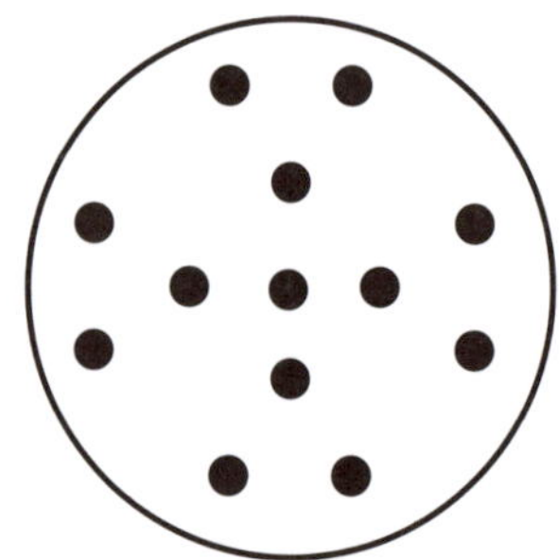

a 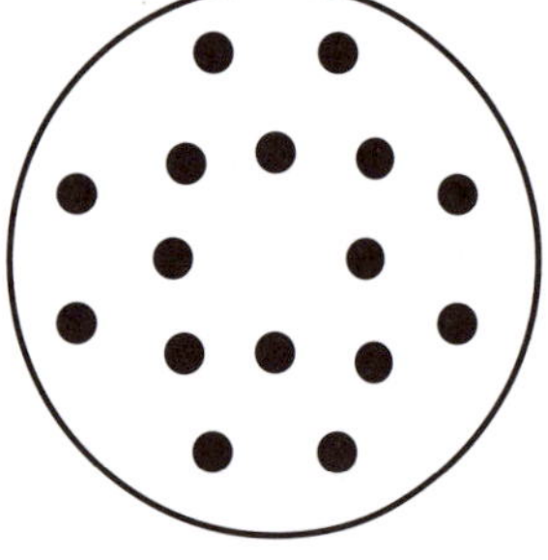

c 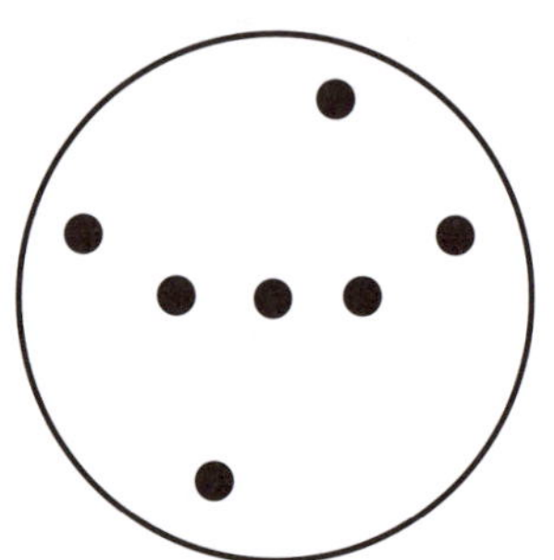

Add 2 Groups

You can add 2 groups together.

Kayla had 4 apples, then she picked 3 more.

Now, she has 7 apples.

4 apples and 3 more apples are 7 apples.

1 Color the squares to match each sentence.

● 2 and 2 is 4.

a 3 and 1 is 4.

b 1 and 4 is 5.

c 1 and 1 is 2.

d 1 and 2 is 3.

When you add 2 groups together, it makes a bigger group!

SELF CHECK Mark how you feel

Got it!	Need help...	I don't get it
 ☐	 ☐	 ☐

Practice

1. Draw lines to make each number bond true.

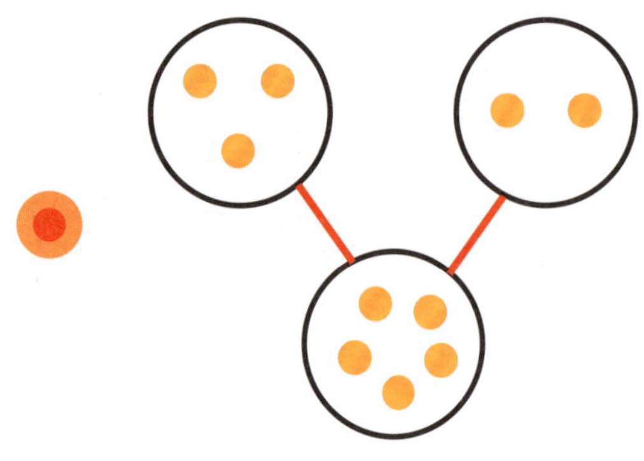

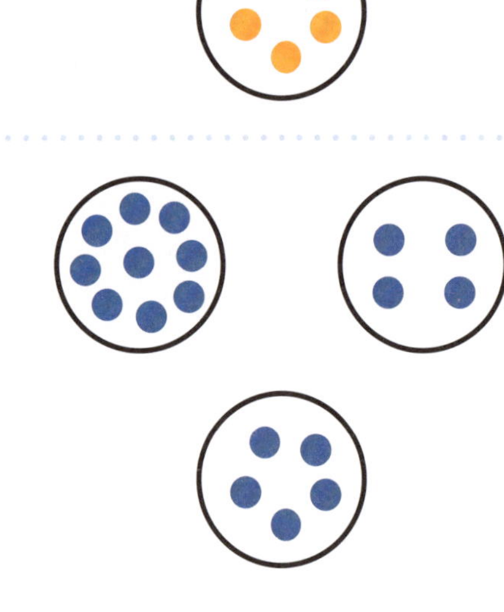

b

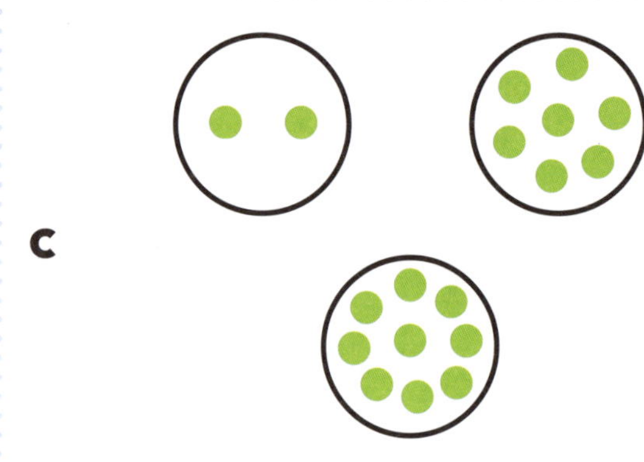

a

c

2. Color the squares to match each sentence.

6 and 3 is 9.

c 1 and 6 is 7.

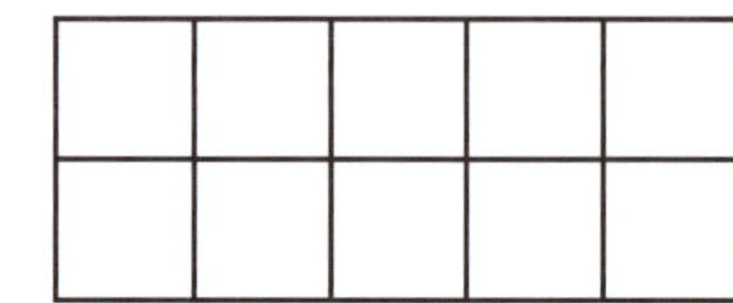

a 5 and 4 is 9.

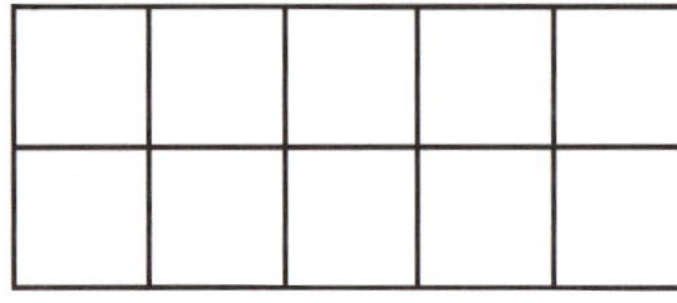

d 4 and 3 is 7.

b 3 and 7 is 10.

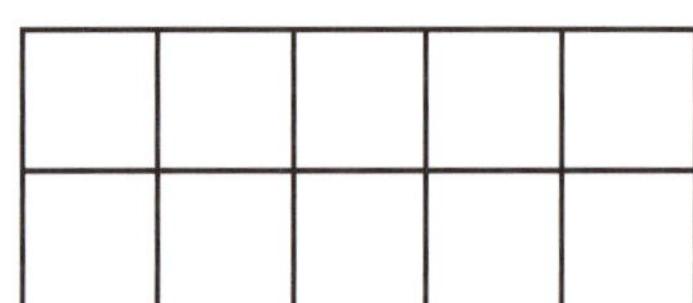

e 2 and 8 is 10.

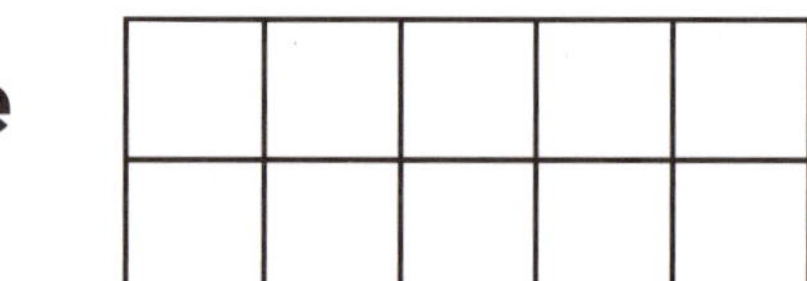

3 Draw lines to make each number bond true.

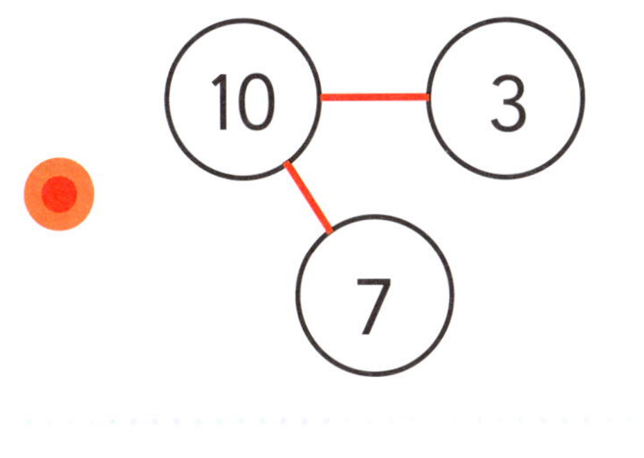

b 3 4 7

a

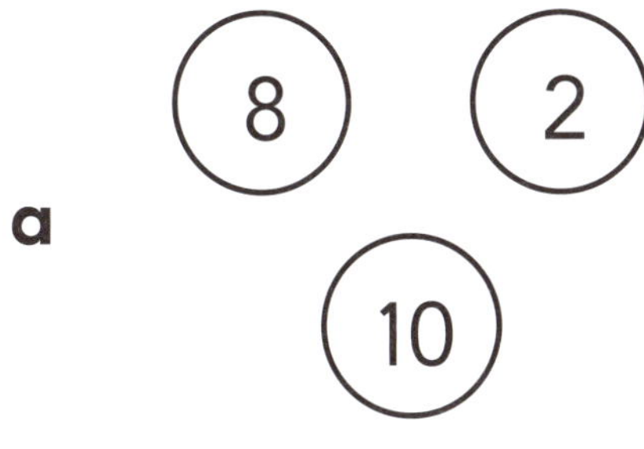

c 8 4 4

4 Add the numbers. Write the total. Draw pictures to match.

2 and 1 make 3. 

a 4 and 2 make ______.

b 2 and 5 make ______.

c 6 and 4 make ______.

d 7 and 2 make ______.

Make 10

You can combine sets to make 10.

Numbers can be combined in different ways to make 10.

3 + 7 = 10

1 + 9 = 10

That is not all! There are many other ways to make 10.

Learning how to make 10 will help you add and subtract.

4 + 6 = 10

Your turn

1 Fill each ten frame to show how to make 10. Use two colors. Then, complete the sentence.

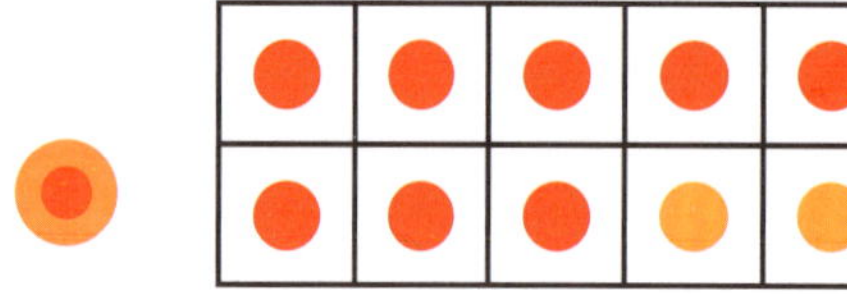

8 and 2 make 10.

a 

6 and ______ make 10.

b 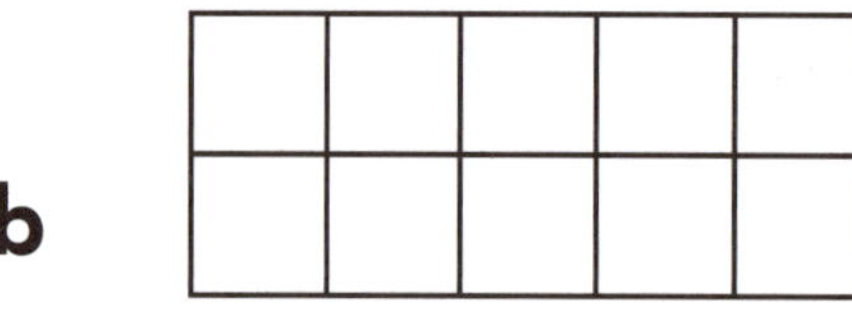

9 and ______ make 10.

c 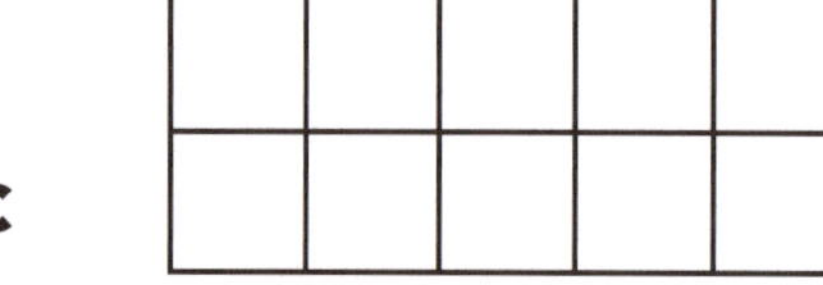

10 and ______ make 10.

SELF CHECK Mark how you feel

Got it!	Need help...	I don't get it

Practice

1 Write the missing number to make 10.

● 2

a

b

c

d

e

f

g

h

i

2 Color the circles to show the 2 sets. Use two colors.

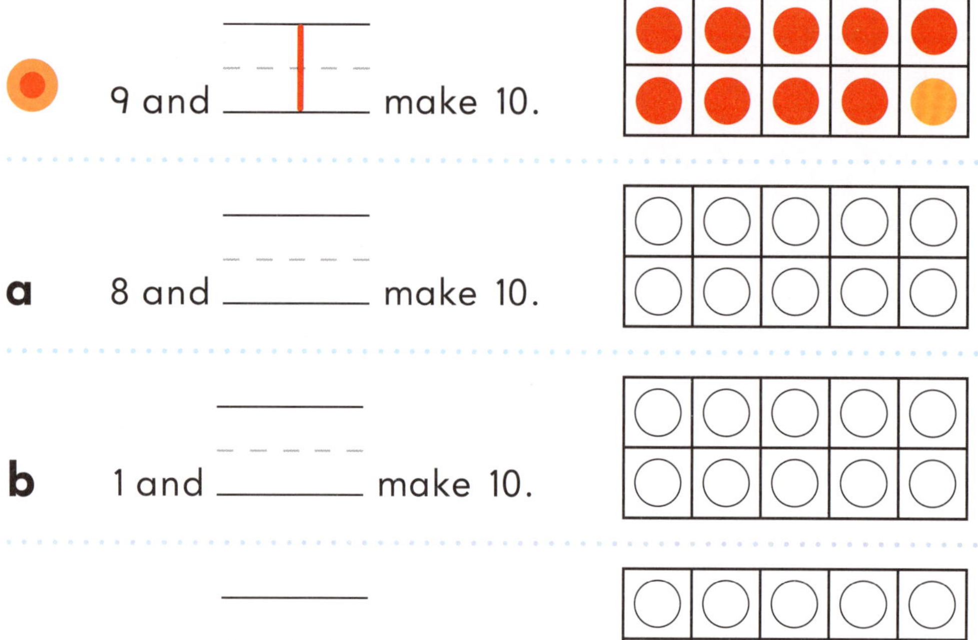

- (example) 9 and 1 make 10.
- **a** 8 and ______ make 10.
- **b** 1 and ______ make 10.
- **c** 4 and ______ make 10.

3 Write the missing number.

- (example) 4 and 6 make 10.
- **a** 1 and ______ make 10.
- **b** 10 and ______ make 10.
- **c** 5 and ______ make 10.
- **d** 4 and ______ make 10.
- **e** 2 and ______ make 10.
- **f** 9 and ______ make 10.
- **g** 6 and ______ make 10.
- **h** 8 and ______ make 10.
- **i** 7 and ______ make 10.

Fluency Within 5

You can add within 5.

Adding is combining two sets to get a bigger set.

1 2 3 4 5

When you add with fluency, you can add quickly. You can think about adding in different ways.

1 2 3 4 5

3 + 2 = 5

1 Color the circles to show the ways to make 5.

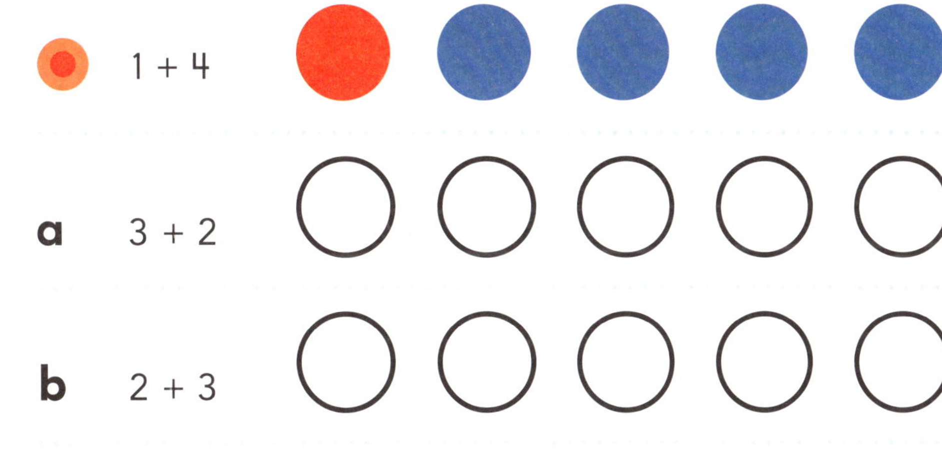

1 + 4

a 3 + 2

b 2 + 3

c 0 + 5

d 4 + 1

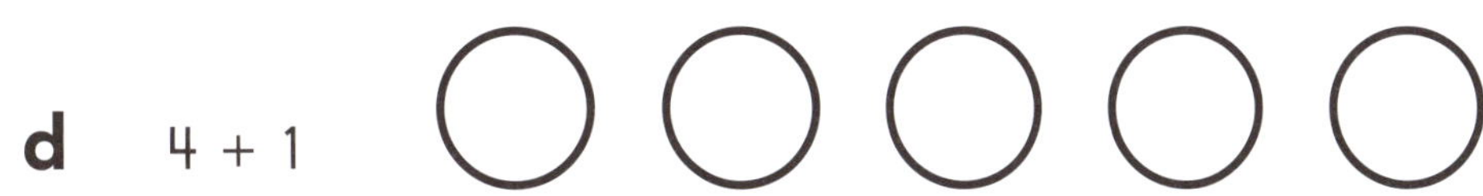

SELF CHECK Mark how you feel

Got it!	Need help...	I don't get it
☐	☐	☐

Practice

1 Draw dots to fill each frame. Write the numbers to show the math fact in the frame.

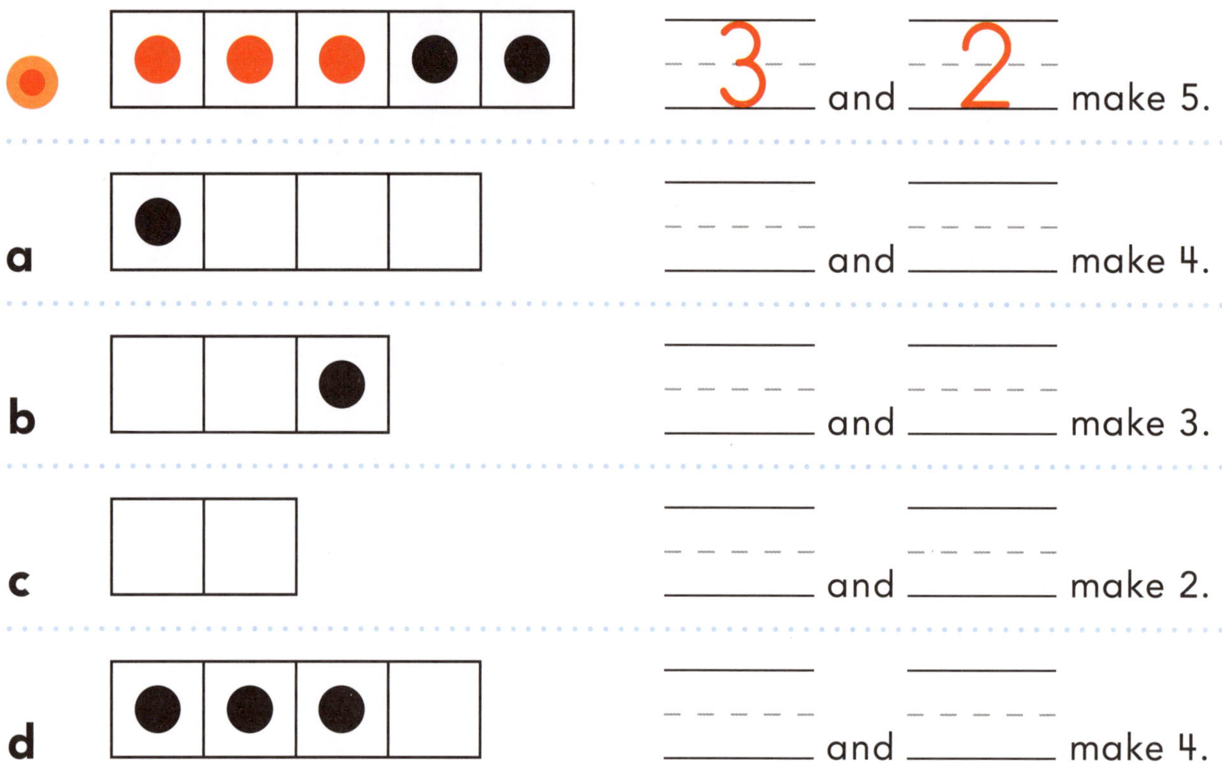

- (example) 3 and 2 make 5.
- a ____ and ____ make 4.
- b ____ and ____ make 3.
- c ____ and ____ make 2.
- d ____ and ____ make 4.

2 Connect the numbers that make 5 when added together.

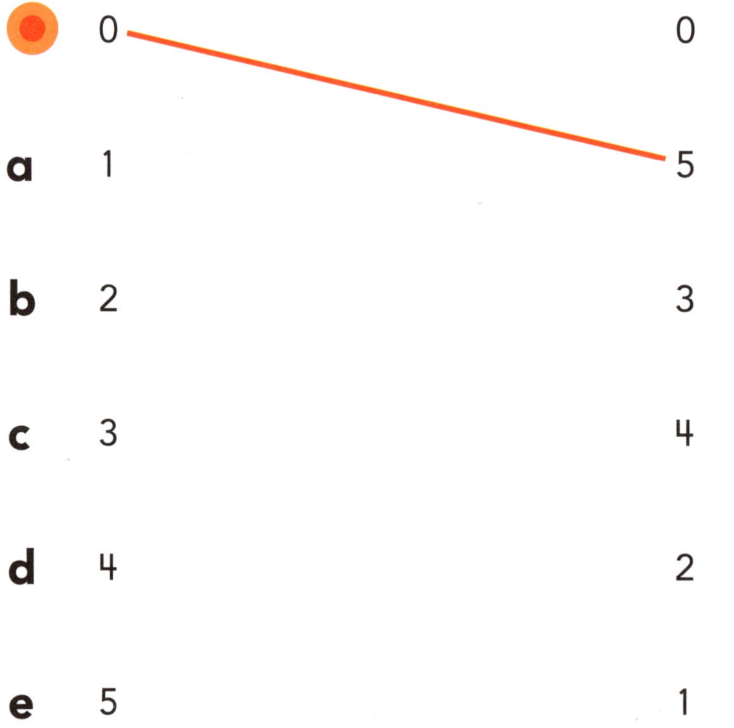

(example)	0	0
a	1	5
b	2	3
c	3	4
d	4	2
e	5	1

3 Connect the five frame to the numbers that match.

3 + 2

a 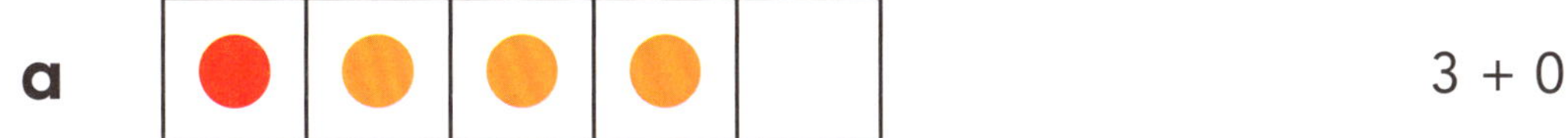

3 + 0

b

3 + 1

c

1 + 3

d

1 + 4

4 Add the numbers. Write the answers.

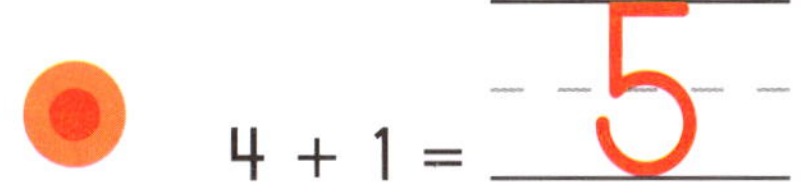

4 + 1 = 5

a 4 + 1 = ______

b 2 + 2 = ______

c 3 + 0 = ______

d 0 + 0 = ______

e 2 + 2 = ______

f 3 + 1 = ______

g 2 + 0 = ______

h 1 + 1 = ______

i 2 + 1 = ______

10 and Some More

By using 10 and some more ones, you can make the numbers 11 to 19.

Teen numbers are a set of 10 plus some more ones.

10 and 4 more makes 14.

10 + 4 = 14

1 Write the missing numbers.

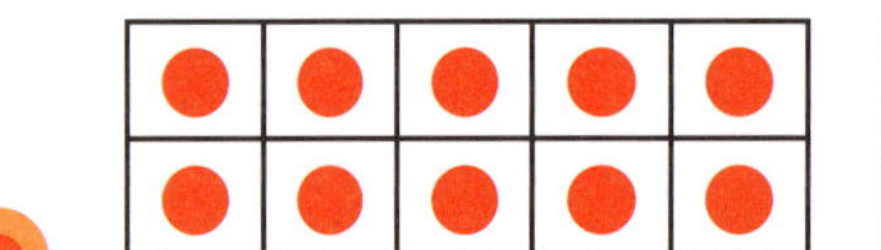

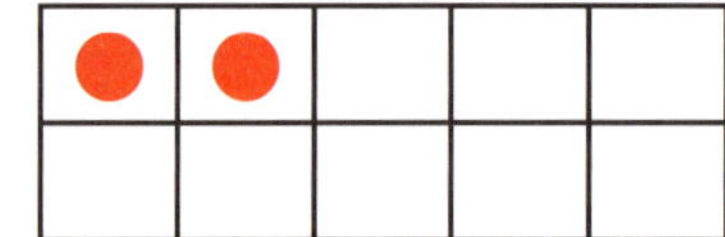

10 and 2 make 12.

a

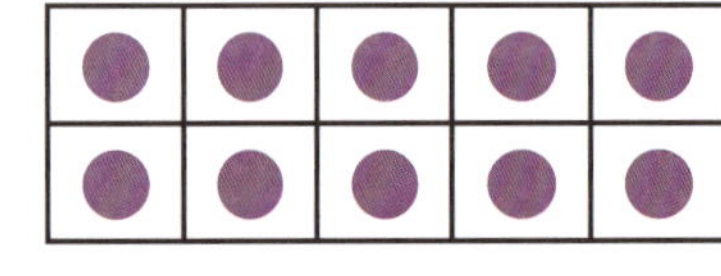

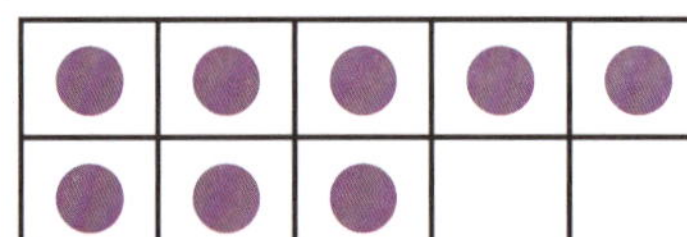

10 and ______ make ______.

In the 14, the 1 stands for the 10 and the 4 stands for some more ones.

b

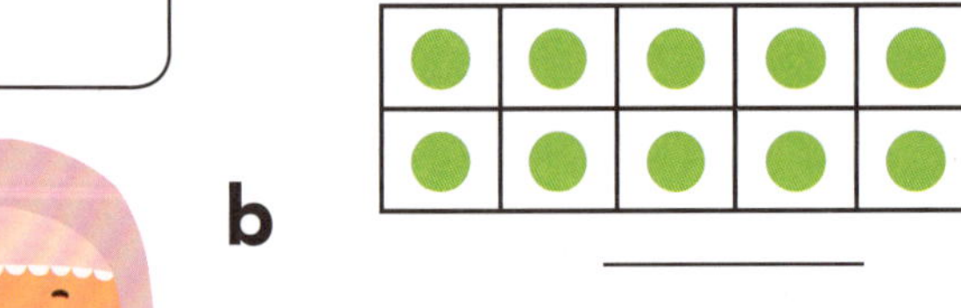

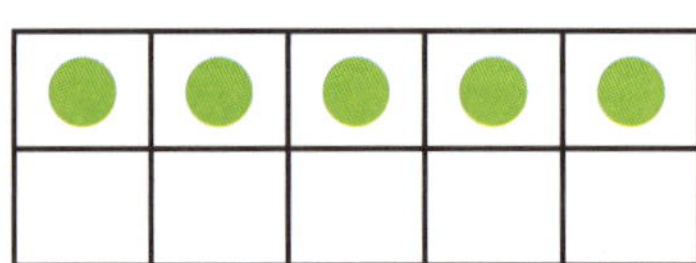

10 and ______ make ______.

Practice

1 Show the numbers in the tens frames. Write the totals.

10 and 3

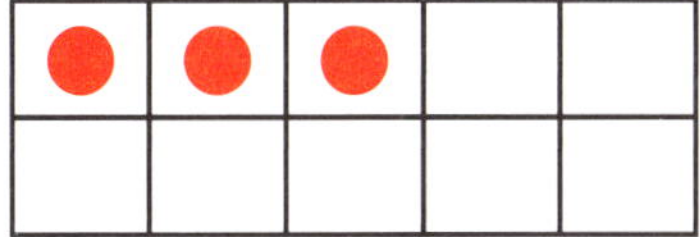

a 10 and 5

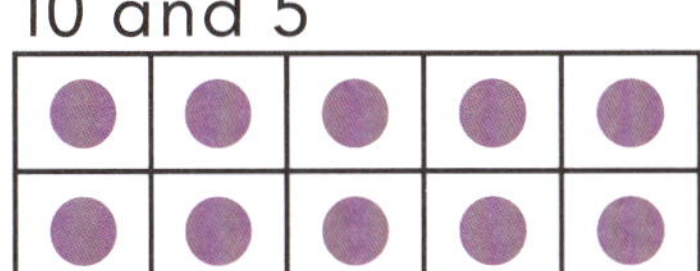

b 10 and 8

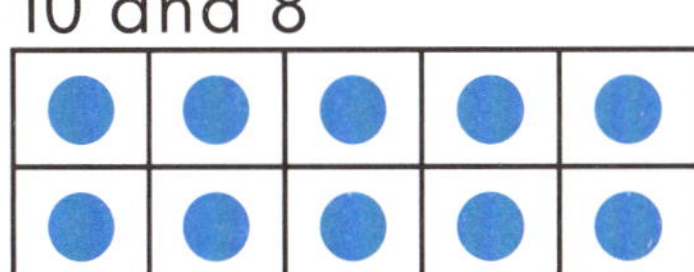

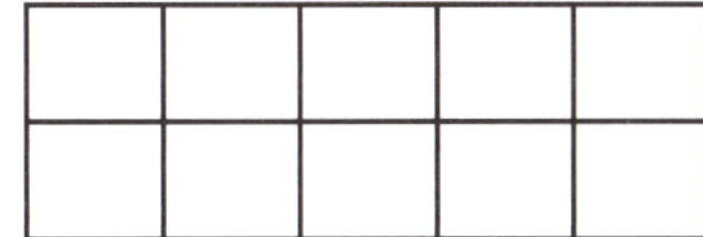

c 10 and 9

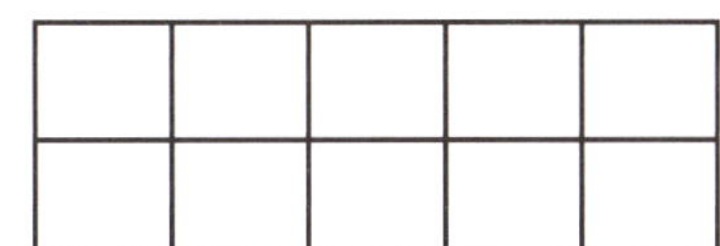

d 10 and 1

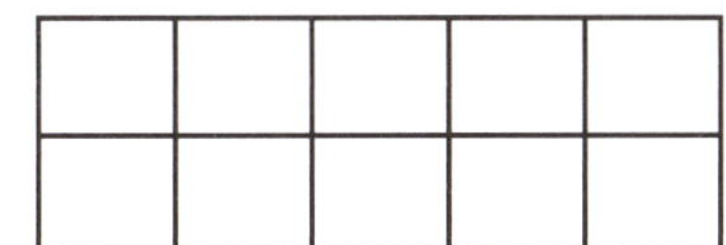

2 Each bundle stands for 10. Write the missing numbers in each equation.

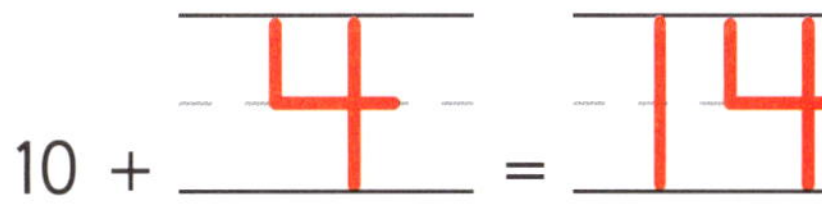

10 + 4 = 14

a

10 + ______ = ______

b

10 + ______ = ______

c

10 + ______ = ______

d

10 + ______ = ______

3 Color the two numbers that make the given number.

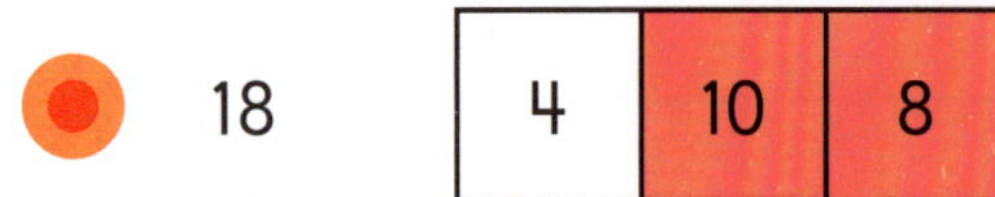

a 12

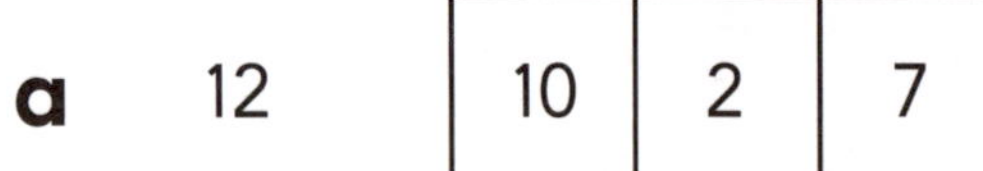

c 19

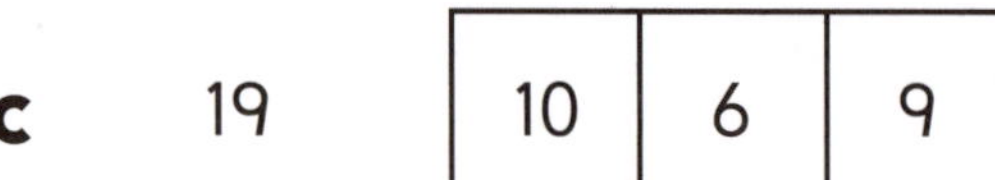

b 16

6	2	10

d 11

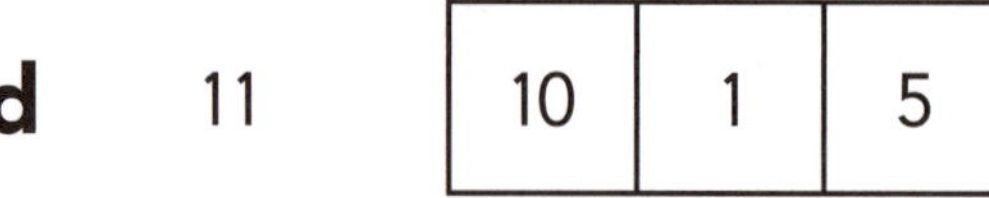

4 Write the missing number in each number bond.

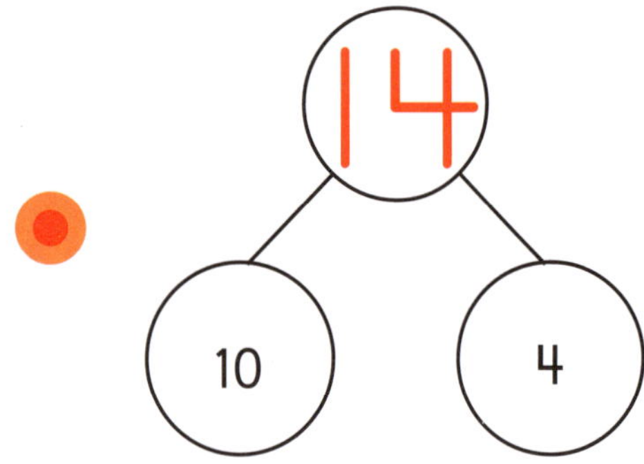

a

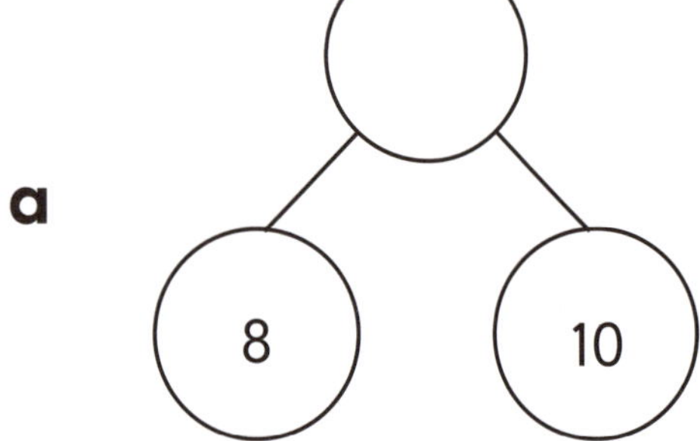

c

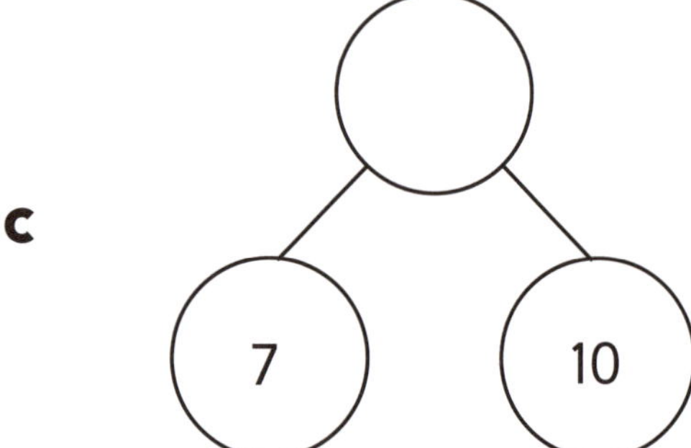

b

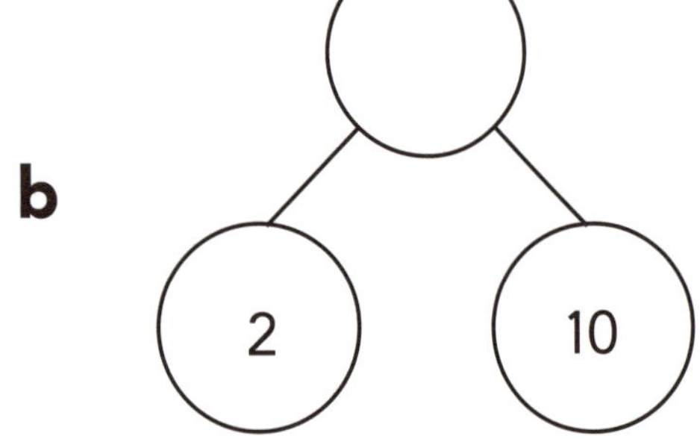

d

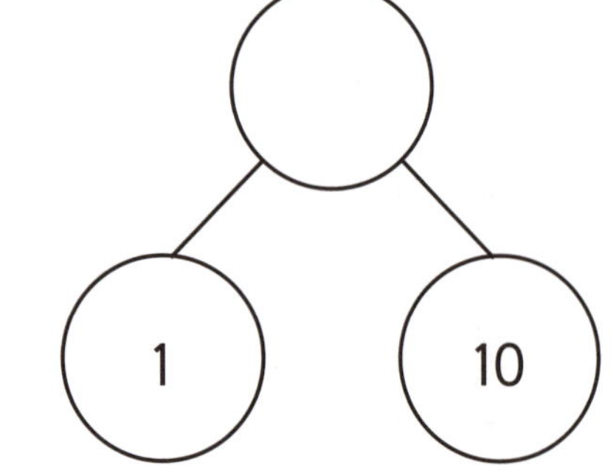

Addition Review

1 Color the squares to show each math fact.

a 1 and 6 is 7.

b 3 and 2 is 5.

c 6 and 3 is 9.

d 4 and 4 is 8.

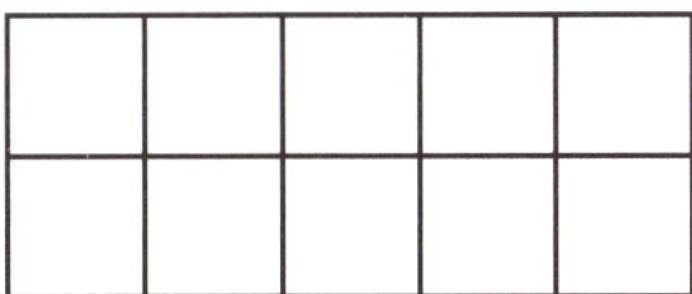

2 Draw one more on each ten frame. Write the new number.

a

b

c

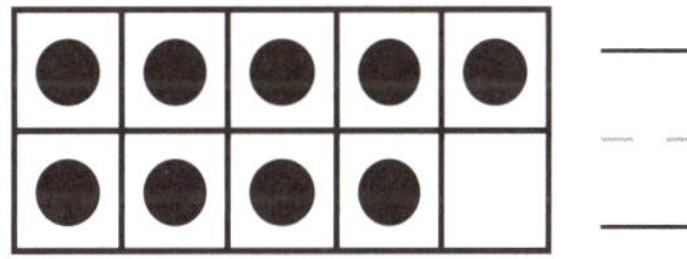

d

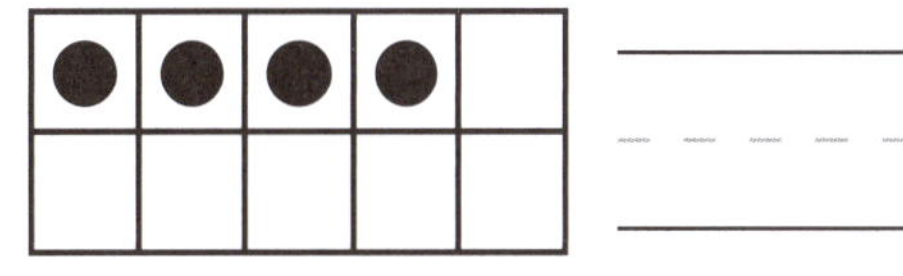

3 Add the numbers. Write the answers.

a 2 + 0 =

b 4 + 1 =

c 0 + 0 =

d 2 + 1 =

Review

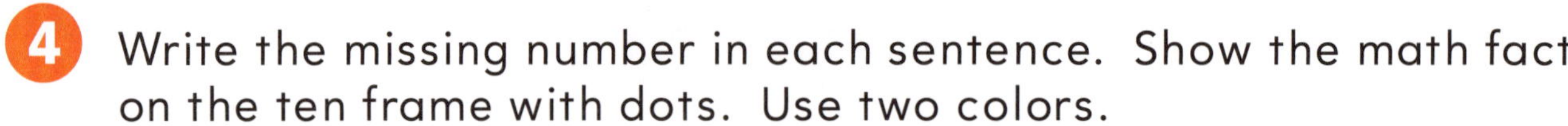

4 Write the missing number in each sentence. Show the math fact on the ten frame with dots. Use two colors.

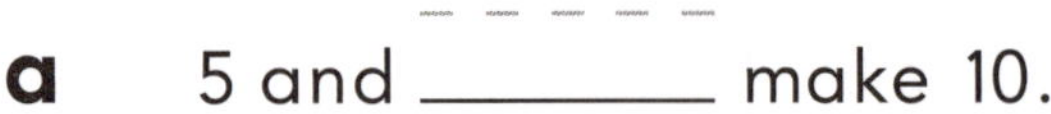

a 5 and ______ make 10.

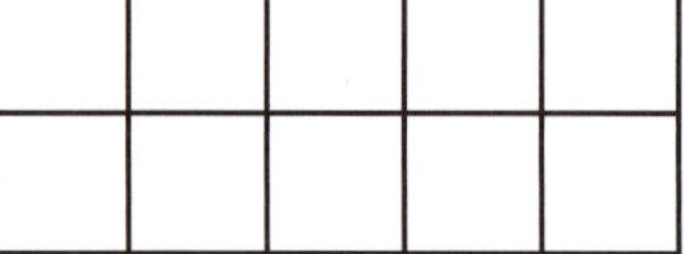

b 6 and ______ make 10.

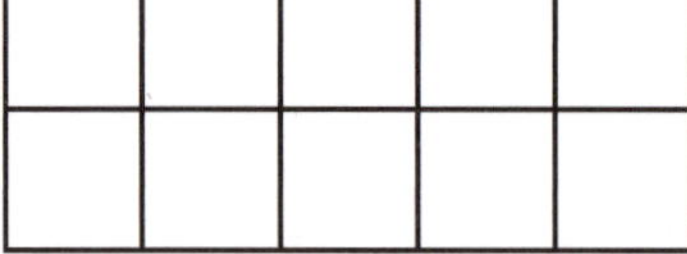

c 2 and ______ make 10.

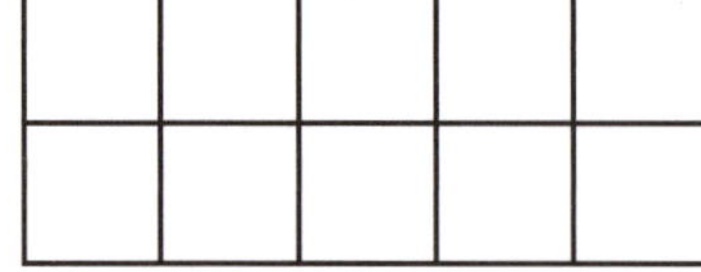

d 7 and ______ make 10.

5 Add the numbers. Write the answers.

a 5 and 4 make ______.

b 9 and 1 make ______.

c 4 and 4 make ______.

d 6 and 2 make ______.

6 Add the numbers. Write the answers.

a $0 + 3 =$ ______

b $2 + 2 =$ ______

c $3 + 1 =$ ______

d $1 + 1 =$ ______

Review

7 Write the missing number to make 10.

a ______

c ______

b ______

d ______

8 Write the missing numbers in each equation.

a 

10 + ______ = ______

b 

10 + ______ = ______

c 

10 + ______ = ______

d 

10 + ______ = ______

e 

10 + ______ = ______

Subtract 1

You can subtract 1 from a number by counting back.

There are 4 ducks, and 1 flies away.
Count backward one number.

1 Count the items. Count back 1 to subtract.
Cross off 1. Write the new number.

SELF CHECK Mark how you feel

Got it!	Need help...	I don't get it
☐	☐	☐

Practice

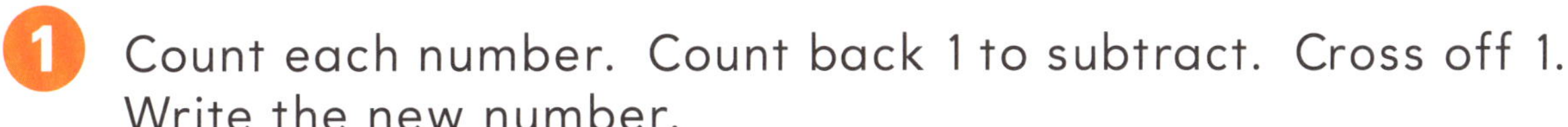

1 Count each number. Count back 1 to subtract. Cross off 1. Write the new number.

● 7

a

b

c

d

2 Count back 1 to subtract. Write the new number.

● 8

a

b

c

d

3 Draw pictures to show each number. Cross off 1 to subtract. Write the new number.

● 8 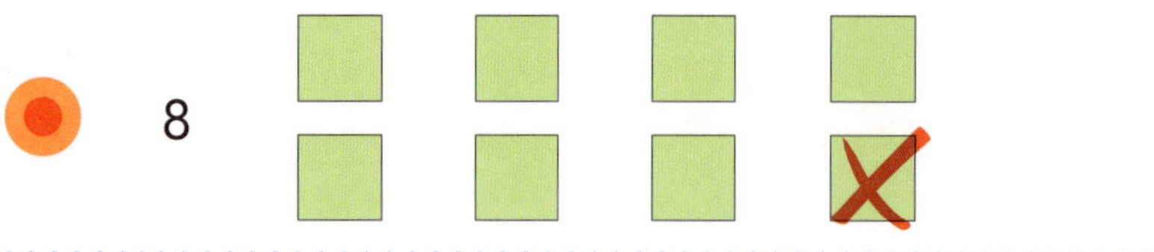 7

a 16

b 11

c 13

d 10

4 Count the dots. Cross off 1 to subtract. Write the new number.

● 13 12

a 18

b 14

c 17

d 9

Subtract 1 Group

You can subtract. You can take a small group from a larger group.

Jamal had 18 cookies. He gave 8 to his friends.

Now, he only has 10 cookies.

18 – 8 = 10

SCAN to watch video

1 Cross off the dots to show each math fact.

● 5 take away 2 is 3.

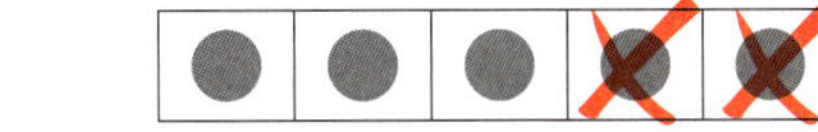

a 3 take away 1 is 2.

b 4 take away 2 is 2.

c 5 take away 4 is 1.

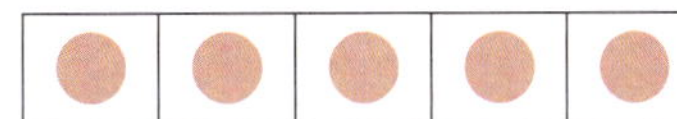

d 2 take away 2 is 0.

When you subtract, or take away, the number gets smaller.

SELF CHECK Mark how you feel

Got it!	Need help...	I don't get it
 ☐	 ☐	☐

Practice

1 Draw lines to make each number bond true.

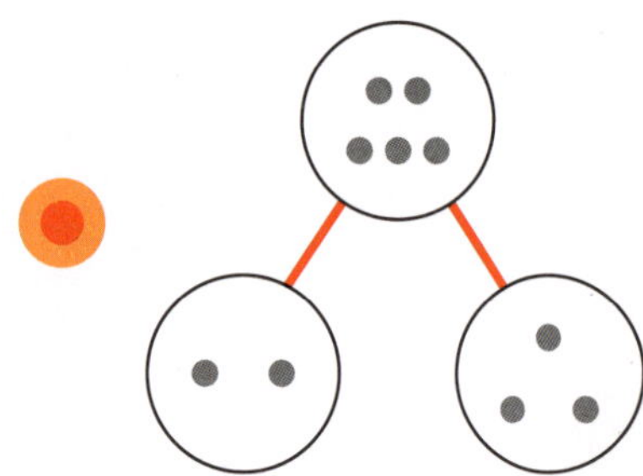

a

e

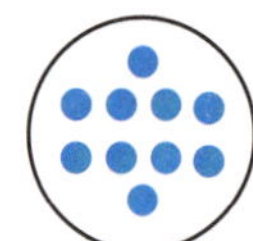

b

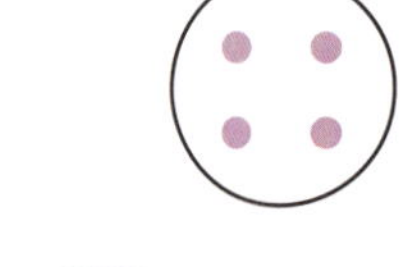

f

5

2 3

c

g

2

4 2

d

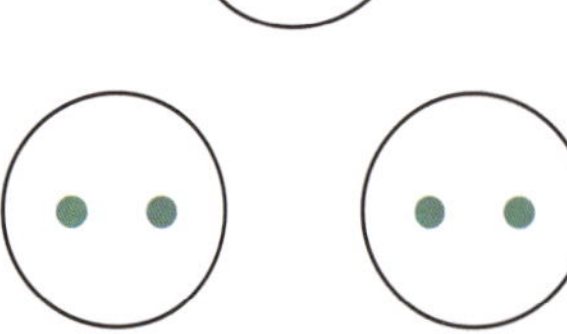

h

1

2 1

2 Cross off the dots to show each math fact.

● 5 take away 3 is 2.

a 2 take away 1 is 1.

b 4 take away 1 is 3.

c 3 take away 1 is 2.

d 5 take away 2 is 3.

3 Cross off the pictures to subtract. Write how many are left.

● 5 take away 2 — 3

a 3 take away 2 ______

b 4 take away 4 ______

c 2 take away 1 ______

d 3 take away 3 ______

Subtract Within 10

When you subtract, you take away some of the things from a group.

10 take away 8 is 2. 

Another way to say this is 10 minus 8 equals 2.

10 – 8 = 2

1 Write the missing symbol and numbers to make each equation true.

a

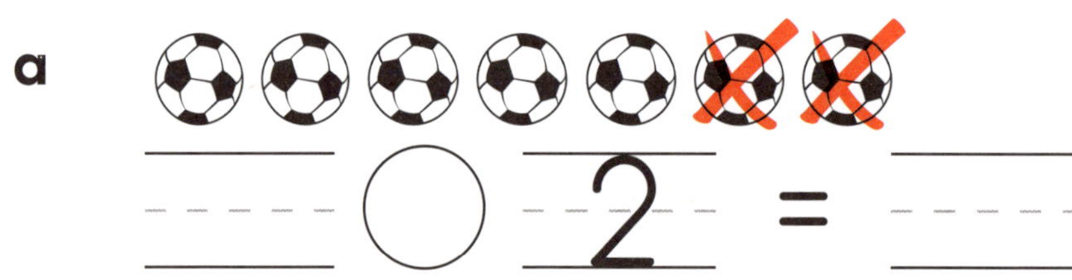

b

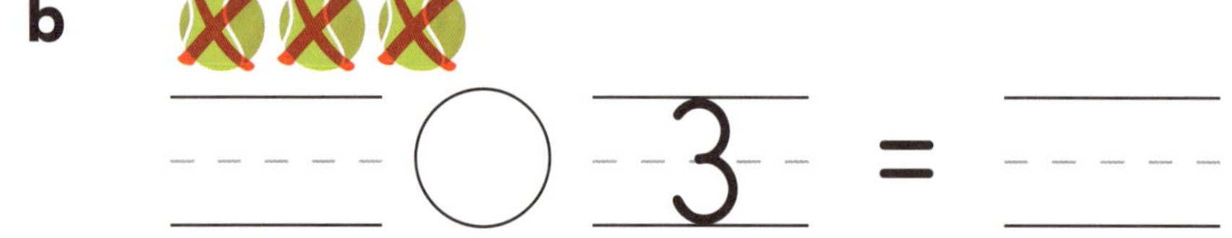

c

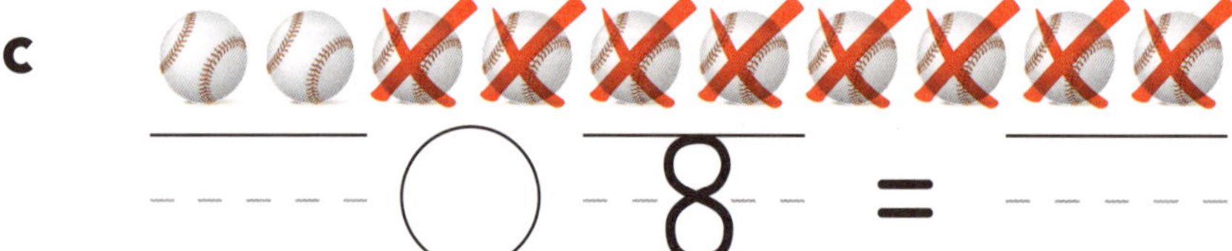

d

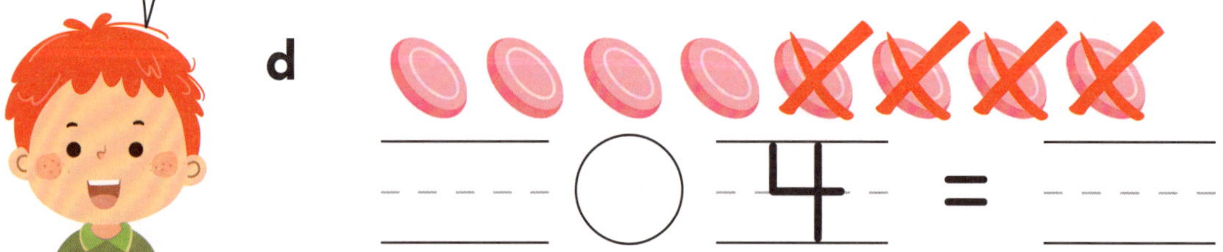

The – means *subtract* or *take away*. The = means *equals* or *is the same as*.

SELF CHECK Mark how you feel

Got it!	Need help...	I don't get it
☐	☐	☐

Practice

1 Subtract using fingers. Write the answers.

● take away 3 is 2

a take away 2 is ____

b take away 3 is ____

c take away 1 is ____

d take away 5 is ____

2 Cross off dots to subtract. Write the answers.

● take away 4 is 2

a take away 2 is ____

b take away 1 is ____

c take away 0 is ____

d take away 3 is ____

3 Write the missing numbers and symbols.

● 8 (–) 5 (=) 3

a

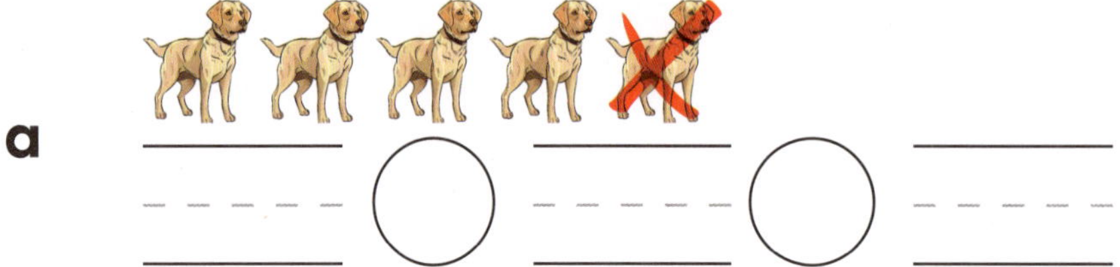

b

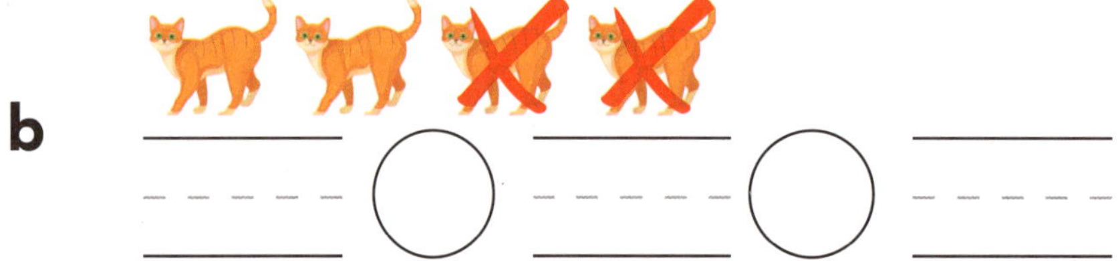

c

4 Draw pictures to subtract. Write the answer for each problem.

● $2 - 2 = 0$

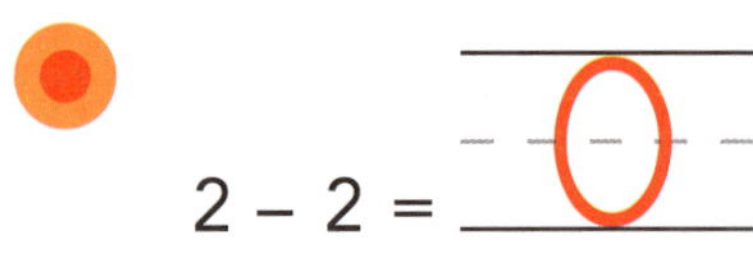

a $10 - 2 =$ ______

b $7 - 1 =$ ______

c $5 - 2 =$ ______

Fluency Within 5

You can fluently subtract within 5.

Subtracting is taking away one group from another. When you subtract with fluency, you can subtract quickly. You can think about subtracting in different ways.

$5 - 3 = 2$

1 Cross off the circles to subtract. Write the answers.

● $5 - 1 =$ 4

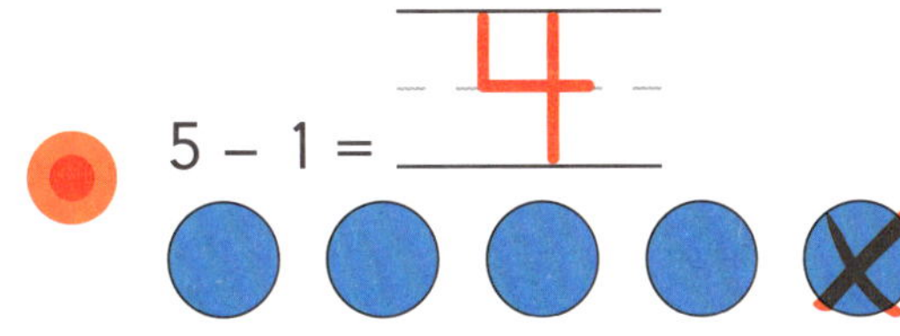

a $5 - 4 =$ ______

○ ○ ○ ○ ○

b $5 - 2 =$ ______

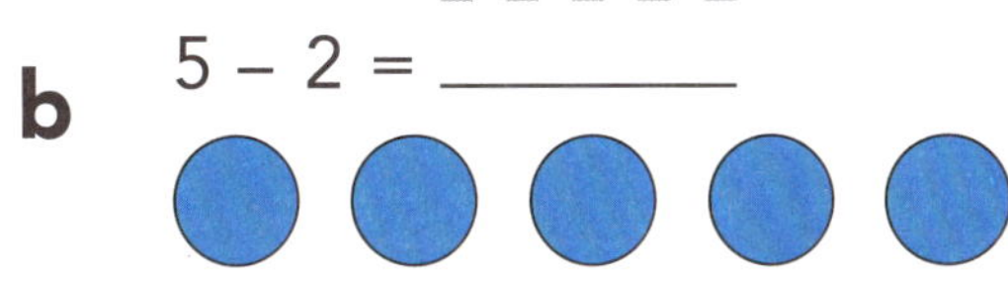

c $5 - 3 =$ ______

○ ○ ○ ○ ○

SELF CHECK	Mark how you feel	
Got it! ☐	Need help... ☐	I don't get it ☐

Practice

1 Write the missing numbers.

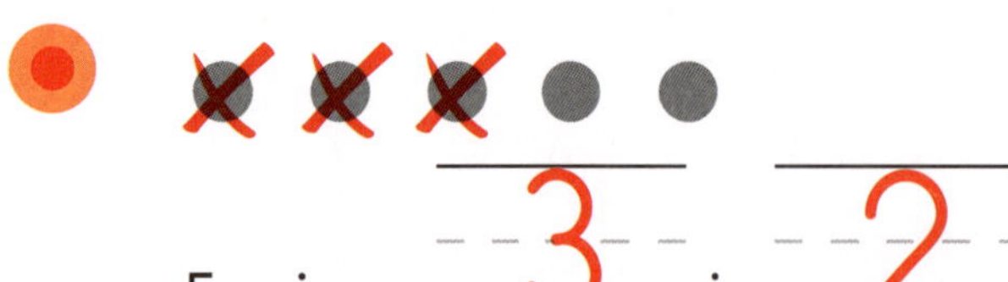

5 minus 3 is 2.

a 3 minus ______ is ______.

b 2 minus ______ is ______.

c 1 minus ______ is ______.

d 4 minus ______ is ______.

2 Draw lines to match the answers with the problems.

●	0	5 – 2
a	4	3 – 1
b	2	5 – 0
c	5	5 – 1
d	3	1 – 1

3 Draw lines to match the five frames to the expressions.

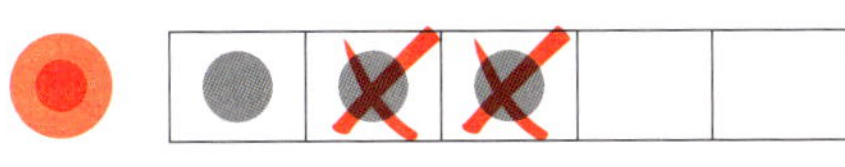

a

b

c

d

5 – 1

2 – 0

4 – 3

3 – 2

2 – 1

4 Subtract the numbers.

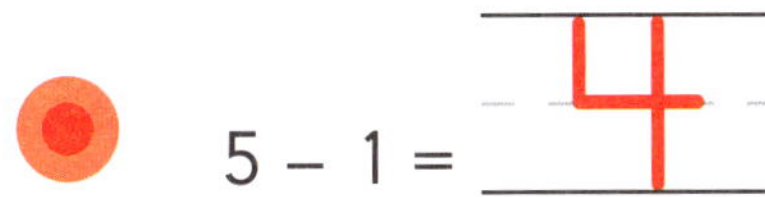

a 5 – 5 = ______

b 2 – 1 = ______

c 0 – 0 = ______

d 4 – 0 = ______

e 3 – 2 = ______

f 5 – 4 = ______

g 4 – 2 = ______

Subtract 10

You can subtract 10 from numbers 11 to 19.

Teen numbers are a set of 10 and some more ones.

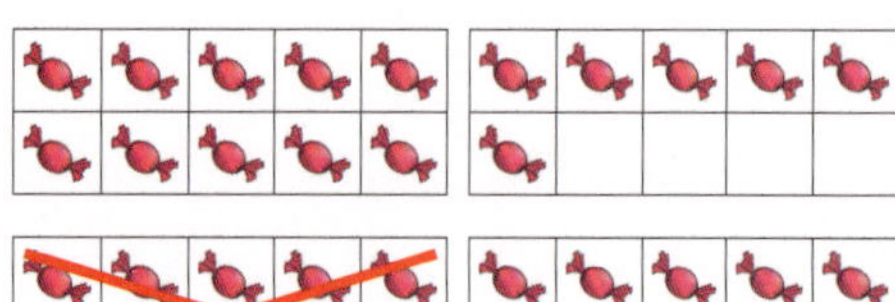

16 is 10 and 6 ones.

16 – 10 = 6

To subtract 10, you can cross off the full ten frame.

1 Write the missing numbers.

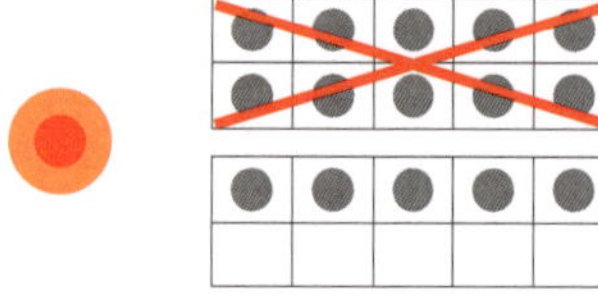

15 minus 10 is 5.

a

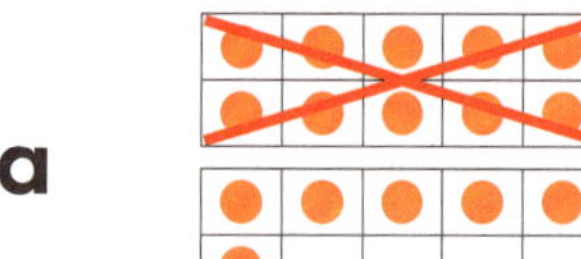

16 minus ______ is ______.

b

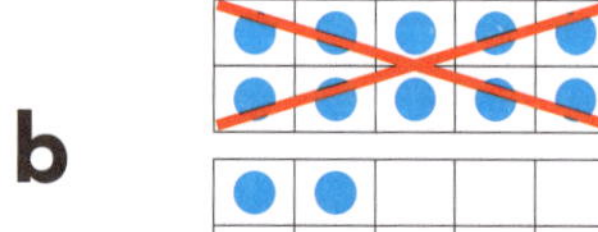

12 minus ______ is ______.

c

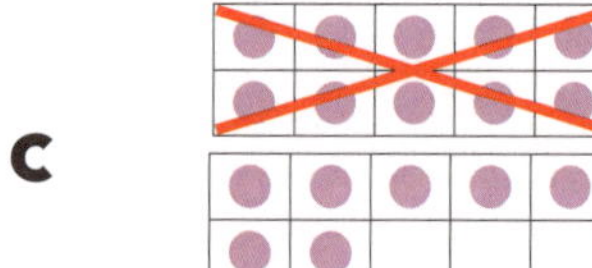

17 minus ______ is ______.

d

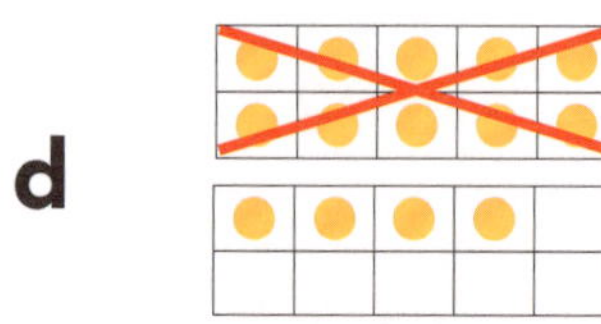

14 minus ______ is ______.

SELF CHECK Mark how you feel

Got it!	Need help...	I don't get it
 ☐	 ☐	☐

Practice

1 Cross off ten frames to subtract. Write the answers.

16 minus 10

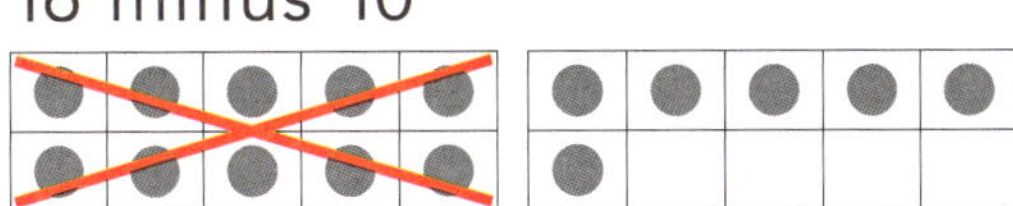

a 18 minus 10

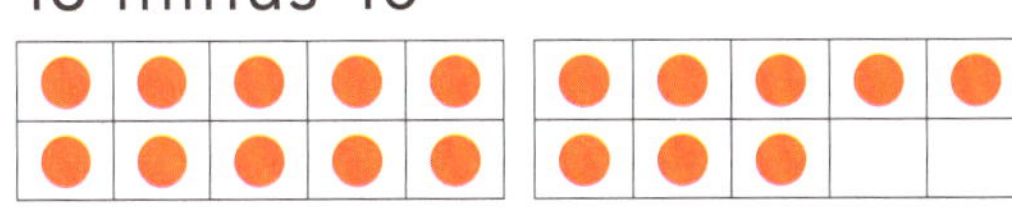

b 13 minus 10

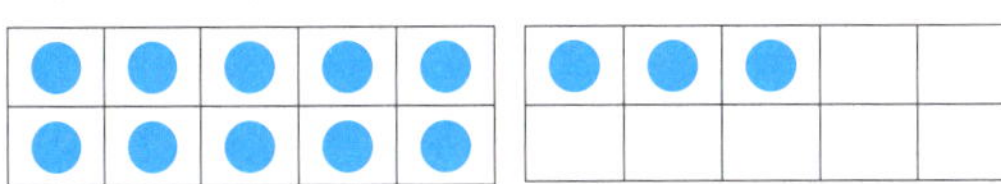

c 11 minus 10

2 Each bundle stands for 10. Write the missing numbers.

16 – 10 = 6

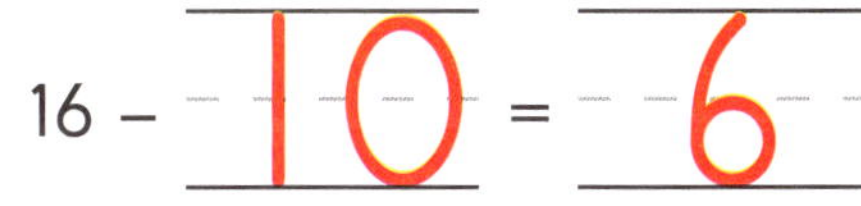

a  14 – ____ = ____

b  13 – ____ = ____

c 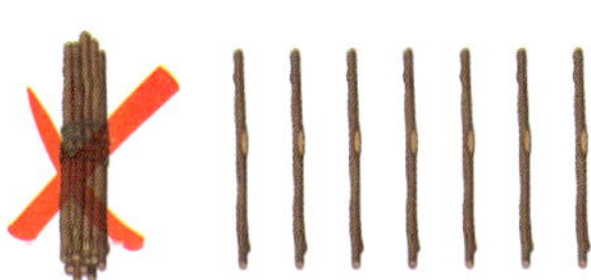 17 – ____ = ____

d  19 – ____ = ____

3 Write the missing number for each number bond.

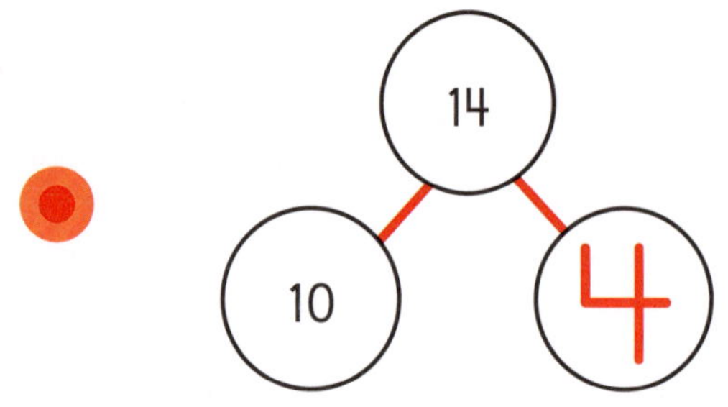

a

18

10

b

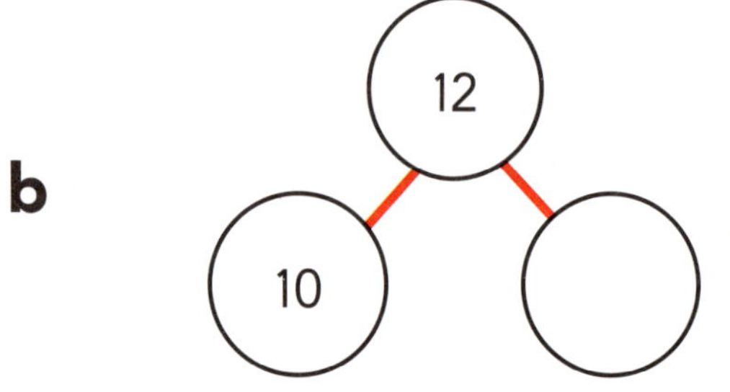

c

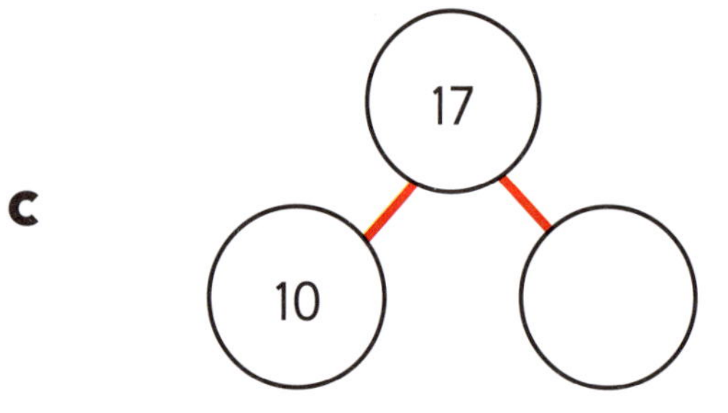

d

11

10

e

15

10

f

16

10

g

13

10

Subtraction Review

1 Cross off the squares to show each math fact.

a 5 take away 1 is 4.

c 4 take away 3 is 1.

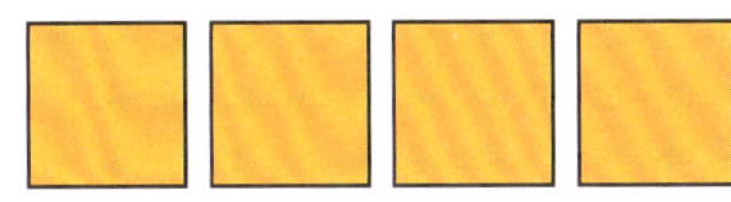

b 2 take away 2 is 0.

d 3 take away 3 is 0.

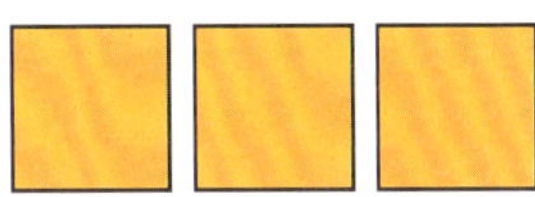

2 Cross off ten frames to subtract. Write the answers.

a 17 minus 10

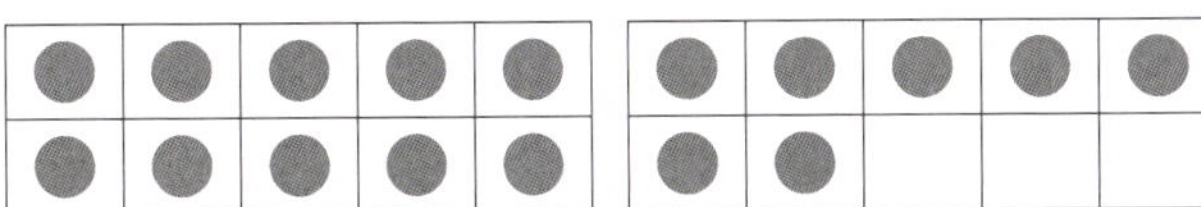

______

b 12 minus 10

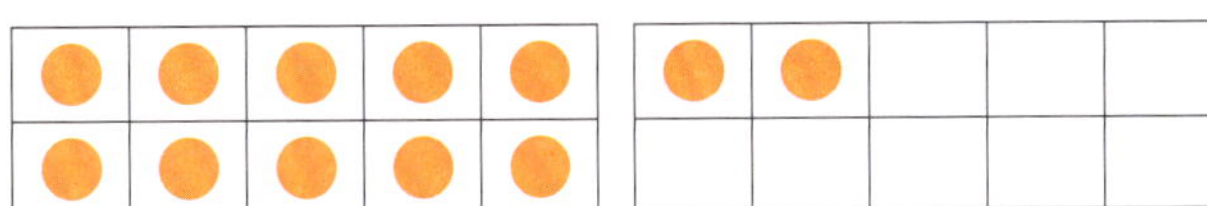

______

c 13 minus 10

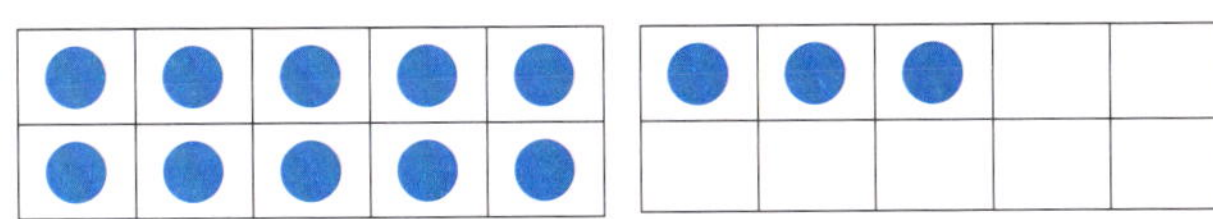

______

d 16 minus 10

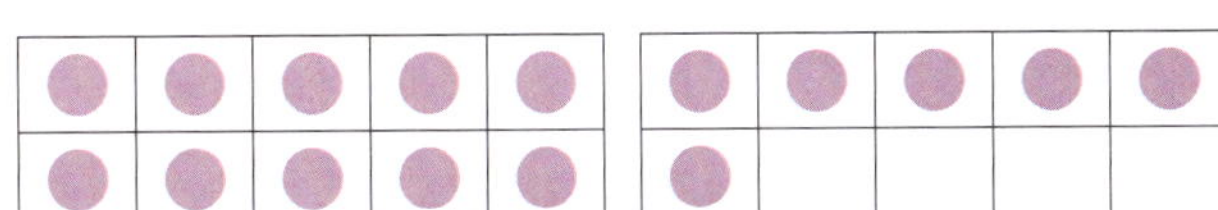

______

Review

3 Subtract using fingers. Write the answers.

a 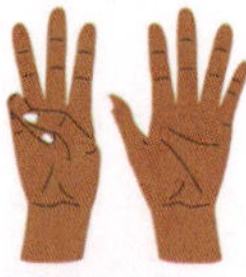 take away 3 is ______

b  take away 2 is ______

c  take away 0 is ______

d 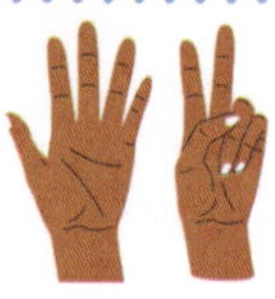 take away 5 is ______

4 Draw pictures to solve the problems. Write the answers.

a 9 – 4 = ______

b 6 – 1 = ______

c 7 – 4 = ______

d 5 – 3 = ______

Review

5 Count each number. Cross off 1 to subtract. Write the new number.

a 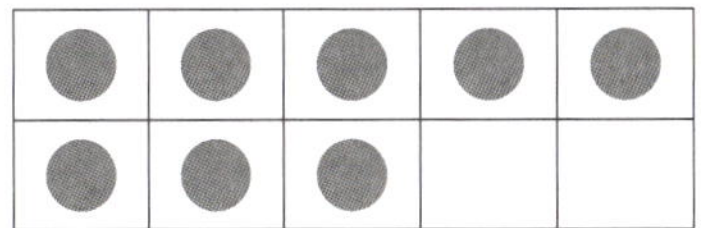 ________

b 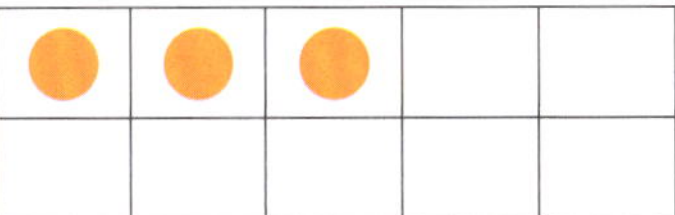 ________

c  ________

d 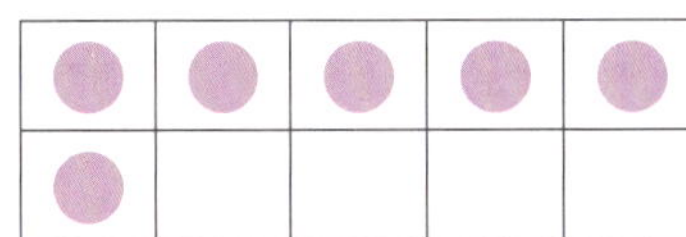 ________

6 Cross off to subtract. Write how many are left.

a 4 take away 3

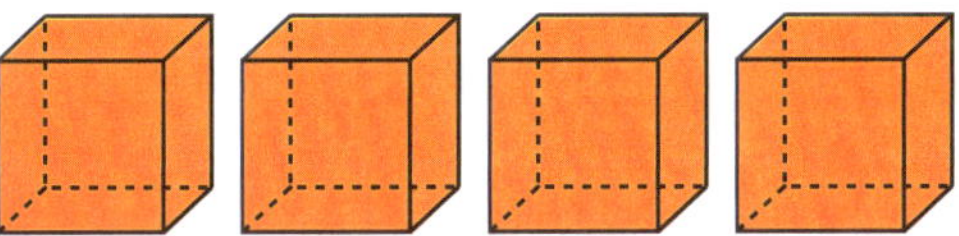 ________

b 4 take away 1

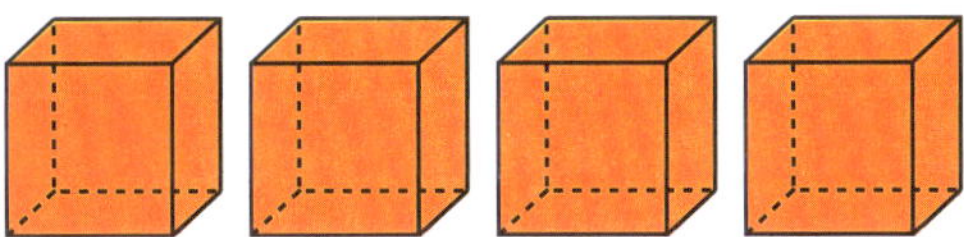 ________

c 3 take away 2

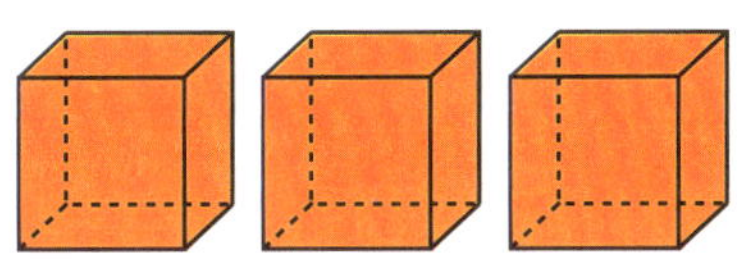 ________

d 5 take away 2

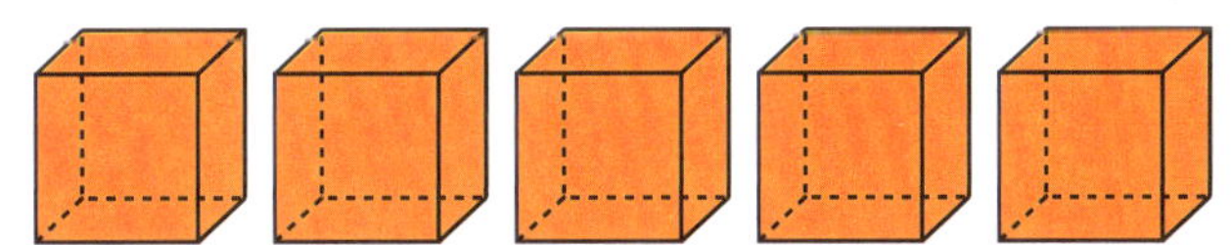 ________

Squares

All squares have certain features. These are called attributes.

This is a **square**. A square has 4 sides.

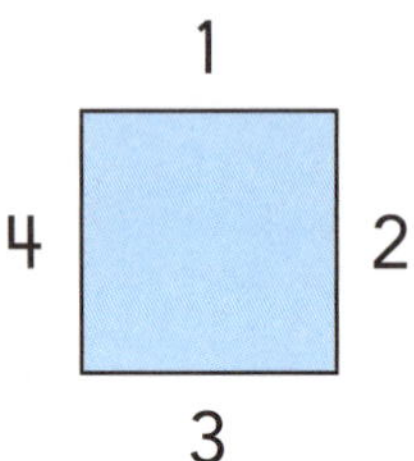

All its sides are the same length.

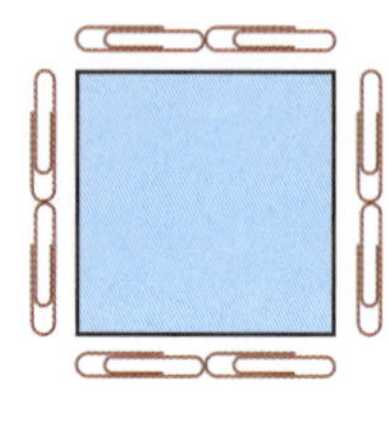

A square has 4 corners, or vertices.

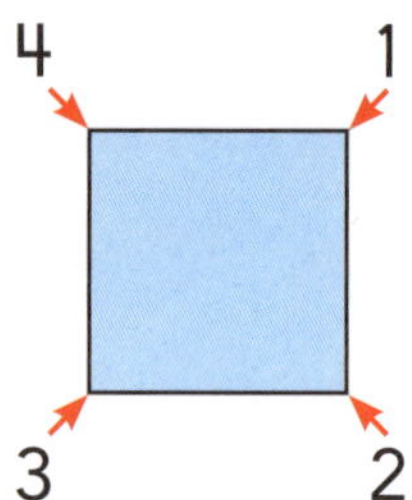

A square can be turned in any direction, and it is still a square.

1 Color the squares.

 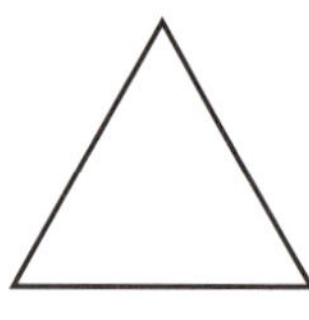  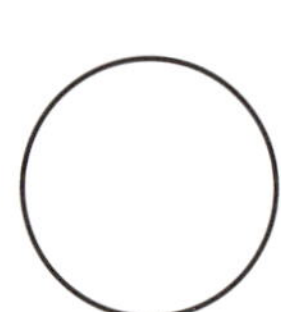 

SELF CHECK Mark how you feel

Got it!	Need help...	I don't get it
 ☐	 ☐	☐

Practice

1 Find the squares. Trace the sides of each square.

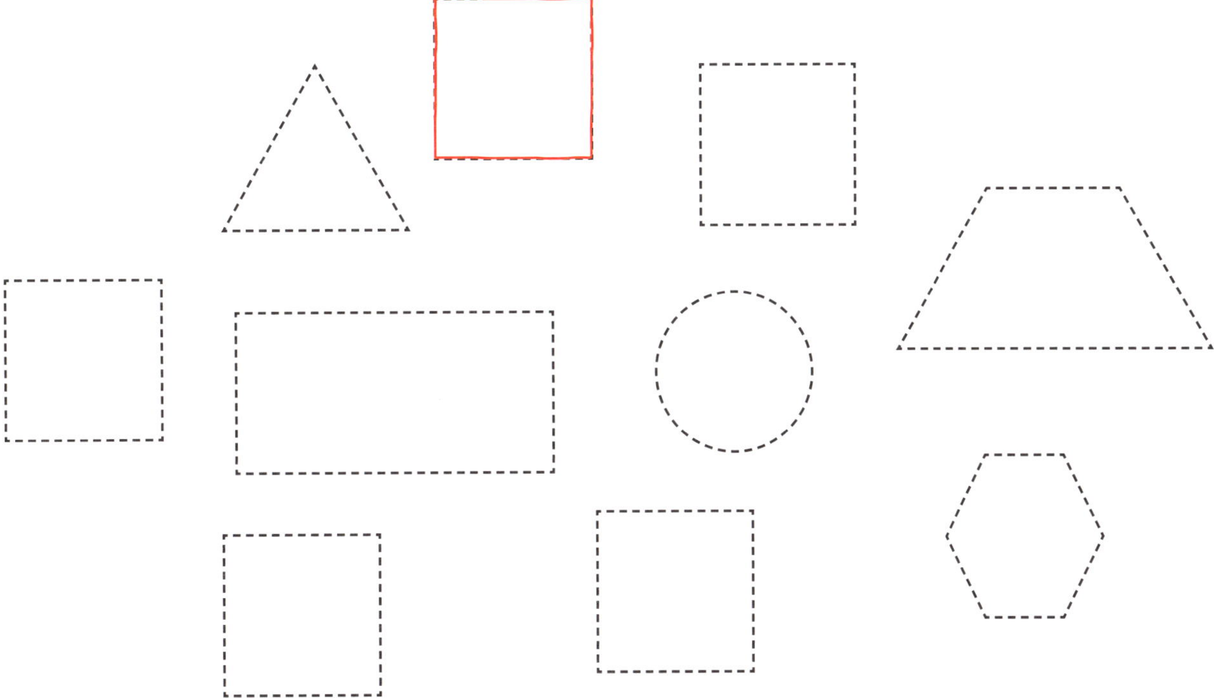

2 Circle all four vertices on each square.

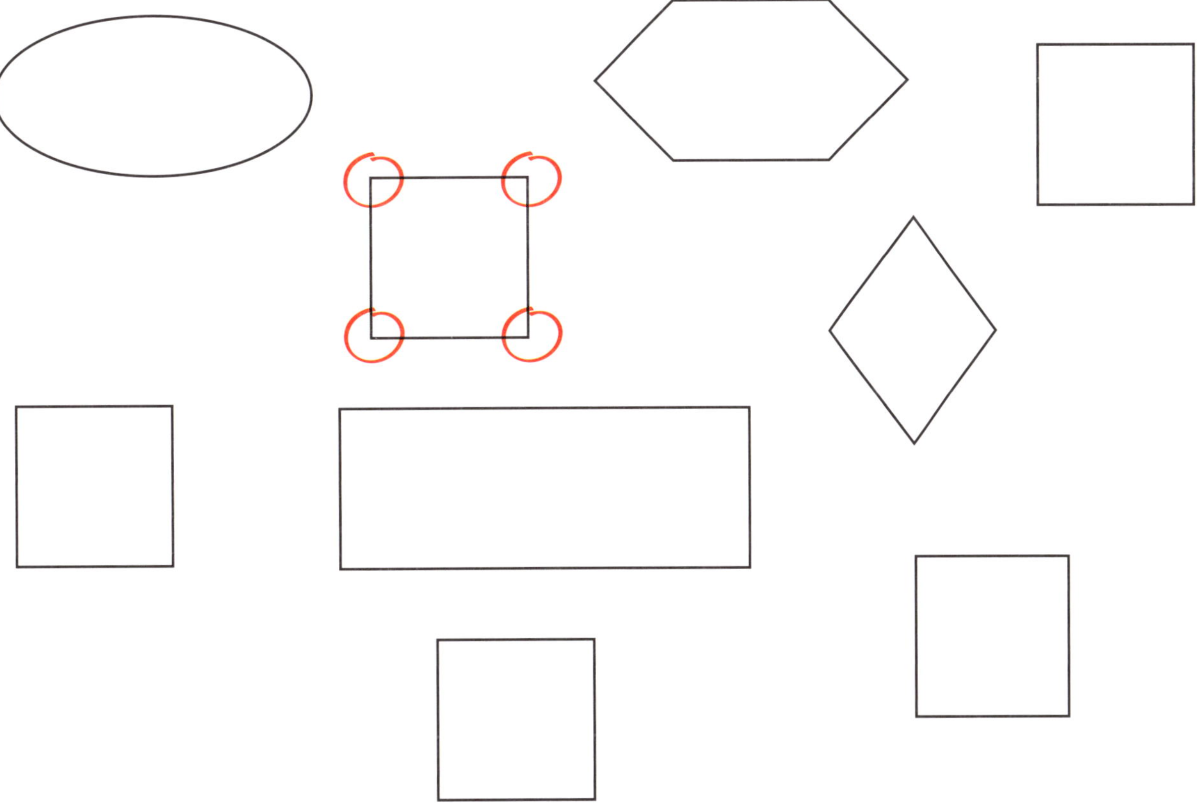

3 Color the square objects.

4 Trace the squares.

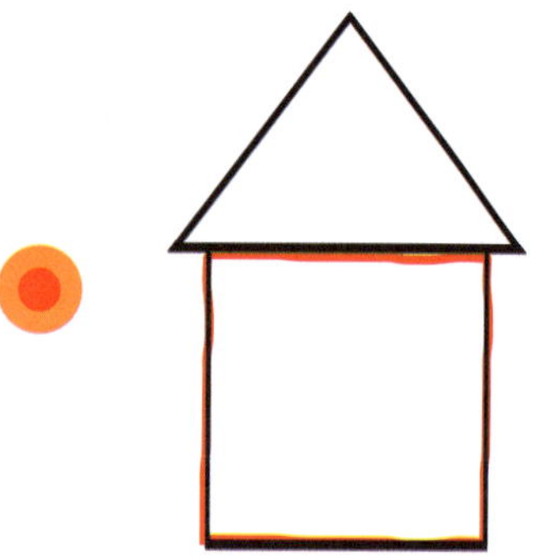

c

a

d

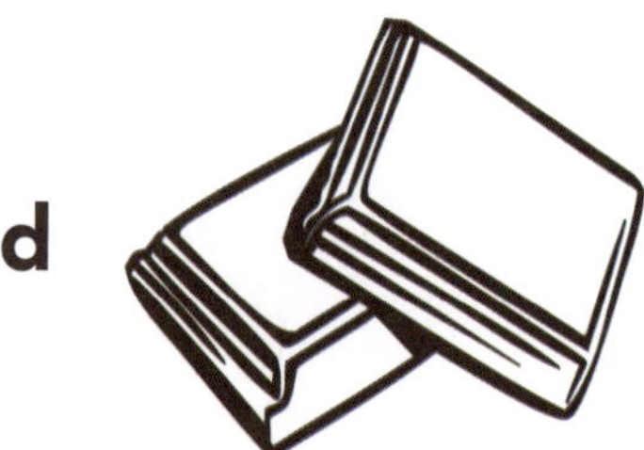

b

e

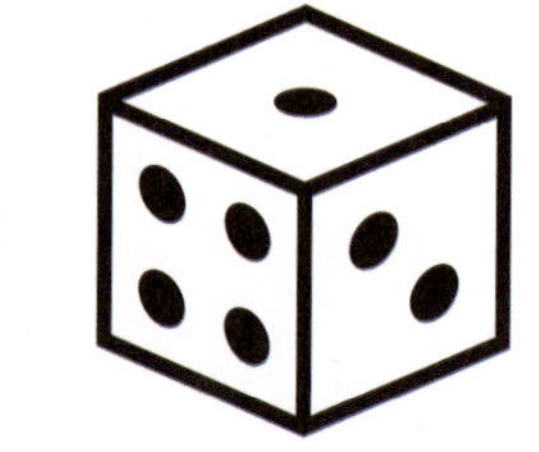

Circles

Circles are flat shapes. They have attributes.

This is a **circle**.
It is a round shape.

It is curved. It does not have any vertices or flat sides.

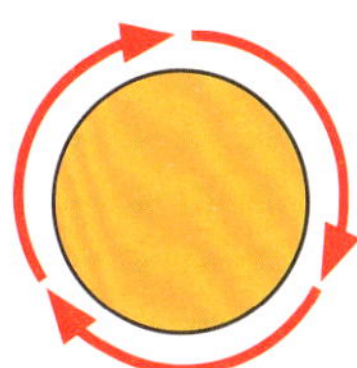

Circles can be any size.

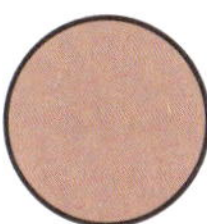
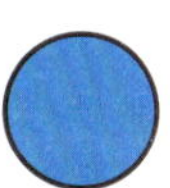
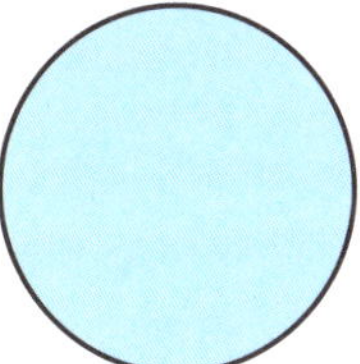

Your turn

1 Color the circles.

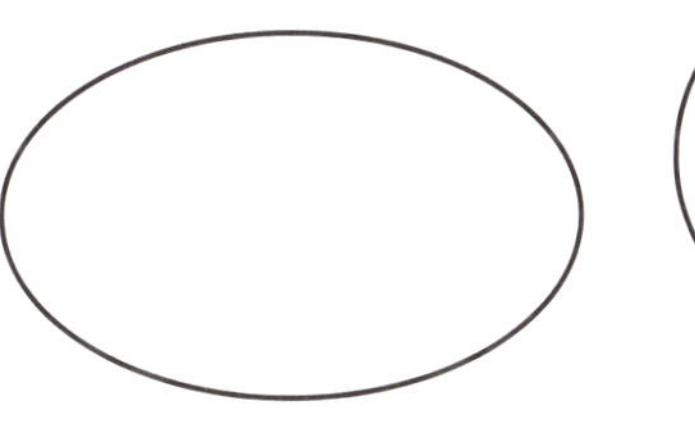
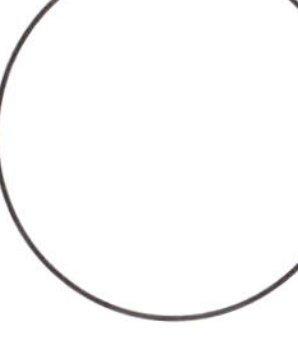

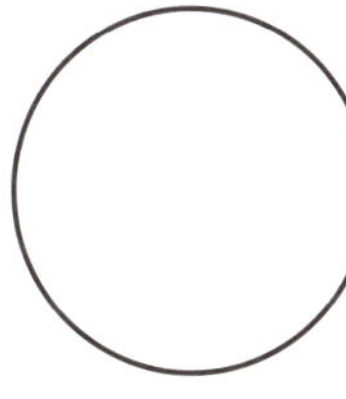

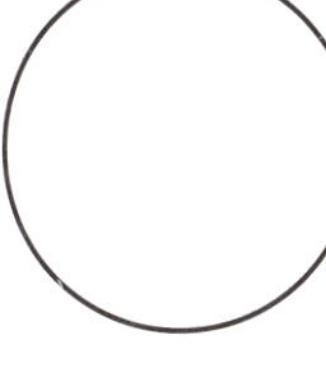

Circles can turn in any direction and still look the same.

SELF CHECK Mark how you feel

Got it!	Need help...	I don't get it

Practice

1 Color all the circles.

2 Trace the circles.

3 Trace the circles.

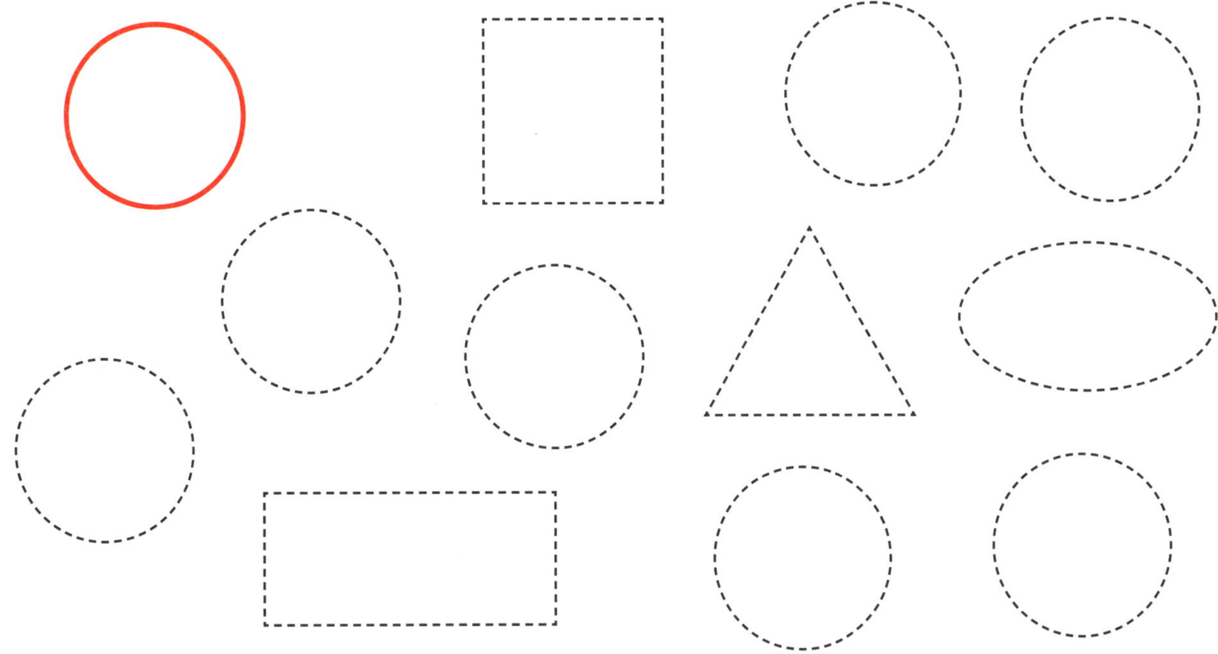

4 Color all the circles.

Triangles

Triangles are flat shapes. They have attributes.

This is a **triangle**. A triangle has 3 sides.

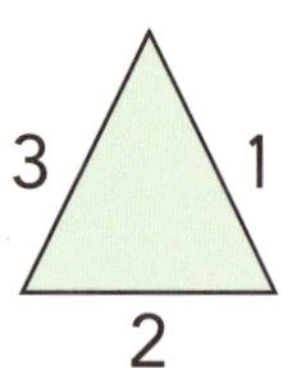

Triangles have 3 vertices.

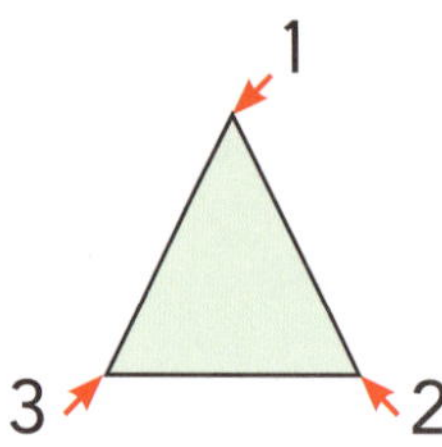

The sides can be different lengths.

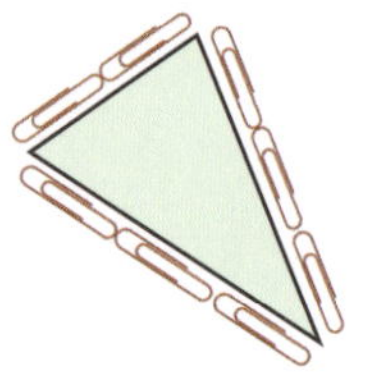

Triangles can be turned in any direction.

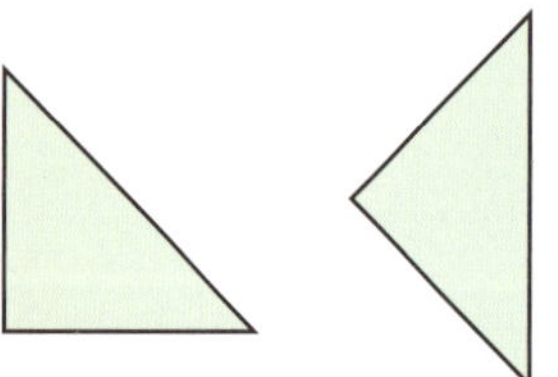

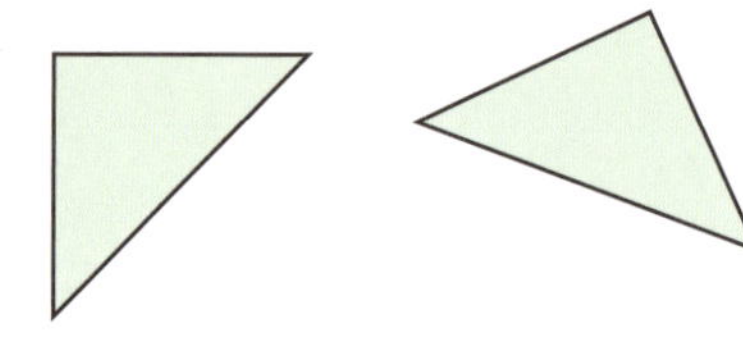

1 Color the triangles.

Practice

1 Trace the triangles.

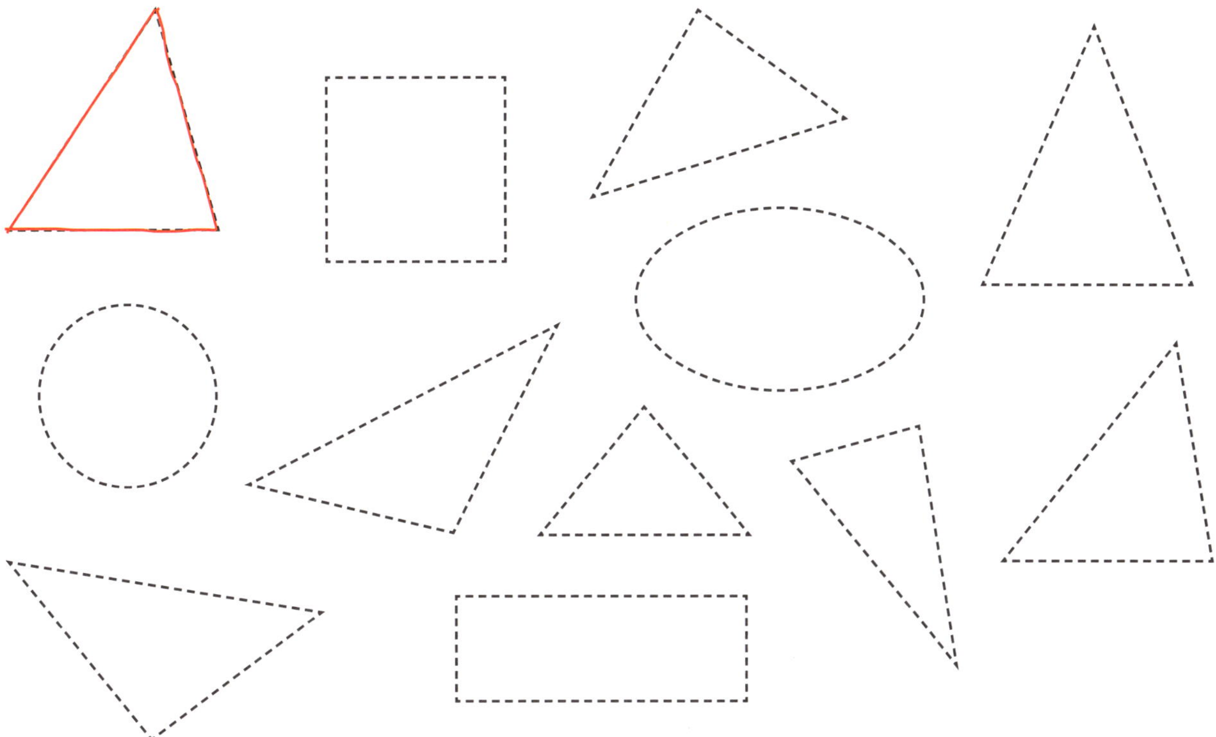

2 Color the triangles.

a

c

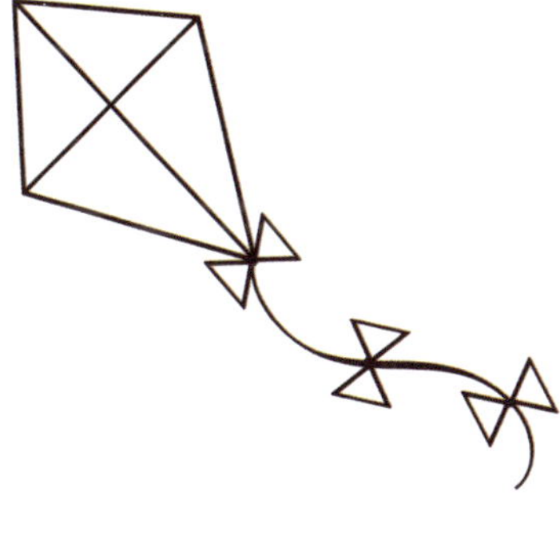

b

d

3 Color the triangles.

4 Circle the 3 vertices on each triangle.

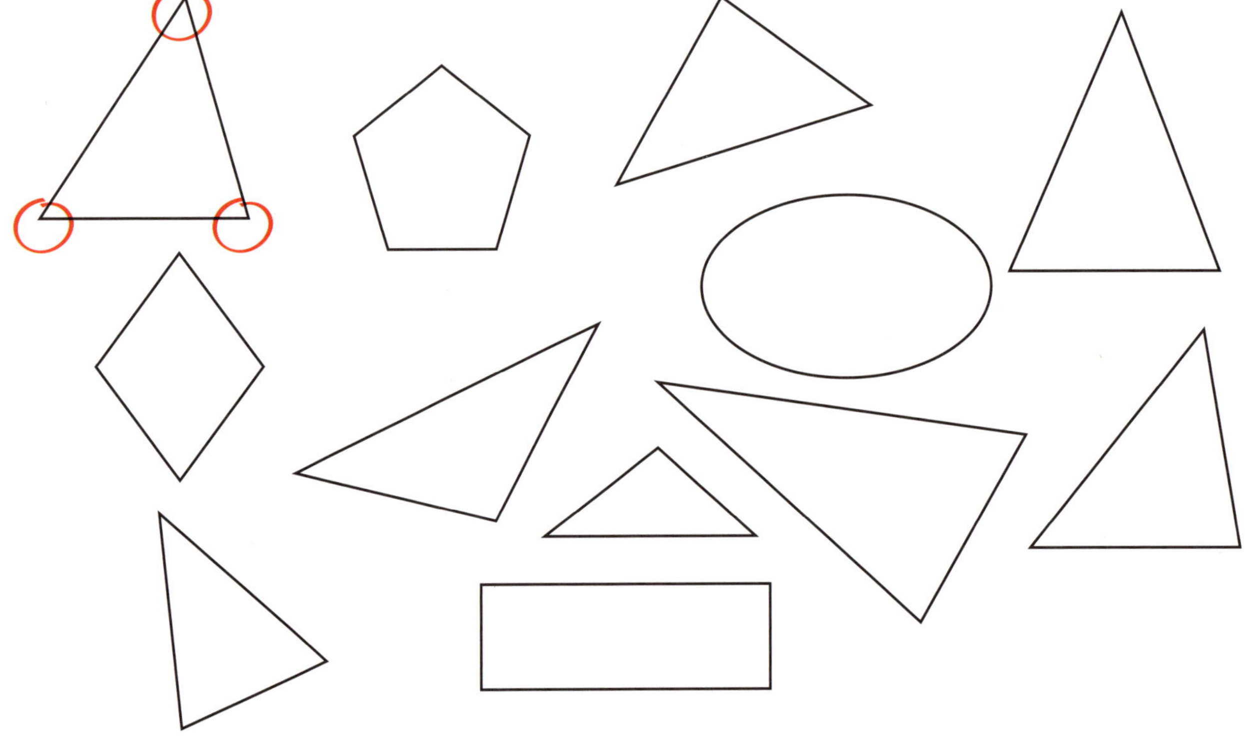

Rectangles

Rectangles are flat shapes. They have attributes.

A **rectangle** has 4 sides.

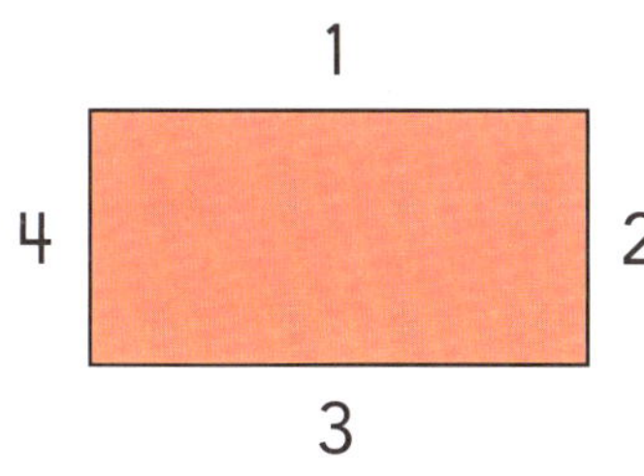

A rectangle has 4 vertices.

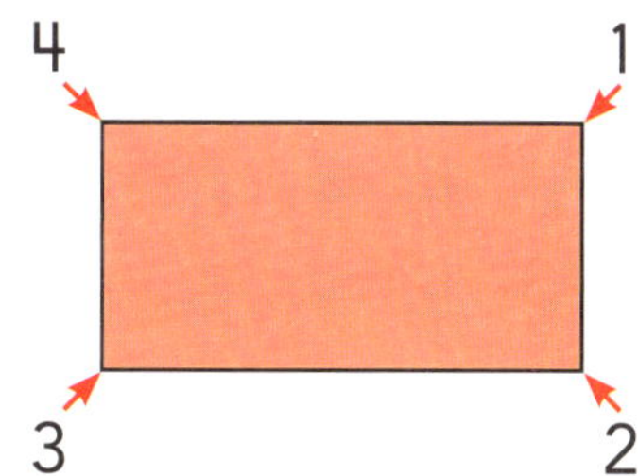

The opposite sides are the same length.

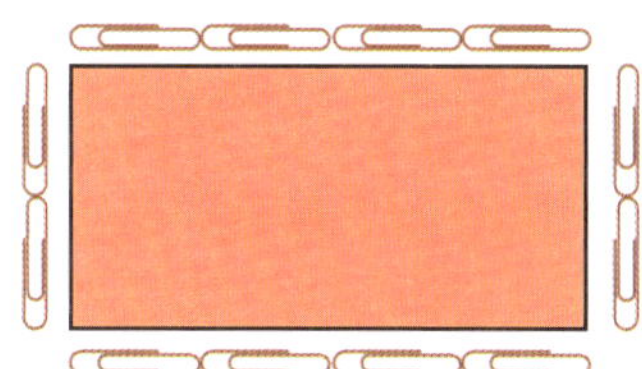

A rectangle can be turned in any direction.

1 Color the rectangles.

SELF CHECK Mark how you feel

Got it!	Need help...	I don't get it

Practice

1 Trace the rectangles.

2 Color the rectangles.

3 Circle all 4 vertices on each rectangle.

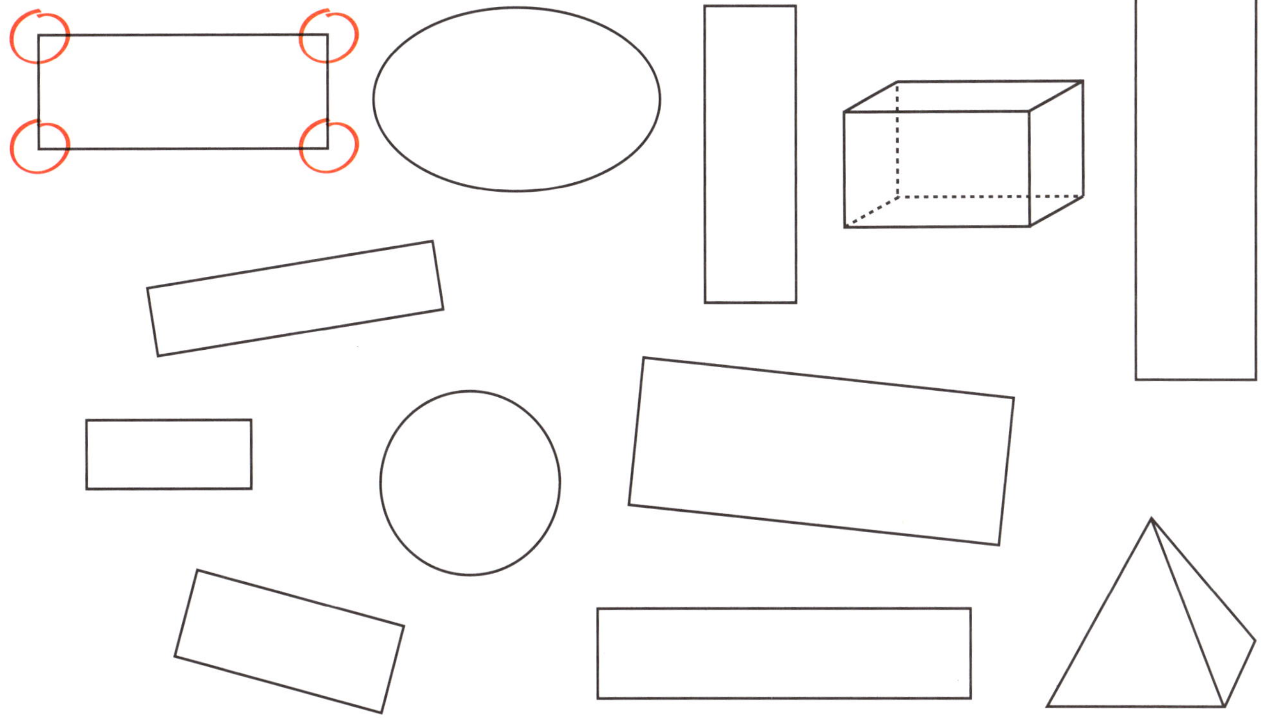

4 Color the rectangles.

a

c

b

d

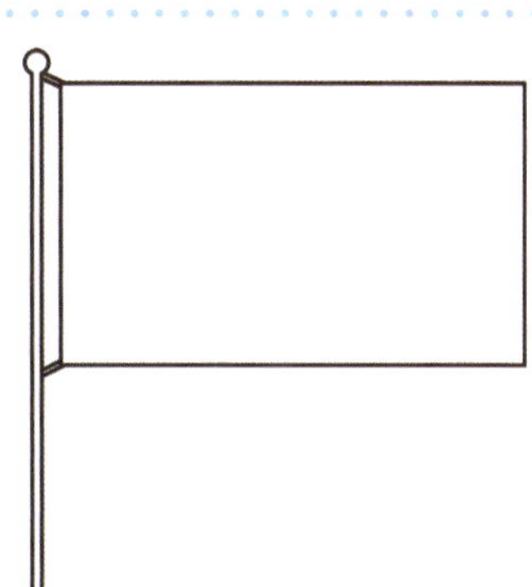

Hexagons and Pentagons

Hexagons and pentagons are flat shapes. They each have attributes.

This is a pentagon.

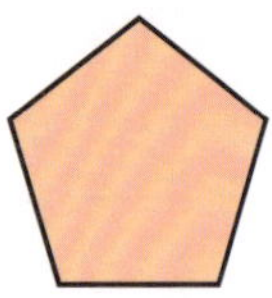

A pentagon has 5 sides. Sometimes they are the same length. Sometimes they are not.

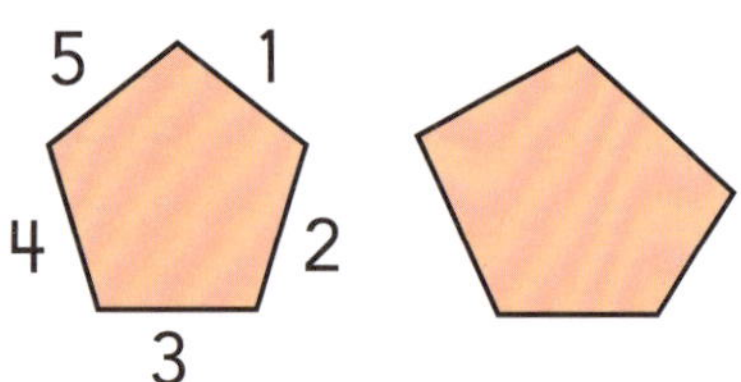

A pentagon has 5 vertices.

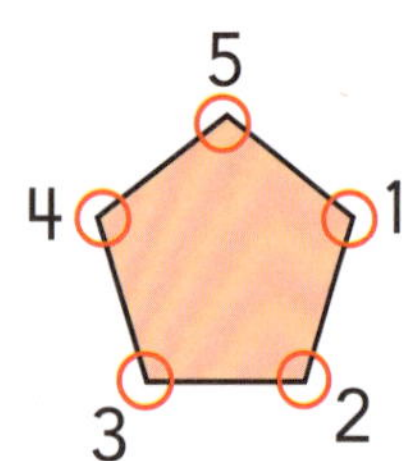

This is a hexagon.

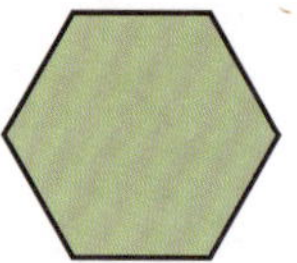

A hexagon has 6 sides. Sometimes they are the same length. Sometimes they are not.

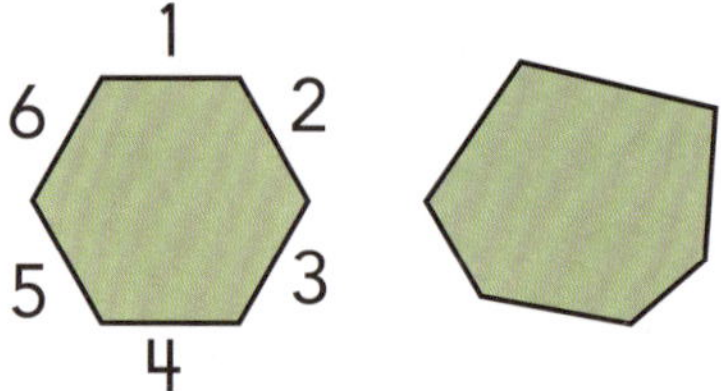

A hexagon has 6 vertices.

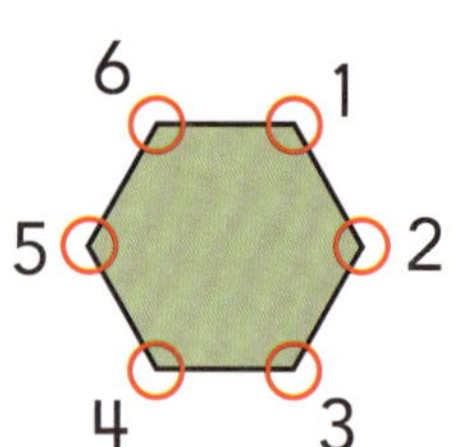

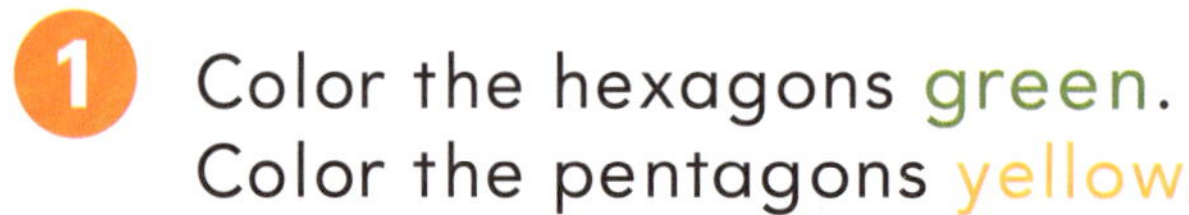

1. Color the hexagons green.
   Color the pentagons yellow.

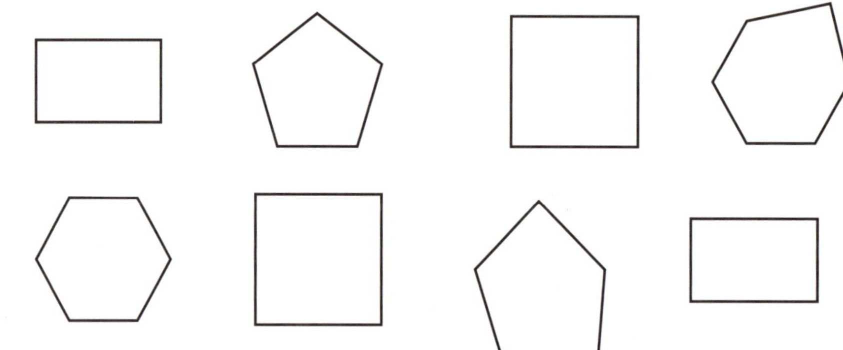

SELF CHECK Mark how you feel

Got it!	Need help...	I don't get it
☐	☐	☐

Practice

1 Trace the hexagons in blue. Trace the pentagons in red.

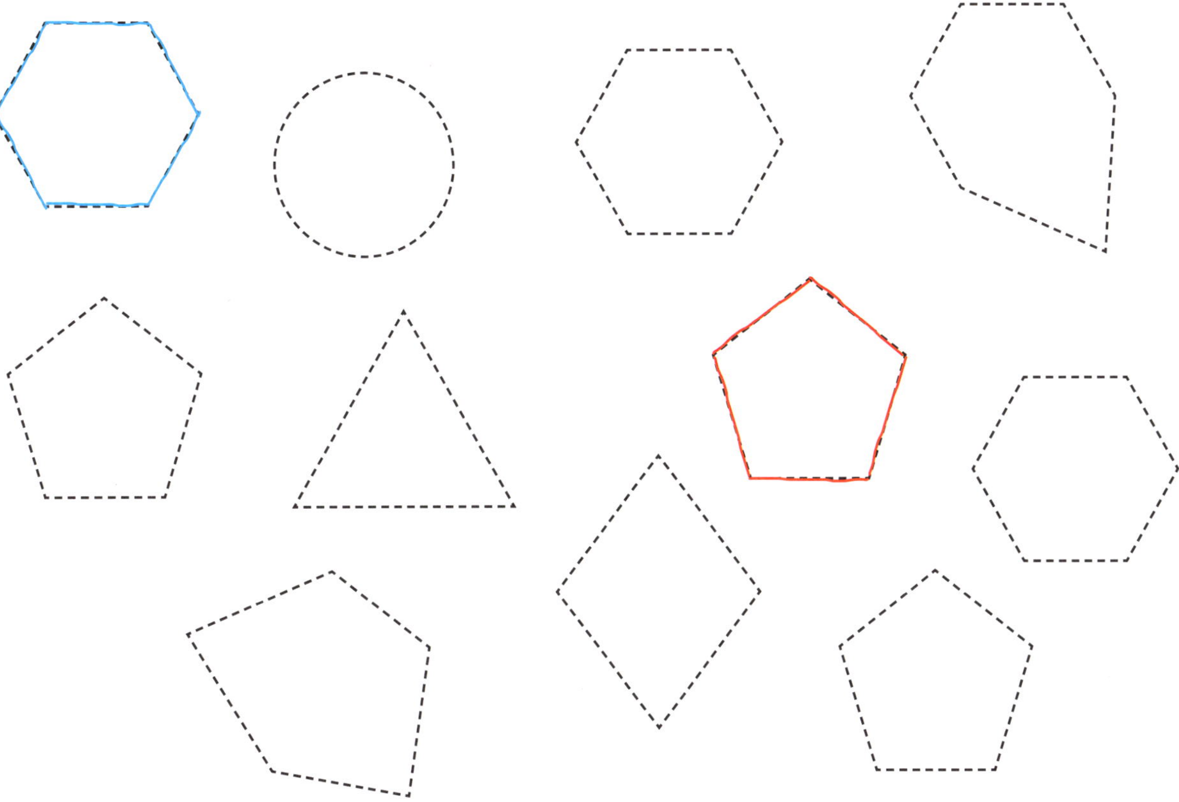

2 Find the hexagons. Circle the vertices in purple.
Find the pentagons. Circle the vertices in green.

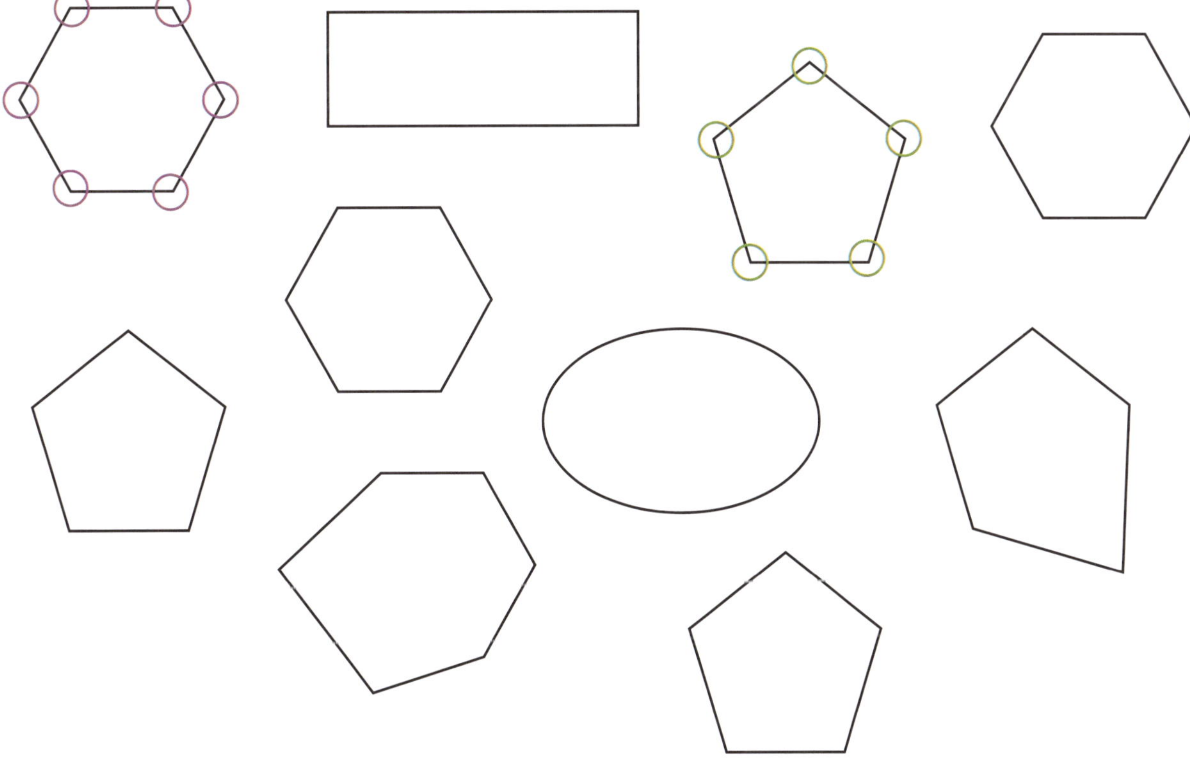

3 Color the objects shaped like hexagons.

4 Color the objects shaped like pentagons.

Describe and Make Shapes

You can describe and make many 2D shapes.

There are many 2D shapes.

square

circle

triangle

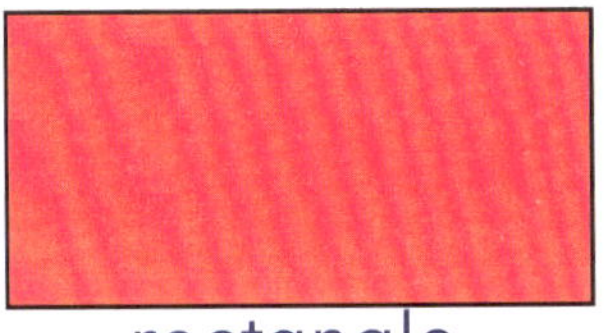
rectangle

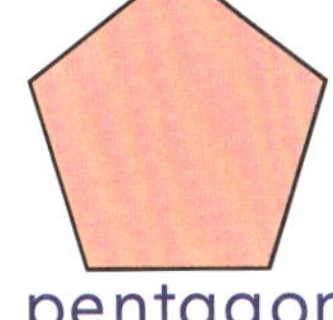
pentagon

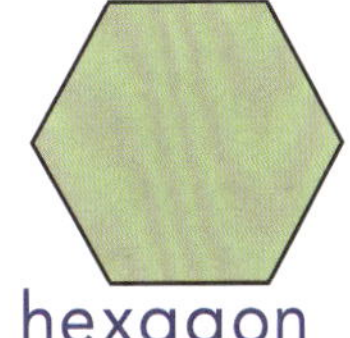
hexagon

They can be turned in any direction.

square

circle

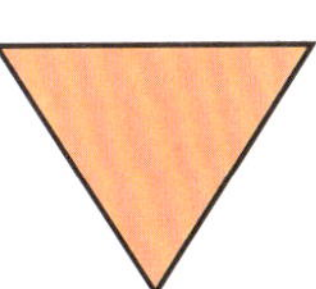
triangle

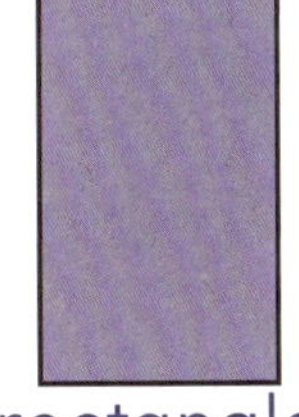
rectangle

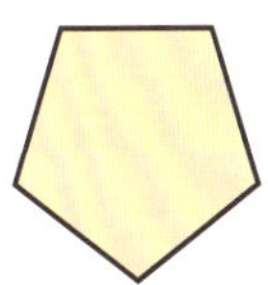
pentagon

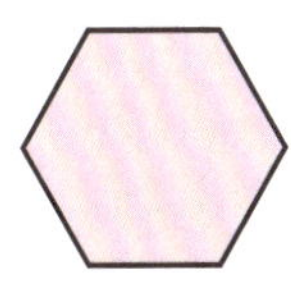
hexagon

All 2D shapes are flat. The shapes below are **not** 2D shapes.

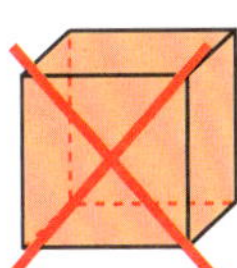
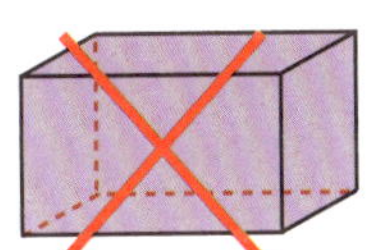
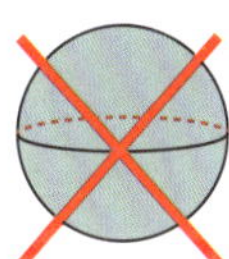

1 Color the flat, 2D shapes.

The things that make a shape special are its attributes.

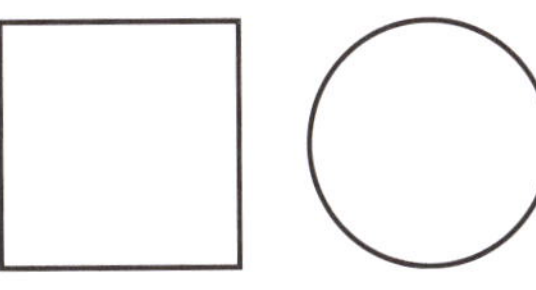
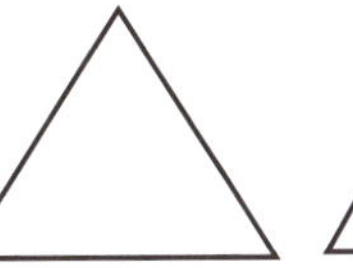

SELF CHECK	Mark how you feel	
Got it!	Need help...	I don't get it

Practice

1 Color each shape. Trace each shape. Draw each shape.

	Color the shape	Trace the shape	Draw the shape
a			
b			
c			
d			
e			
f			

2 Draw a line to match each shape to its name.

rectangle

square

triangle

circle

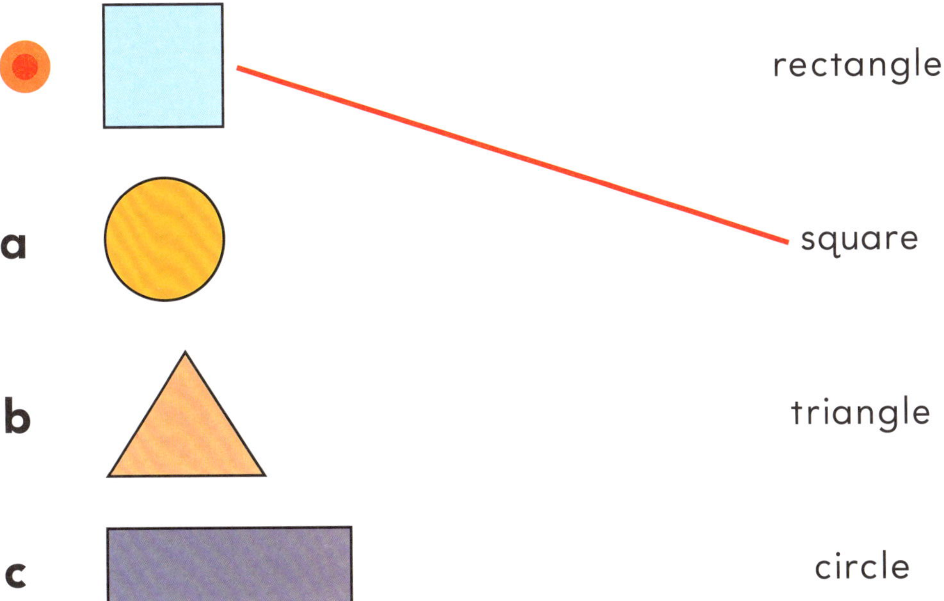

3 Color the objects that match the shapes in the top row.

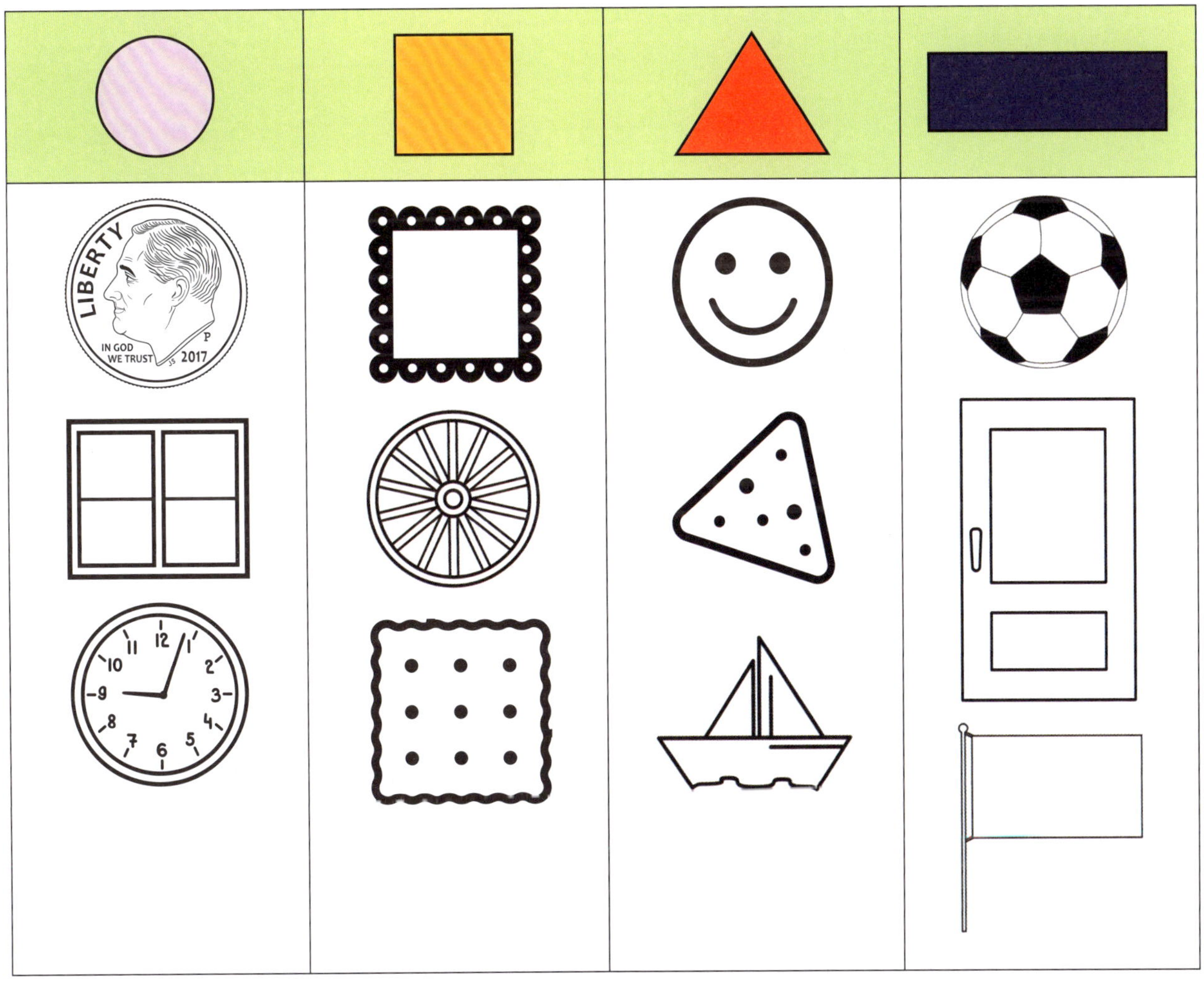

Combine Shapes

You can combine shapes to make a larger shape or a picture.

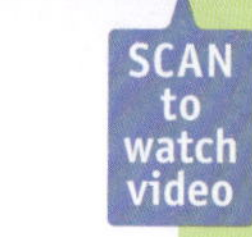

Shapes can be combined to make new shapes.

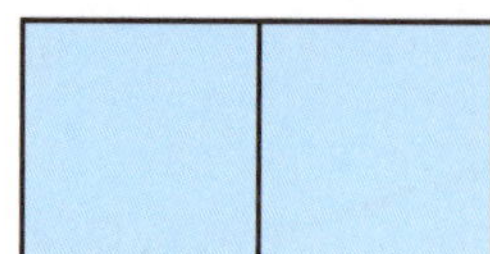
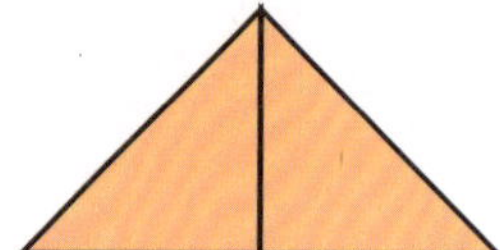
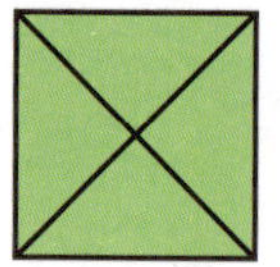

Shapes can also be combined to make pictures.

1 Trace the shapes to make new shapes.

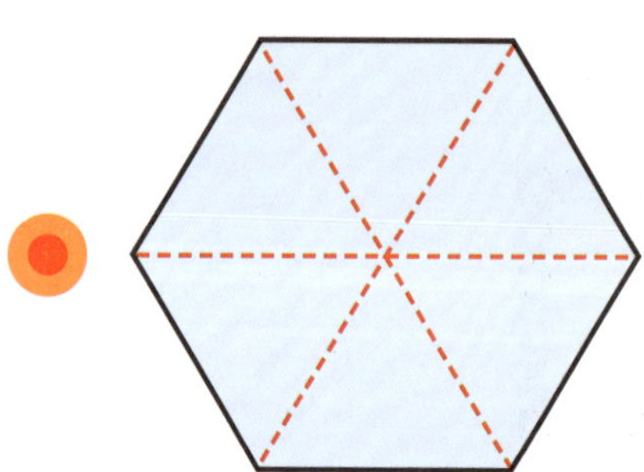

b

a

c

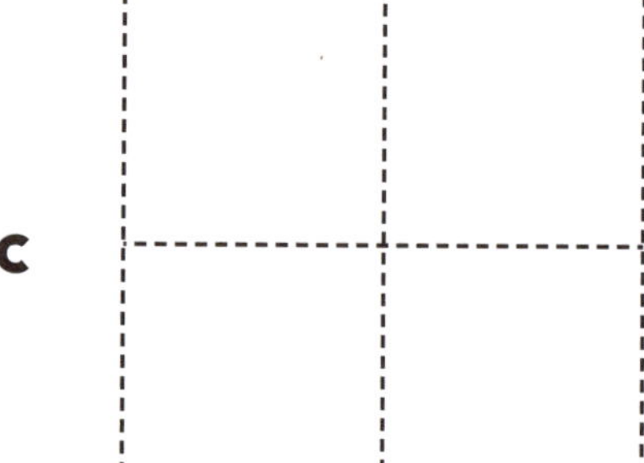

SELF CHECK Mark how you feel

Got it!	Need help...	I don't get it

Practice

1 Draw lines to match the shapes to what they make together.

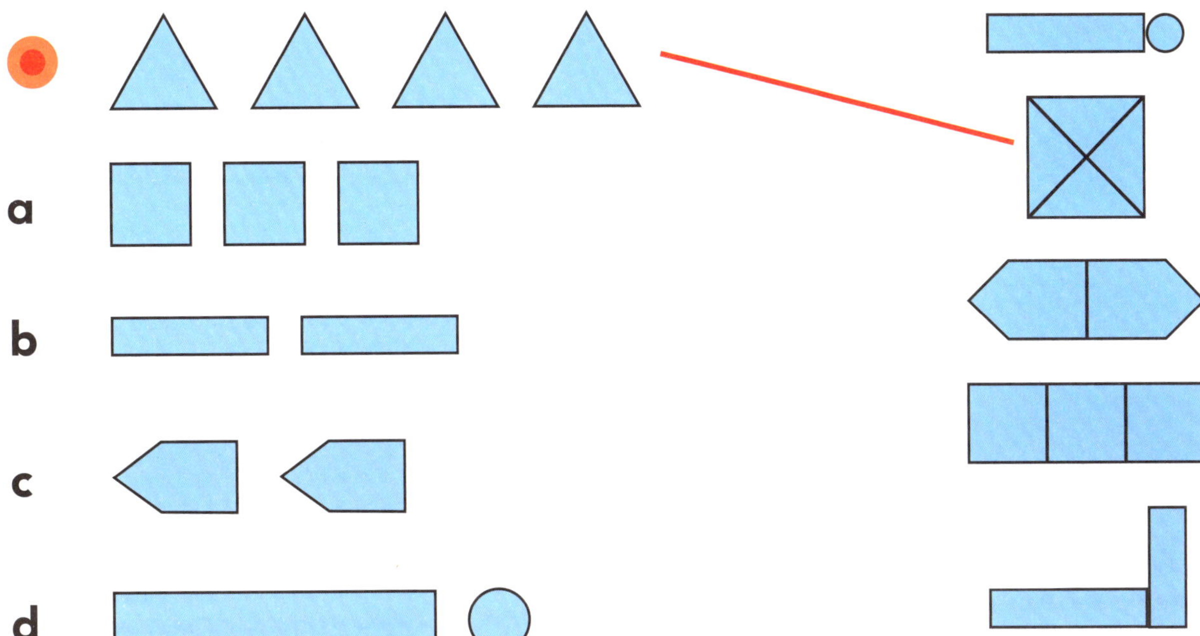

2 Combine shapes to make new ones.

What can you make with a rectangle and a square?

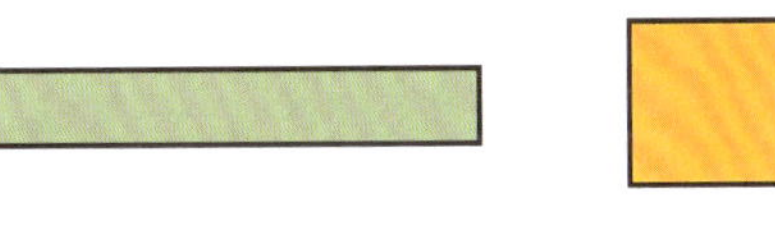

b What can you make with a pentagon and a triangle?

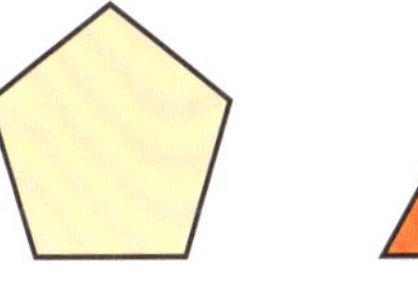

a What can you make with a circle and a triangle?

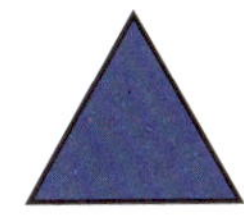

c What can you make with a hexagon and a square?

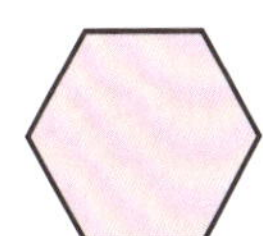

3 Use shapes to make pictures.

It is not just a circle, it is a...

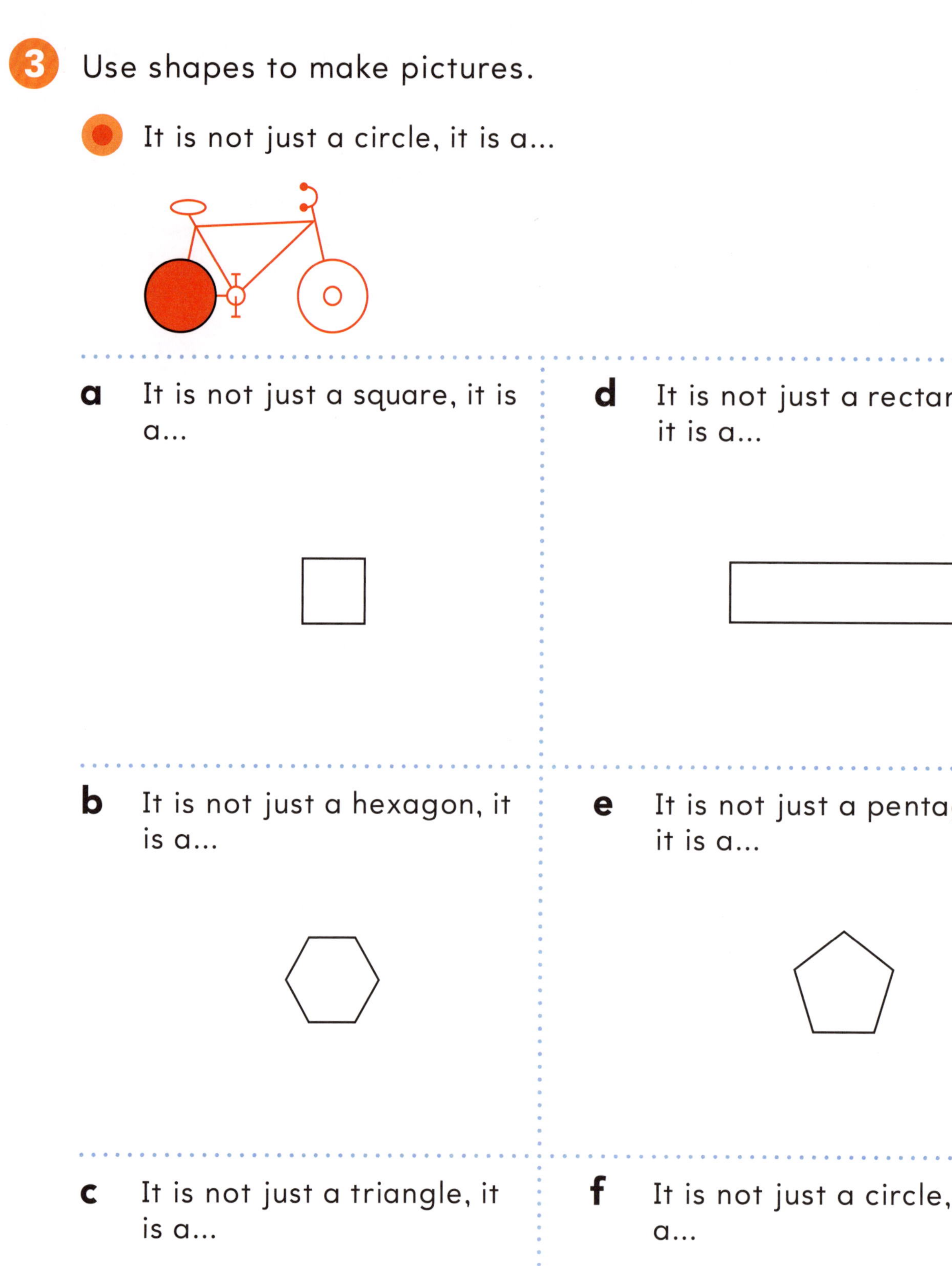

a It is not just a square, it is a...

d It is not just a rectangle, it is a...

b It is not just a hexagon, it is a...

e It is not just a pentagon, it is a...

c It is not just a triangle, it is a...

f It is not just a circle, it is a...

2D Shapes Review

1. Circle the rectangles.

2. Circle the triangles.

3. Circle the squares.

4. Color the flat, 2D shapes.

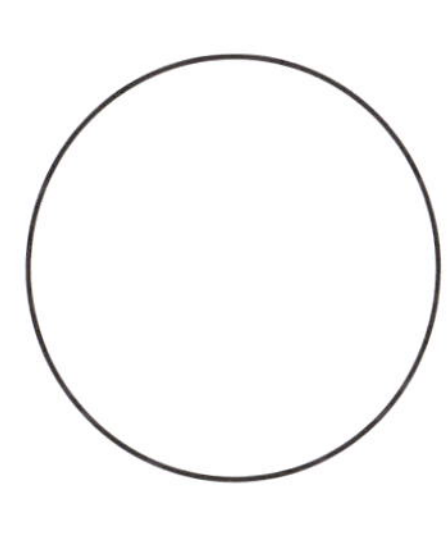

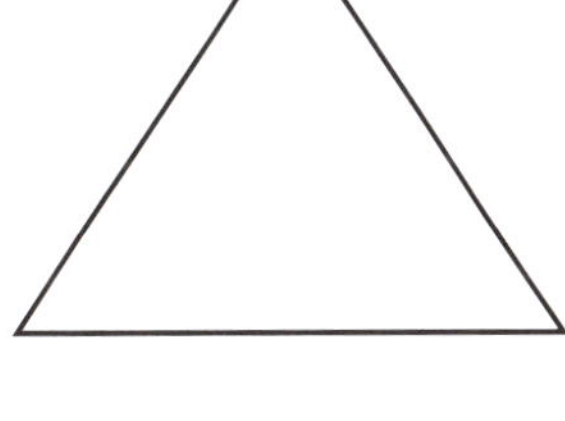

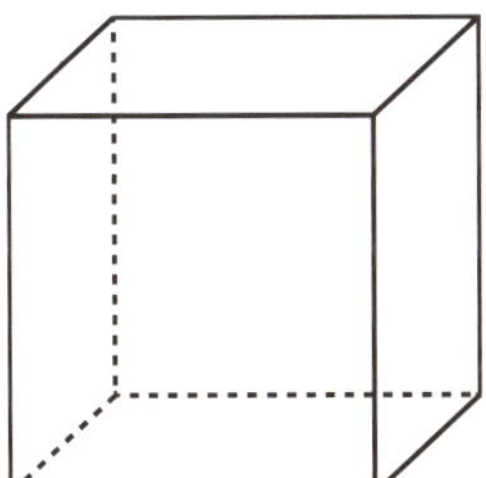
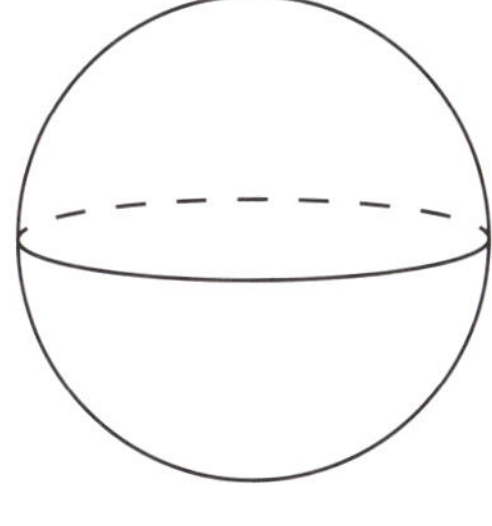
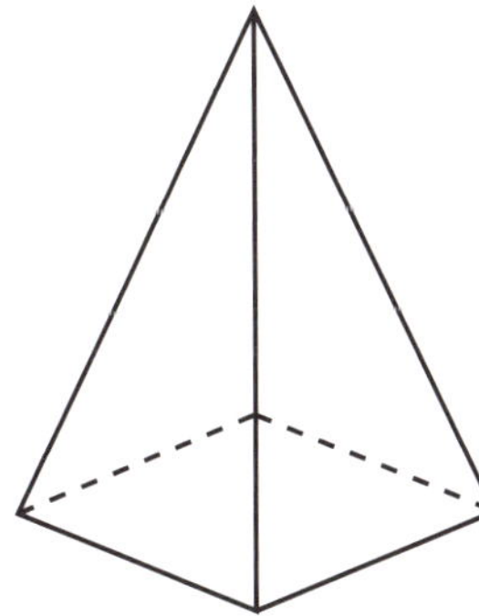
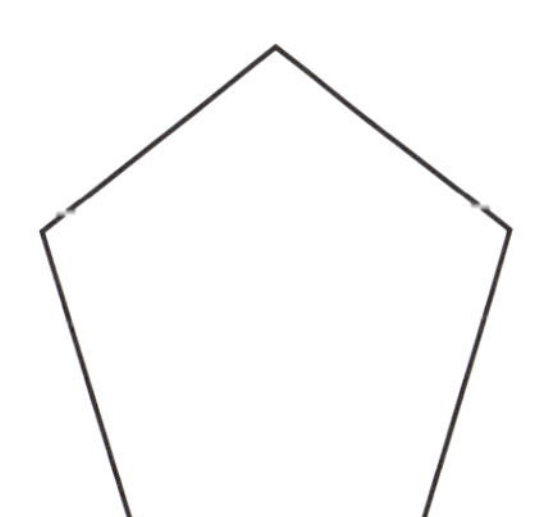
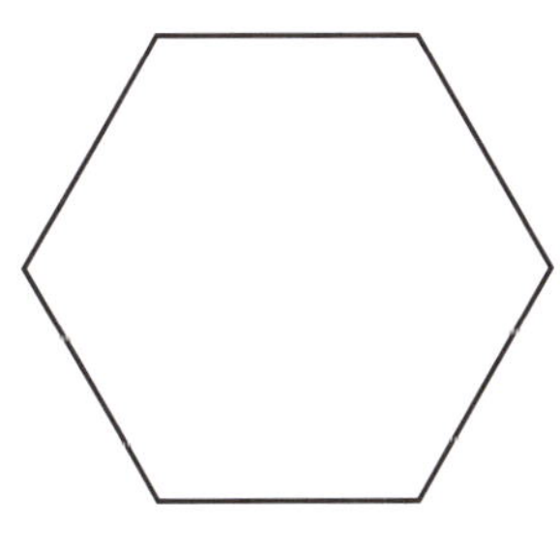

Review

5 Circle the circles.

  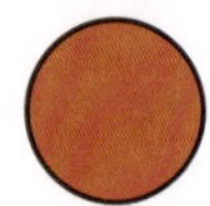 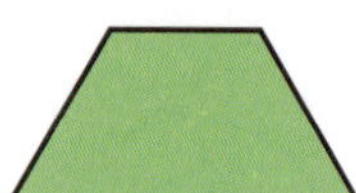 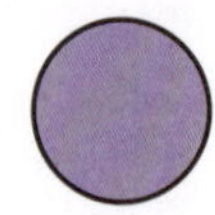

6 Circle the squares.

7 Draw pictures to answer the questions.

a What shape can you make with 2 triangles?

b What shape can you make with a square and a triangle?

c What shape can you make with a pentagon and a square?

d What shape can you make with 2 squares?

8 Color the hexagons pink. Color the pentagons purple.

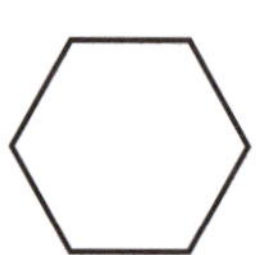  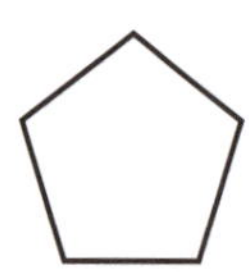  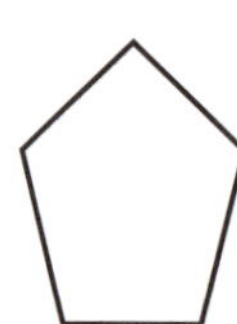 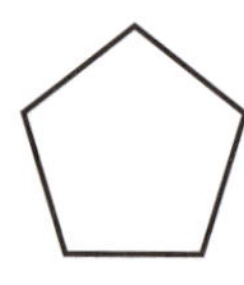 

Cubes

Cubes are solid shapes. They have attributes.

This is a **cube**. It looks like a box.

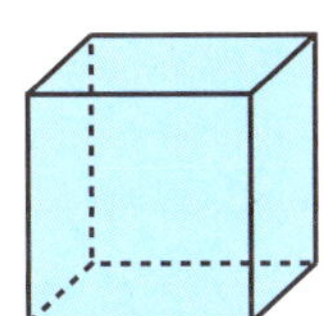

A cube has 12 edges.

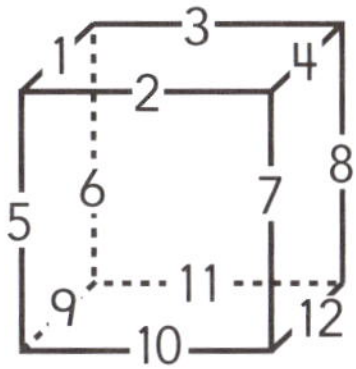

A cube has 6 square faces.

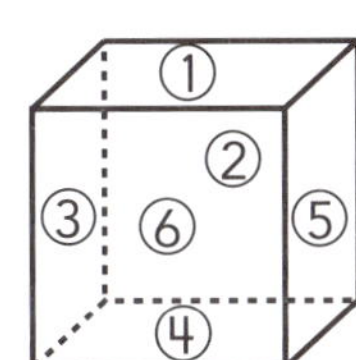

A cube has 8 vertices, or corners.

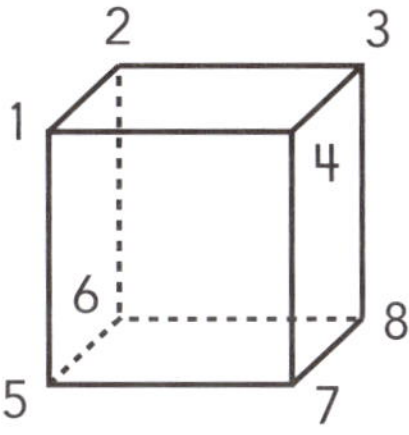

Cubes are 3D. They are solid shapes.

square

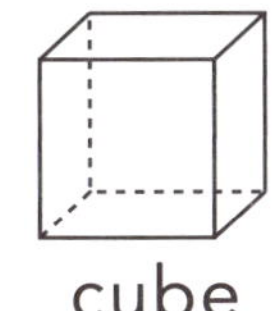

cube

3D shapes are not flat. They are solid. They have thickness.

1 Color the cubes.

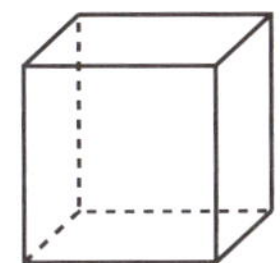 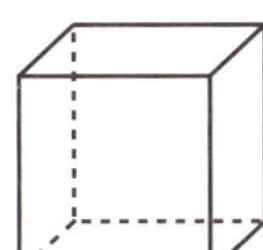  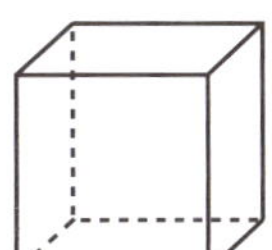 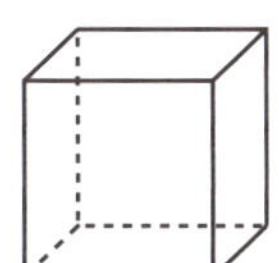 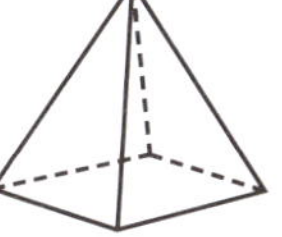

SELF CHECK	Mark how you feel	
Got it!  	Need help...  	I don't get it 

Practice

1 Color the cubes.

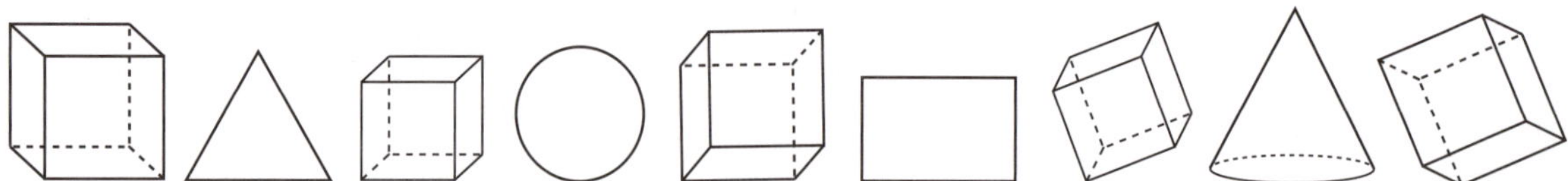

2 Answer the questions about the cube.

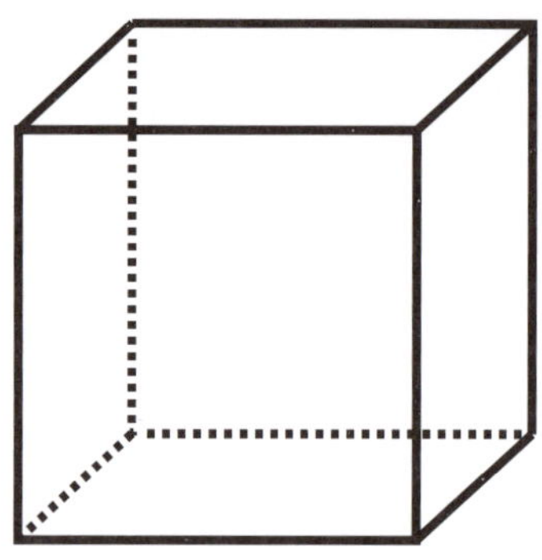

How many faces does a cube have?

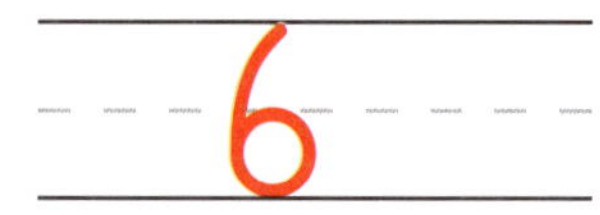

a How many vertices does a cube have?

c How many edges does a cube have?

b What shape are a cube's faces?

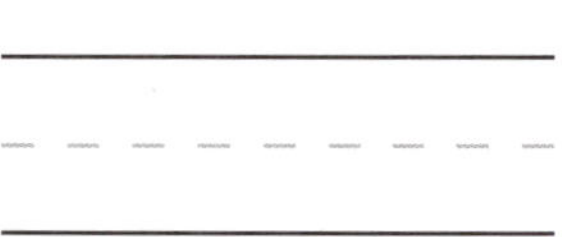

d Is a cube a solid or flat shape?

3 Circle the objects shaped like cubes.

4 Find or think of 4 objects that are shaped like cubes. Draw them.

a

c

b

d

Cones

Cones are solid shapes. They have attributes.

This is a **cone**. It looks like a birthday hat.

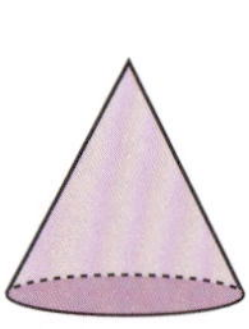

A cone has 2 faces. One is a flat face. One is a curved face.

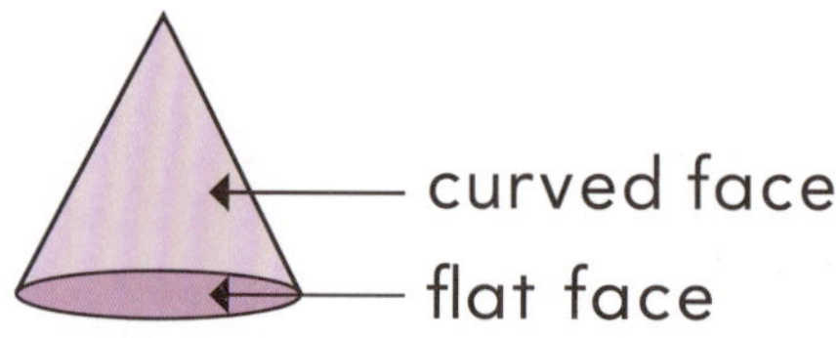

A cone has 1 round edge. It has 1 vertex.

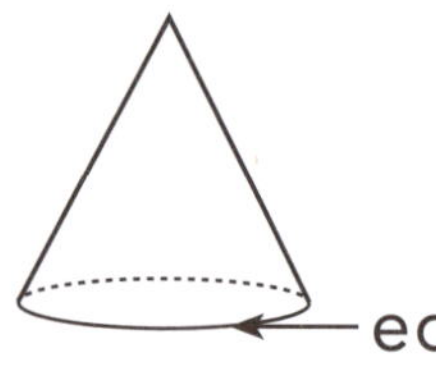

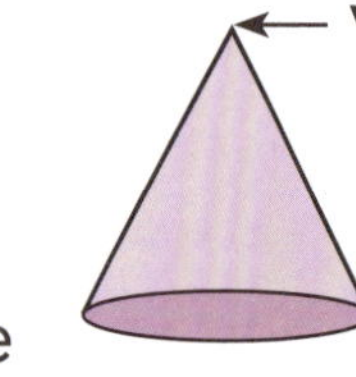

Cones are 3D, or solid shapes.

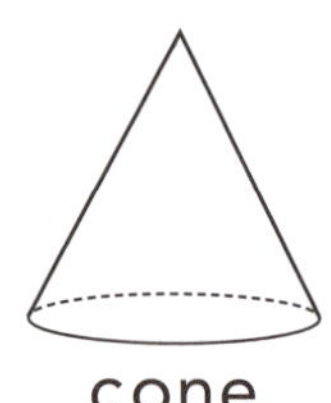

Your turn

 Color the cones.

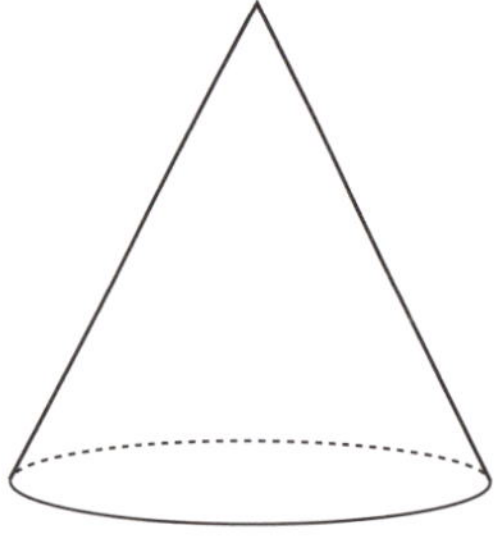

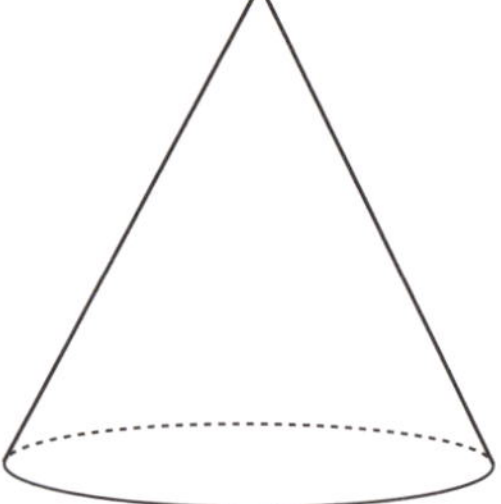
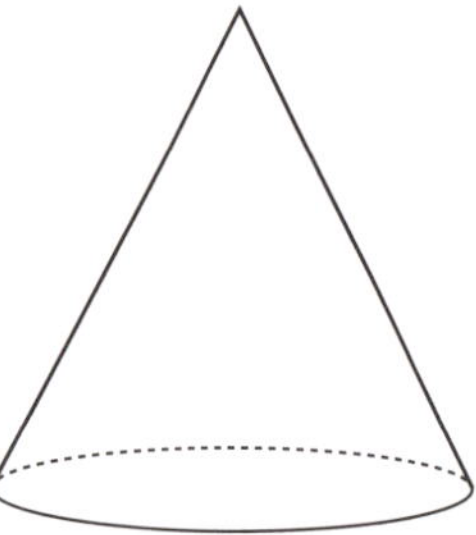
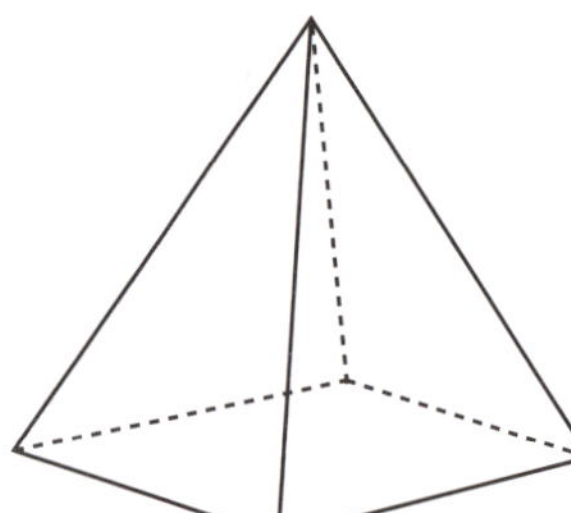
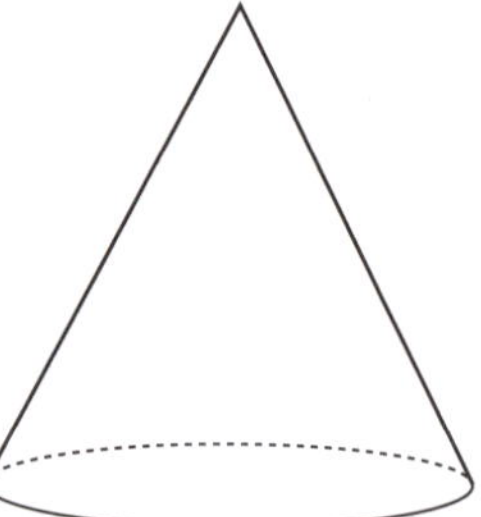

SELF CHECK Mark how you feel

Got it!	Need help...	I don't get it
 ☐	 ☐	 ☐

Practice

1 Color the cones.

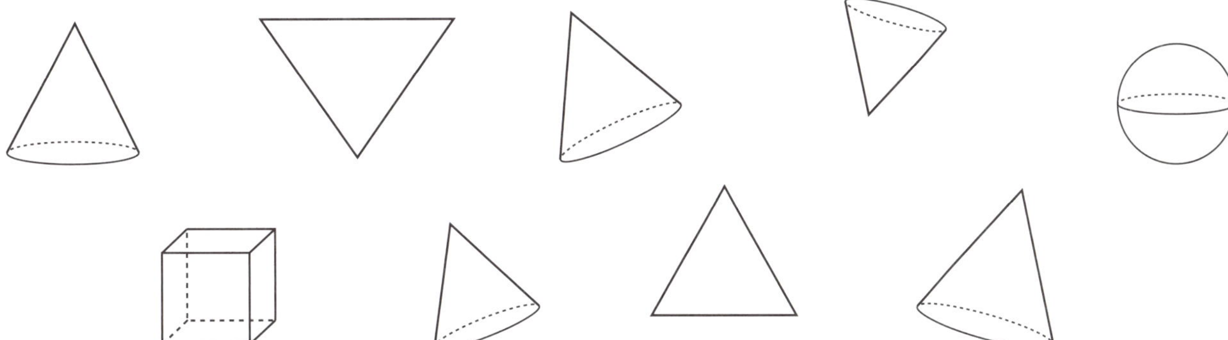

2 Answer the questions about the cone.

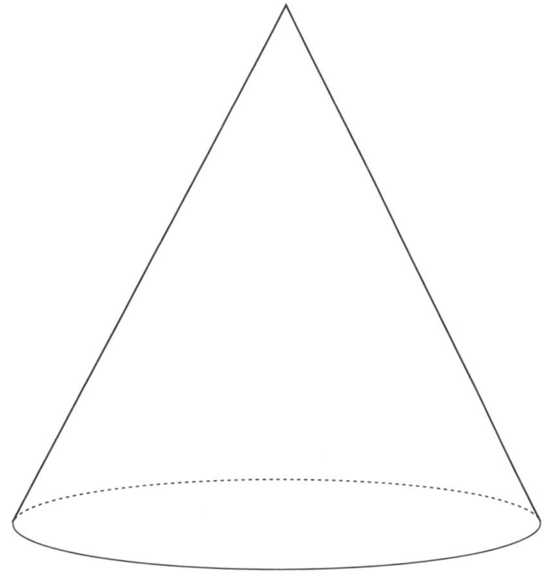

How many vertices does a cone have?

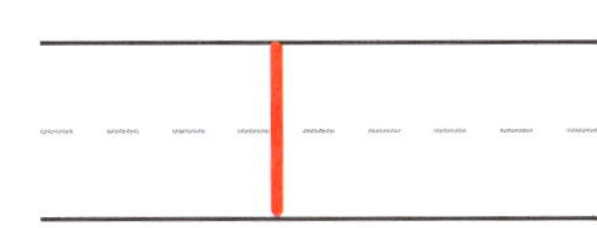

b How many edges does a cone have?

a How many faces does a cone have?

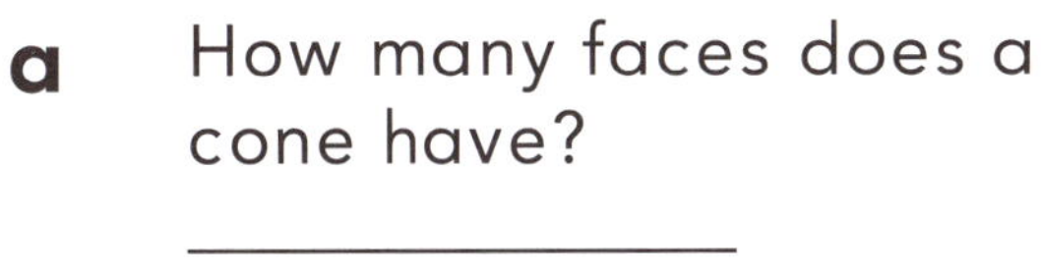

c Is cone a solid or a flat shape?

3. Circle the objects shaped like cones.

4. Find or think of 2 objects that are shaped like cones. Draw them.

a

b

Cylinders

Cylinders are solid shapes. They have attributes.

This is a **cylinder**. It looks like a can.

A cylinder has 3 faces. Two are shaped like a circle. One is on top. One is on the bottom. It also has a curved face.

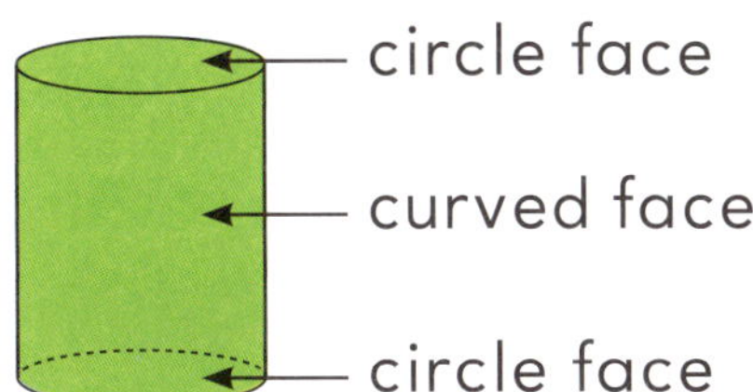

A cylinder has 2 round edges.

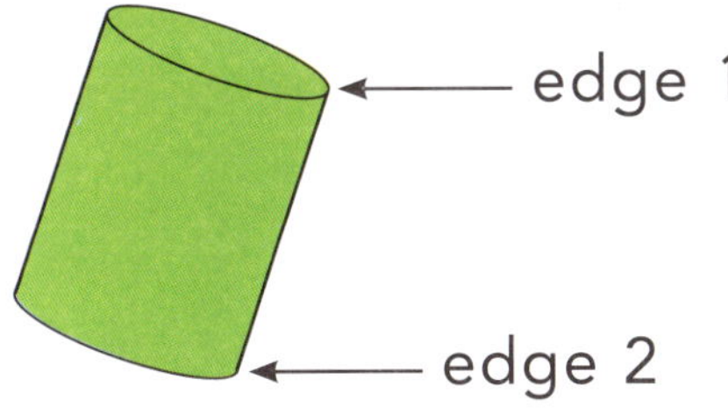

Cylinders are 3D. They are solid shapes.

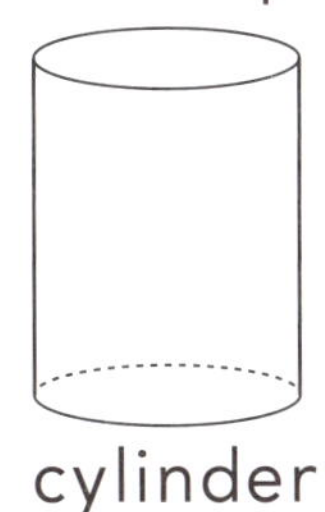

cylinder

rectangle

Your turn

1 Color the cylinders.

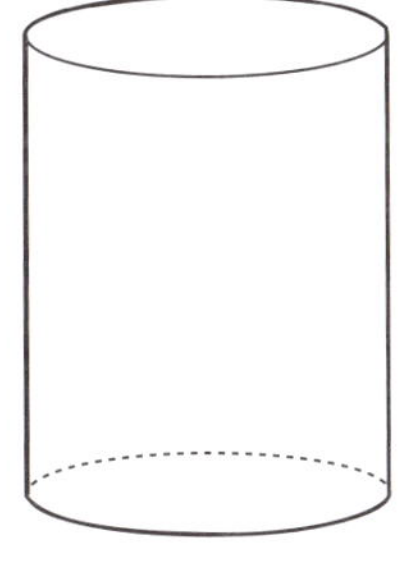

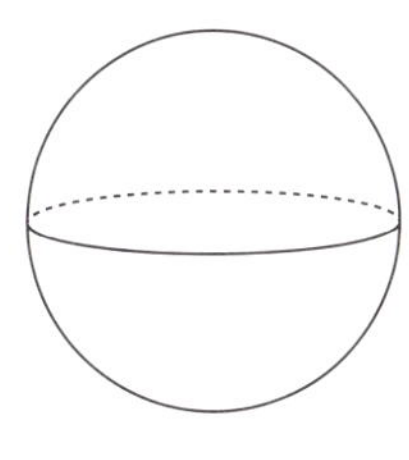

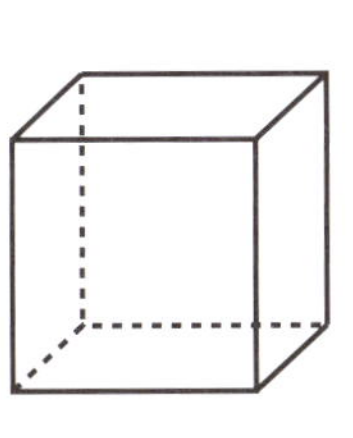

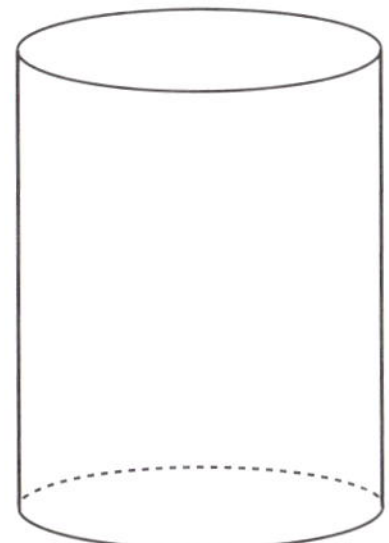

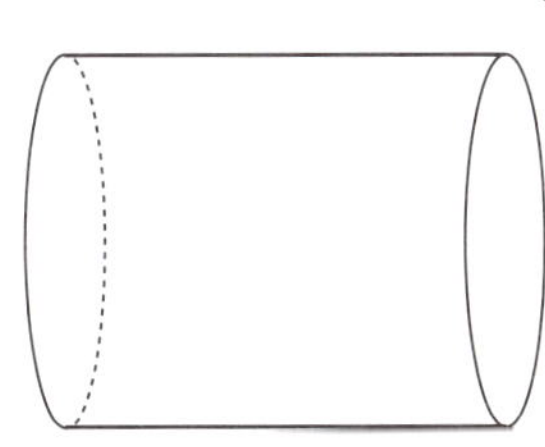

Cylinders do not have any vertices. All the edges are round.

SELF CHECK Mark how you feel

Got it!	Need help...	I don't get it

Practice

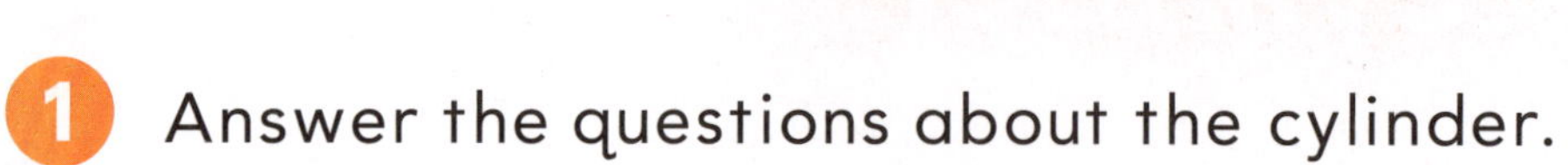

1 Answer the questions about the cylinder.

Is the cylinder a solid or a flat shape?

a How many faces does a cylinder have?

b What shape are a cylinder's faces?

c How many edges does a cylinder have?

d How many vertices does a cylinder have?

2 Color the cylinders.

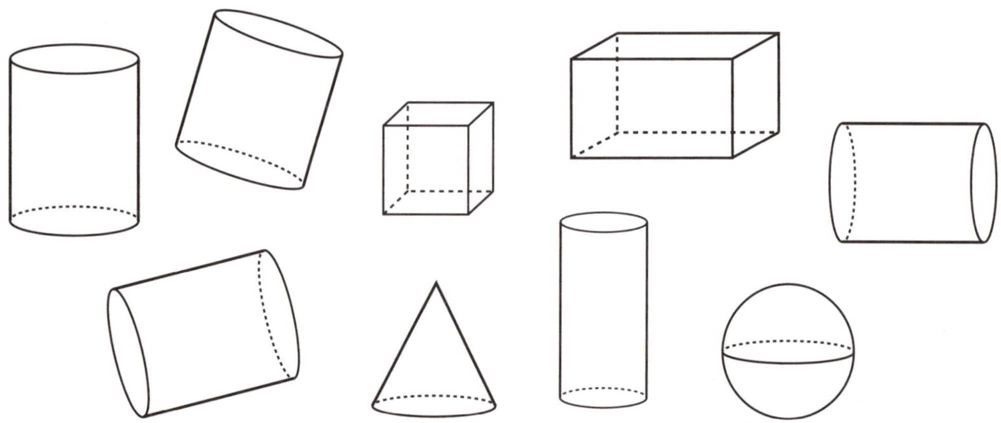

3. Circle the objects shaped like cylinders.

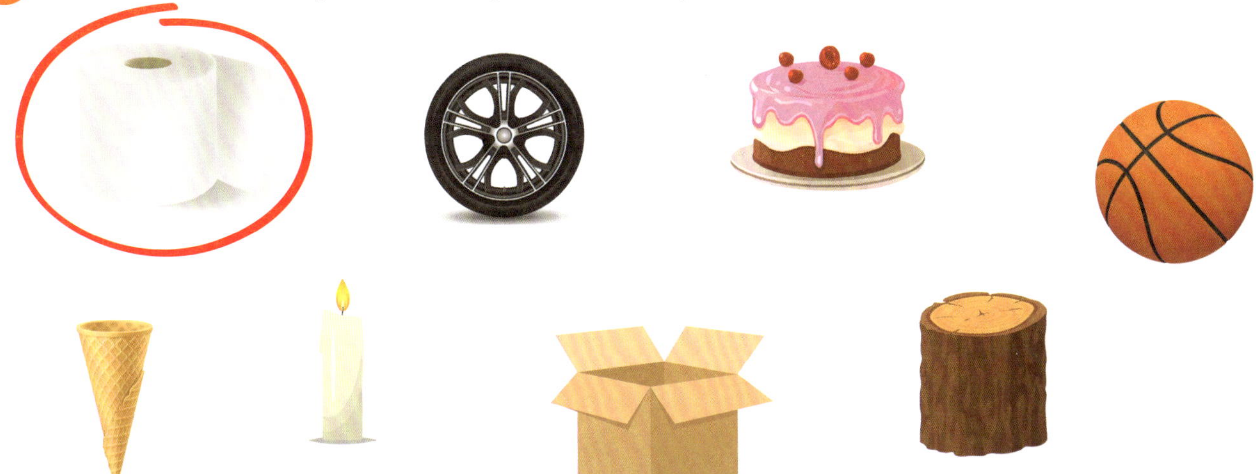

4. Find or think of 4 objects that are shaped like cylinders. Draw them.

a

c

b

d

Spheres

Spheres are solid shapes. They have attributes.

This is a **sphere**. It looks like a ball.

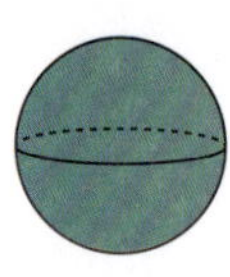

A sphere has 0 flat faces.

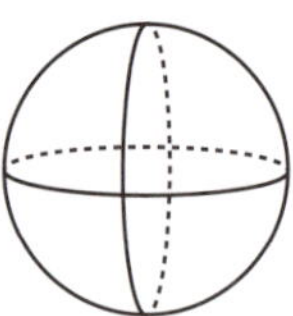

The curved surface wraps all the way around. There are no edges, breaks, or vertices.

Spheres are 3D. They are solid shapes. They are not flat.

sphere

circle

1 Color the spheres.

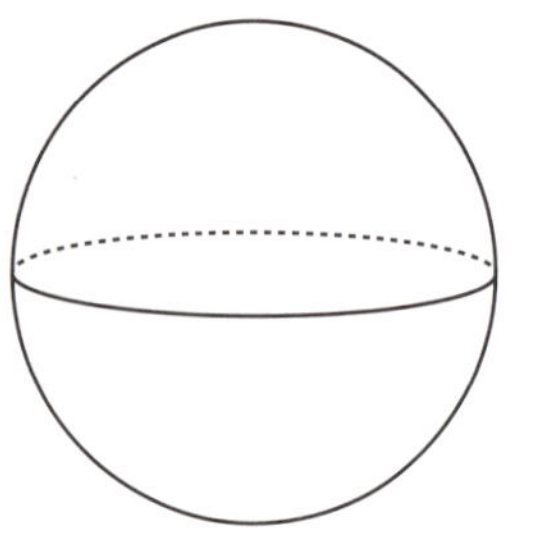
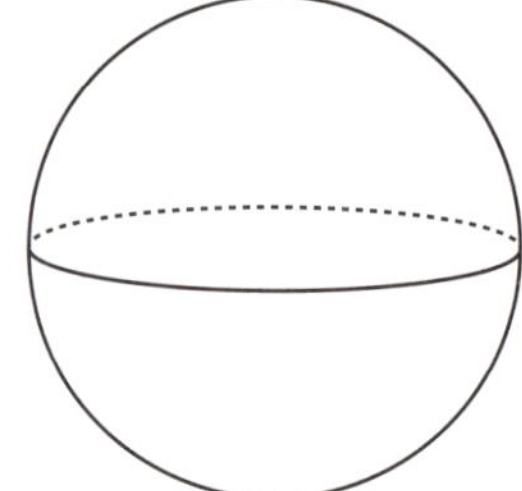
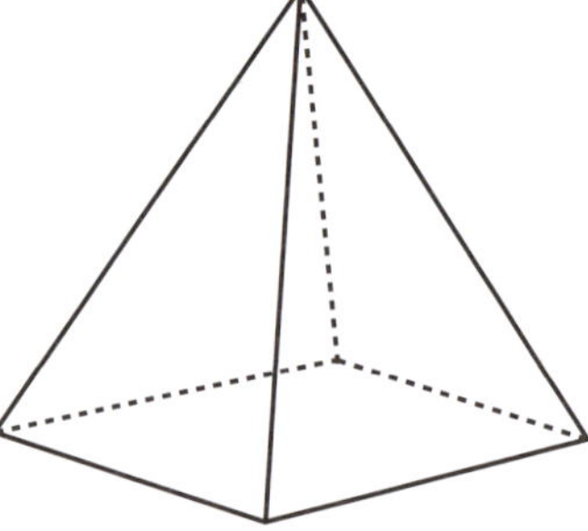
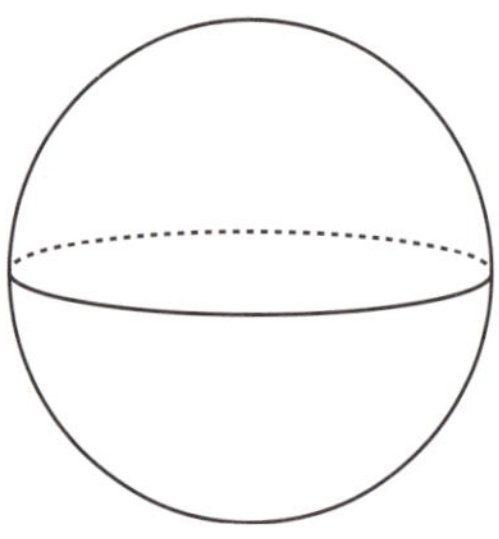
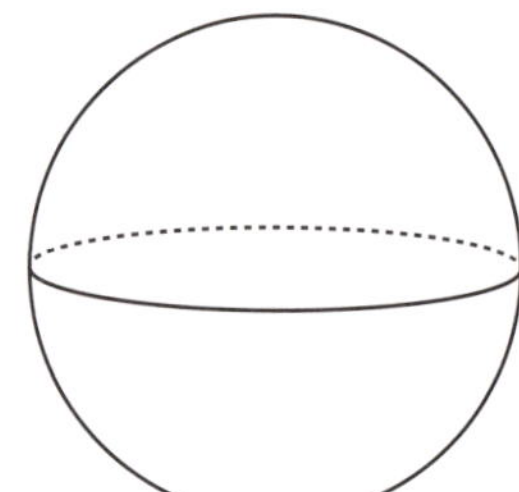
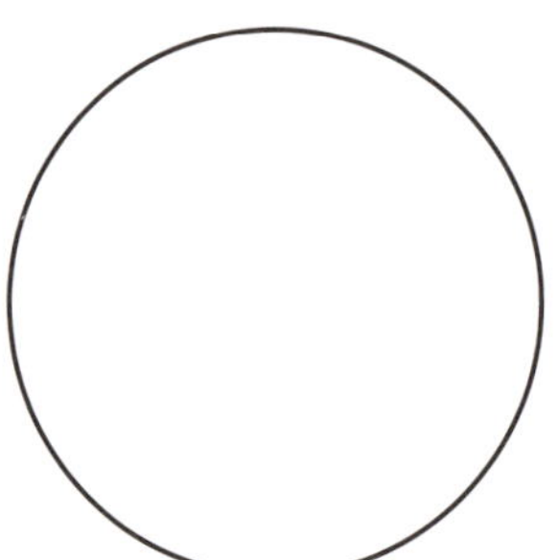

SELF CHECK	Mark how you feel	
Got it!	Need help...	I don't get it

Practice

1 Answer the questions about the sphere.

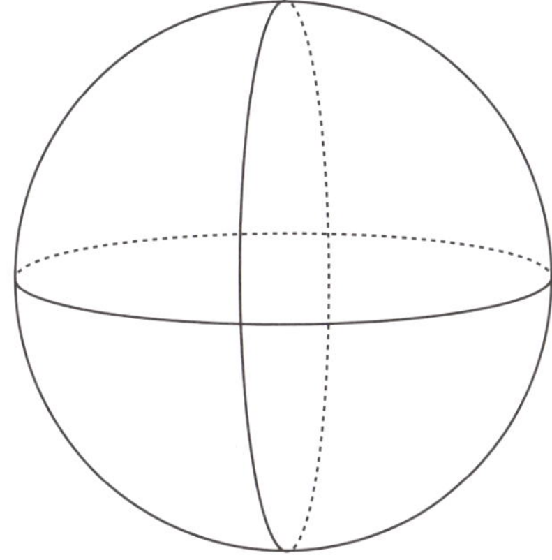

a How many vertices does a sphere have?

____

____

b How many faces does a sphere have?

____

____

c How many edges does a sphere have?

____

____

d Is a sphere a solid or flat shape?

____

____

2 Circle the objects shaped like spheres.

3 Color the spheres.

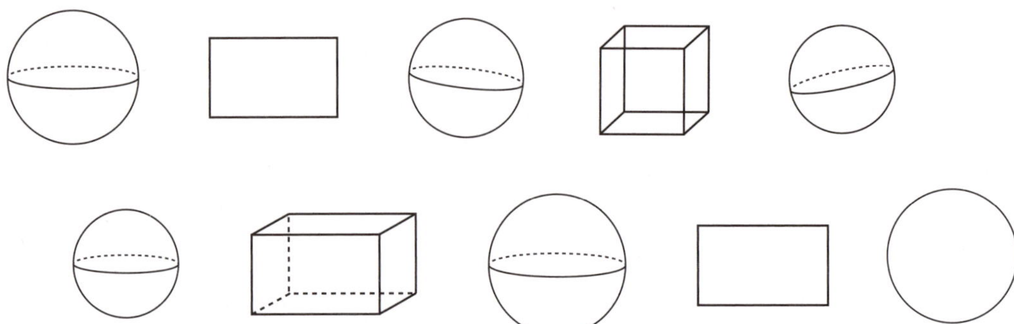

4 Find or think of 4 objects that are shaped like spheres. Draw them.

a

c

b

d

Rectangular Prisms

Rectangular prisms are solid shapes. They have attributes.

This is a **rectangular prism**. It looks like a box.

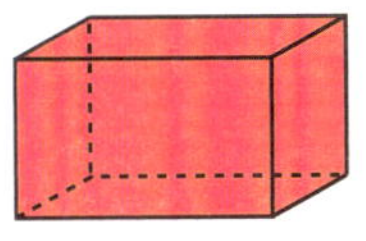

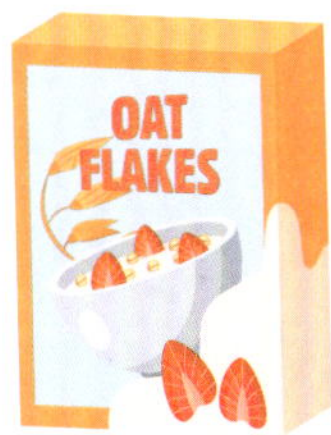

A rectangular prism has 6 faces. The faces are rectangles.

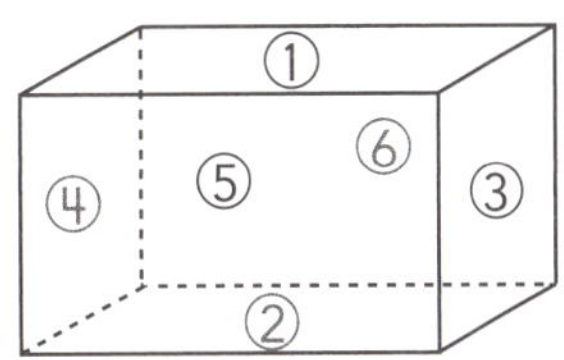

A rectangular prism has 12 edges. It has 8 vertices. Can you count them all?

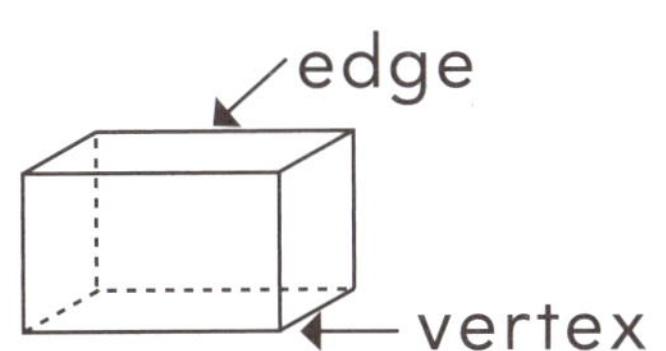

Rectangular prisms are 3D. They are solid shapes.

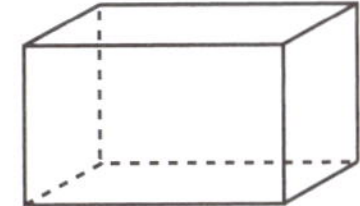

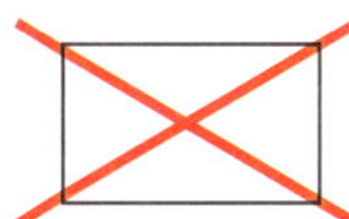

rectangular prism   rectangle

1 Color the rectangular prisms.

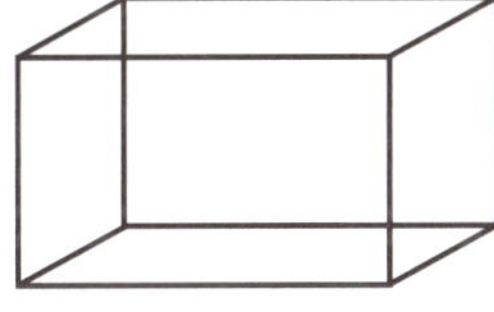

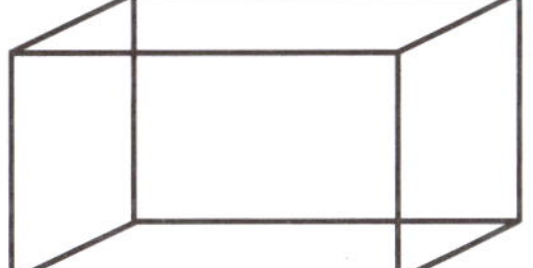

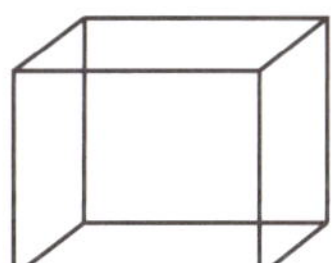

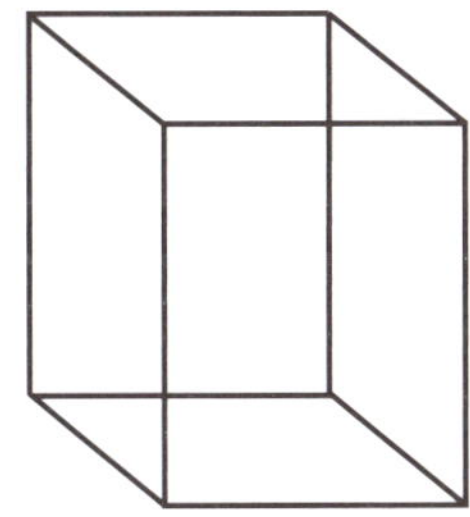

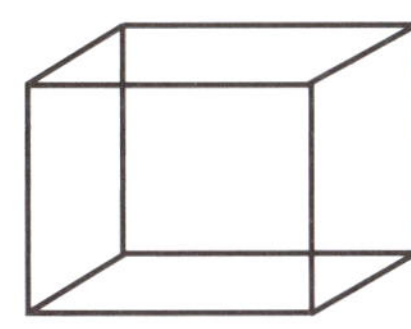

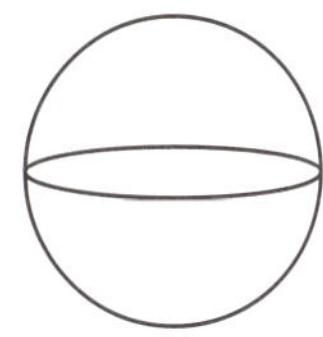

The faces opposite each other are the same size and shape.

SELF CHECK Mark how you feel

Got it!	Need help...	I don't get it

Practice

1 Color the rectangular prisms.

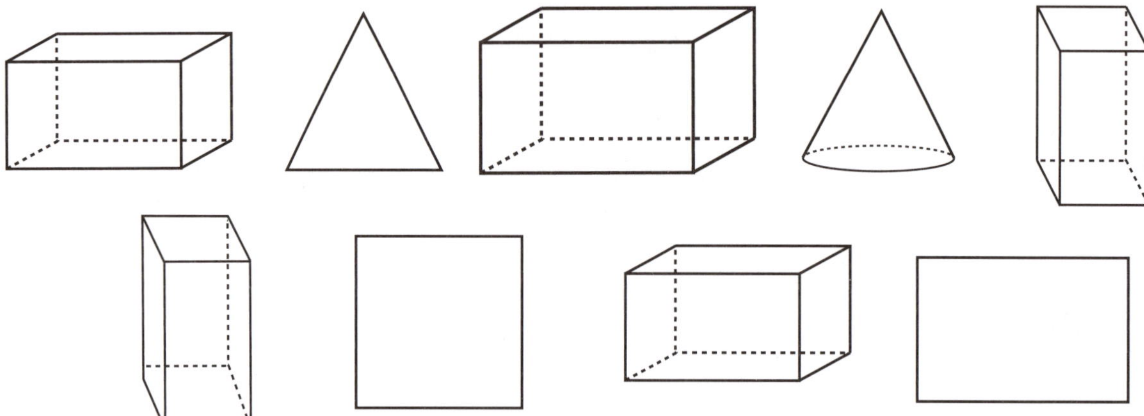

2 Answer the questions about the rectangular prism.

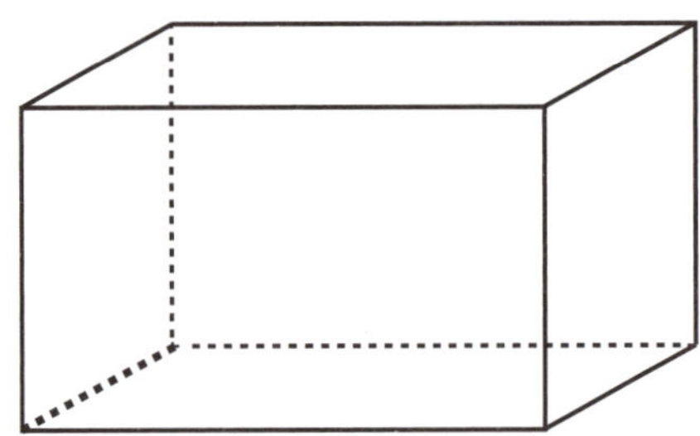

Is a rectangular prism a flat or solid shape?

solid

a How many corners does a rectangular prism have?

b What shape are the faces?

c How many edges does a rectangular prism have?

d How many faces does a rectangular prism have?

3 Circle the objects shaped like rectangular prisms.

4 Find or think of 4 objects that are shaped like rectangular prisms. Draw them.

a

c

b

d

Describe 3D Shapes

You can describe 3D shapes.

There are many 3D shapes.

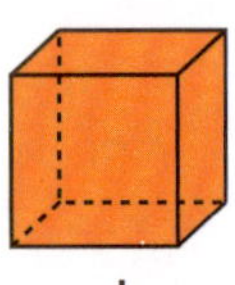
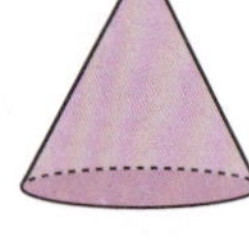
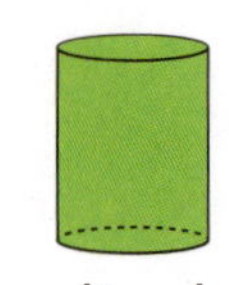
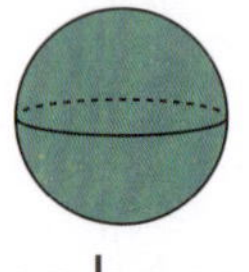
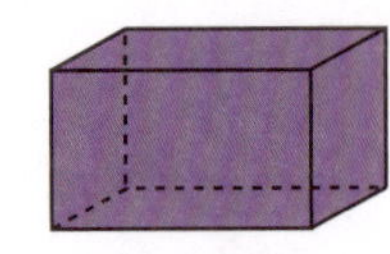

cube cone cylinder sphere rectangular prism

A shape is a shape, no matter its size or which way it is turned.

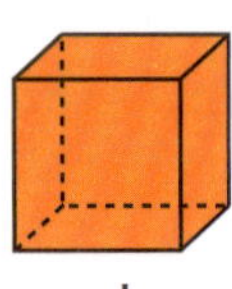
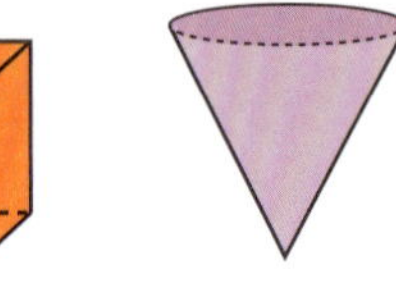
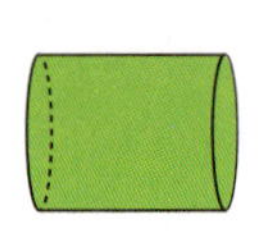
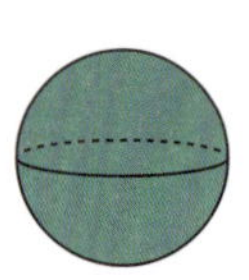
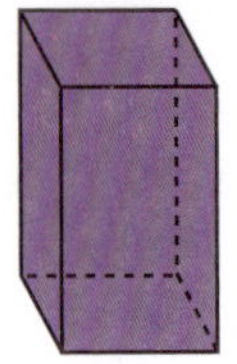

cube cone cylinder sphere rectangular prism

All 3D shapes are solid. This means they have thickness.

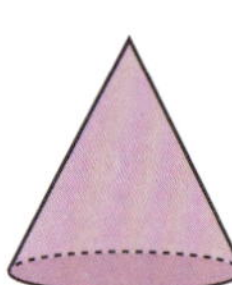

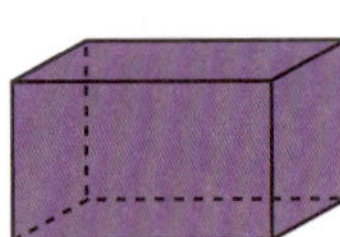

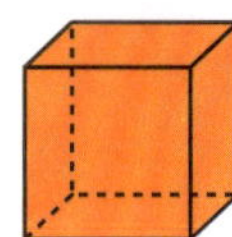

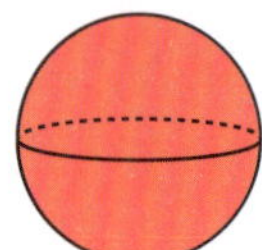

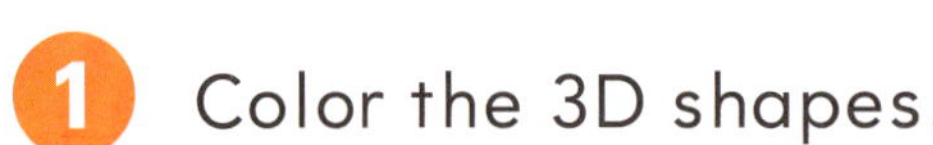

1 Color the 3D shapes.

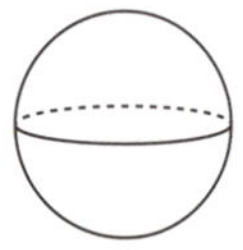

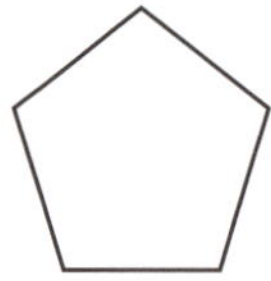
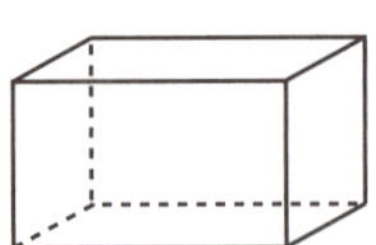
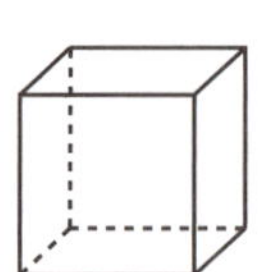

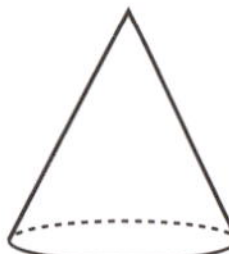

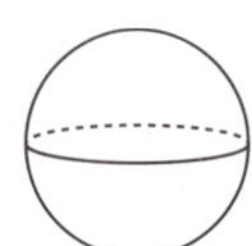

SELF CHECK	Mark how you feel	
Got it!	Need help...	I don't get it
 ☐	 ☐	 ☐

Practice

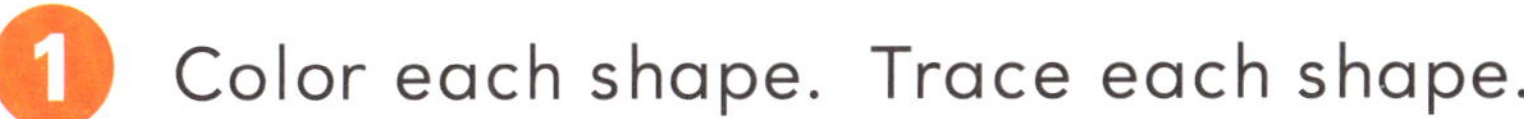

1 Color each shape. Trace each shape.

	Color the Shape	Trace the Shape
a		
b		
c		
d		
e		

2 Circle the answer to each question.

● I have one flat face shaped like a circle. What shape am I?

a I have six square faces. What shape am I?

b I have two circle faces. What shape am I?

c I have six rectangle faces. What shape am I?

d I have no flat faces, edges, or vertices. What shape am I?

3 Draw lines to match the shapes to their names.

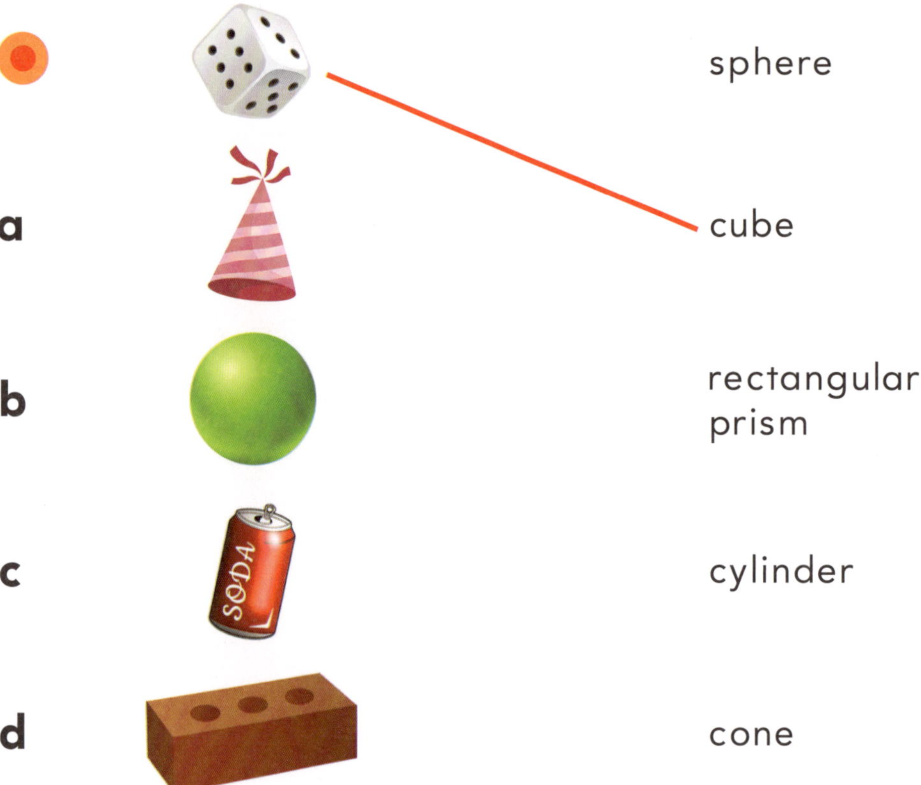

4 Color the objects that have the same shape as the one on the left.

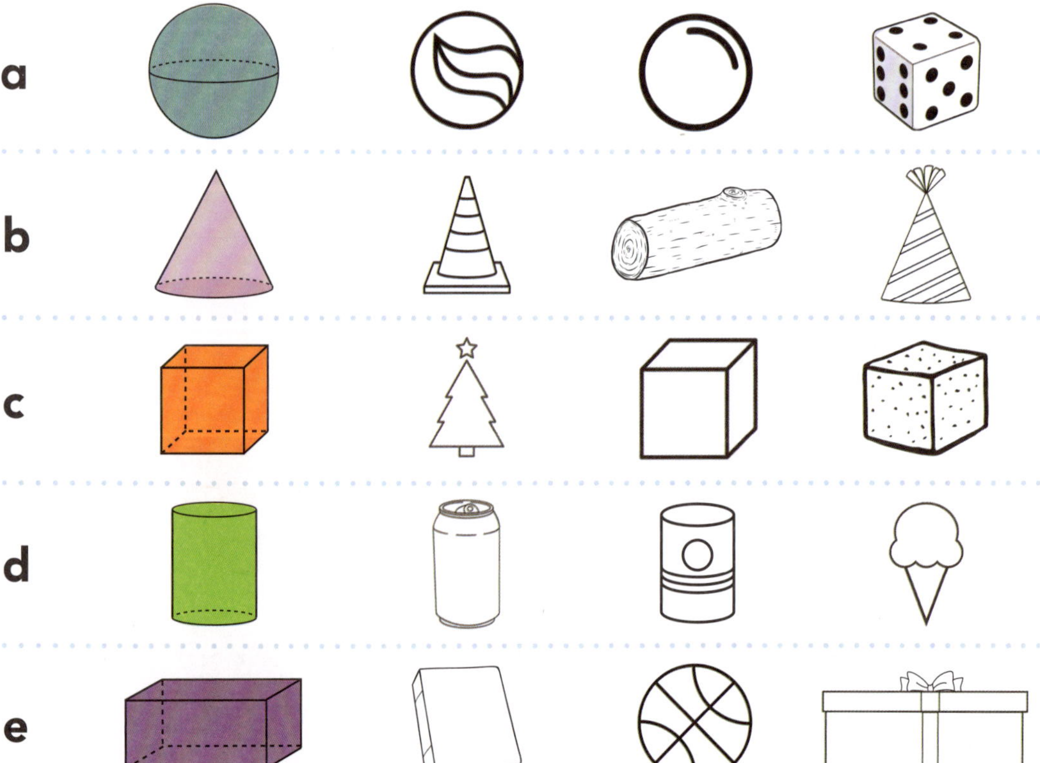

3D Shapes Review

1 Circle the 3D (solid) shapes.

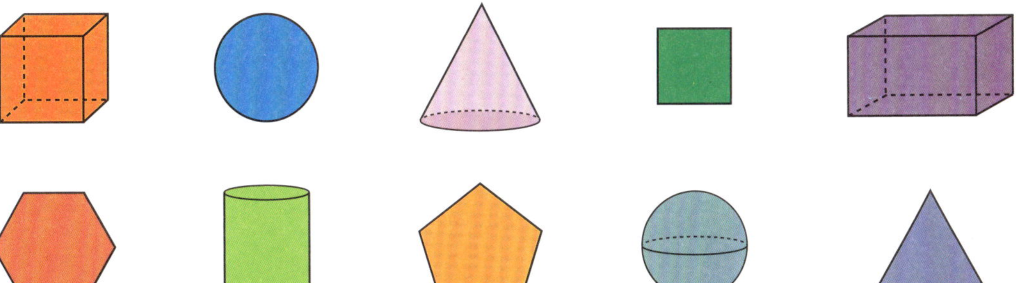

2 Color one face on each shape.

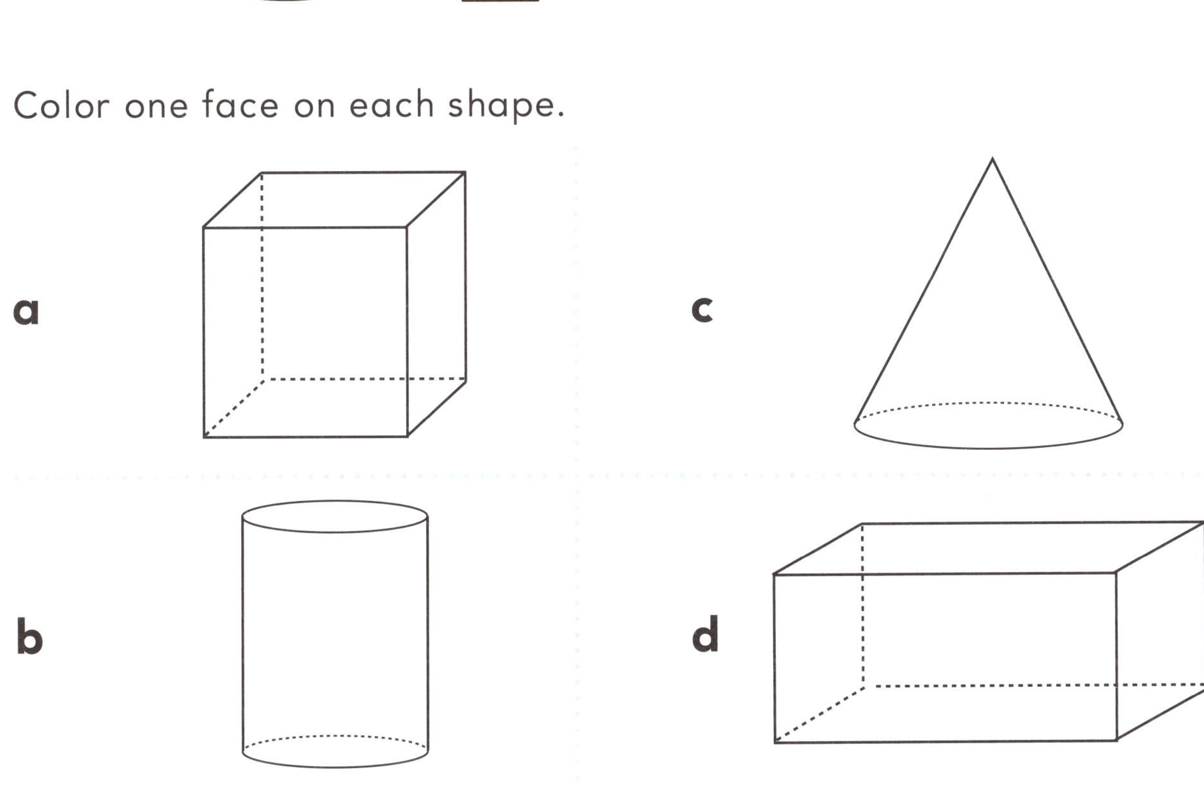

3 Circle the 3D (solid) objects.

Review

4 Match each shape to its name.

a 

b 

c 

d 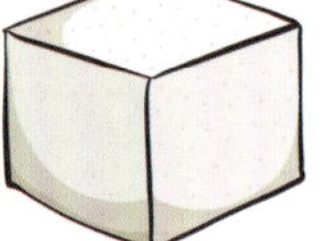

e 

rectangular prism

cone

cube

sphere

cylinder

5 Write how many vertices each shape has.

a  ______

d  ______

b 

______

e  ______

c  ______

Length

You can measure and compare the lengths of objects.

Length is a kind of measurement. It tells how long something is. It measures from one side to the other.

You can measure length with a ruler. You can use other objects, too.

The book is 5 paper clips long.

You can compare the lengths of objects. You can see which is longer and which is shorter.

longest

shortest

1 Circle the longest object.

a

b

SELF CHECK Mark how you feel		
Got it!  ☐	Need help...  ☐	I don't get it ☐

Line up objects at one end when you compare their lengths.

Practice

1 Circle the shortest object.

a

c

b

d

2 Measure each object with connecting cubes. Write how long it is.

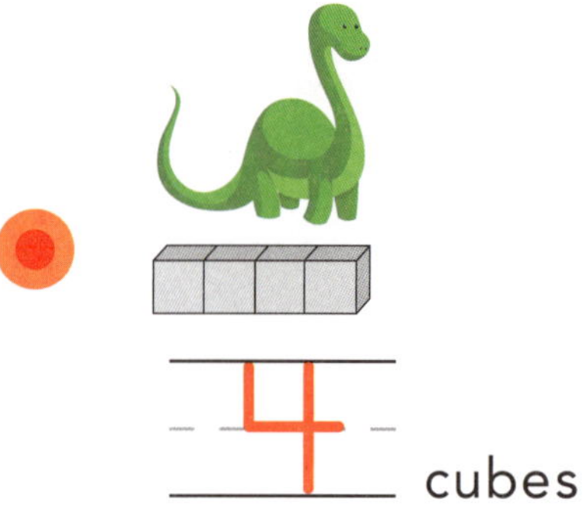

4 cubes

a

_____ cubes

c

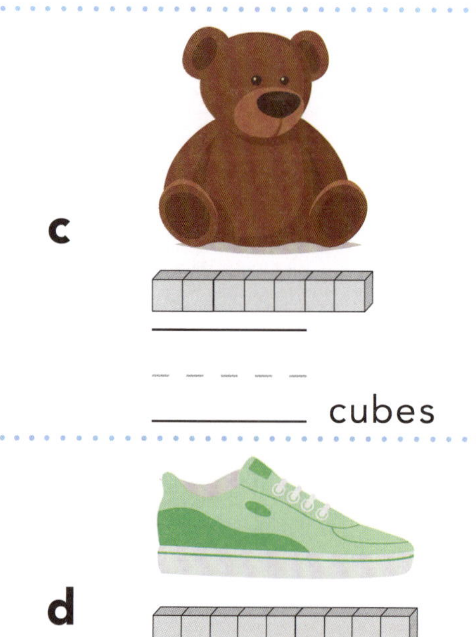

_____ cubes

b

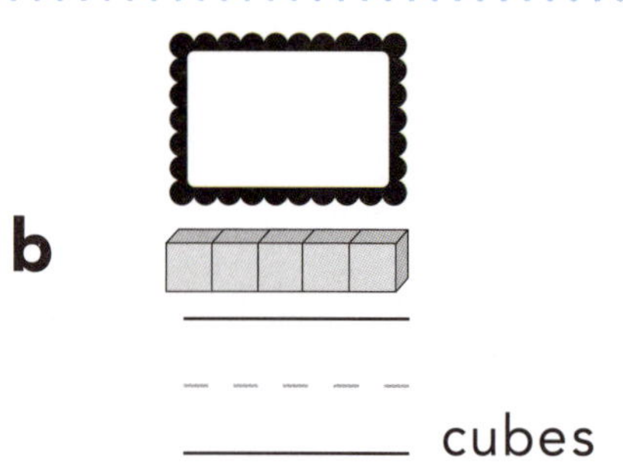

_____ cubes

d

_____ cubes

Height

You can measure and compare the heights of objects.

Height is a measurement. It tells you how tall something is.

To measure height, start at the bottom and go to the top.

You can measure how tall things are. You can find the height of a tree, a building, or even a toy.

You can compare the heights of objects. You can see which is taller and which is shorter.

shortest tallest

Your turn

1 Circle the tallest object.

a

b

What is your height? How can you find out?

SELF CHECK	Mark how you feel	
Got it! ☐	Need help... ☐	I don't get it ☐

1 Circle the shortest object.

b

a

c

2 Circle the objects that are the same height.

b

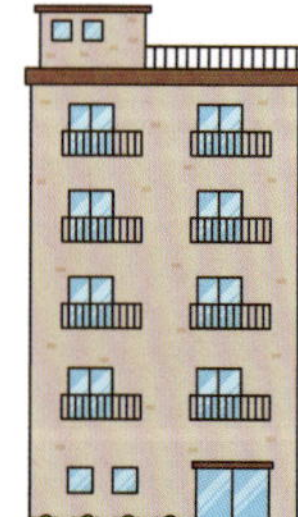

a

c

3 Write how tall each object is.

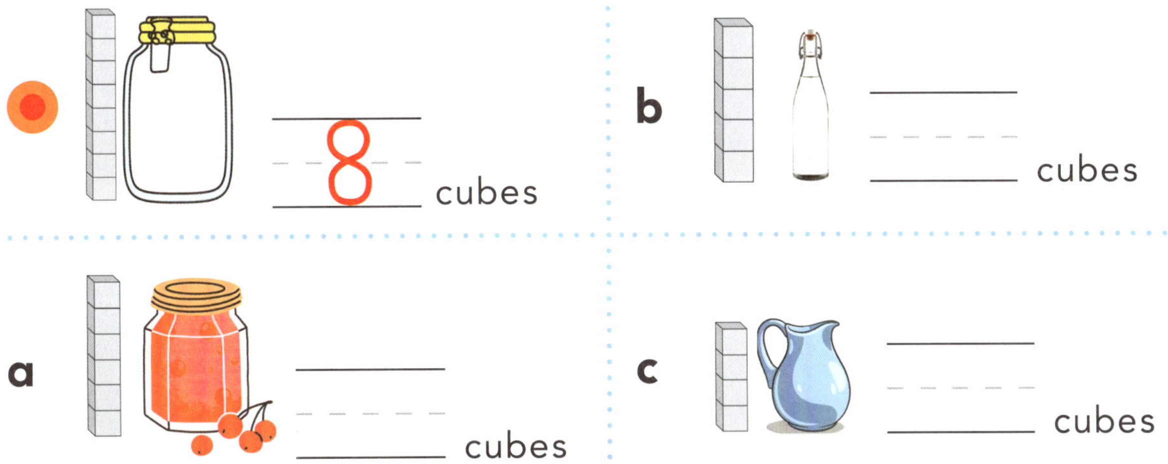

4 Compare the heights of the objects. Write 1, 2, and 3 to order them from tallest to shortest. The tallest is 1. The shortest is 3.

Width

You can measure and compare the widths of objects.

Width is a measurement. It tells you how wide something is. It measures from one side to the other.

You can compare the width of objects. You can see which is narrower and which is wider.

width

widest

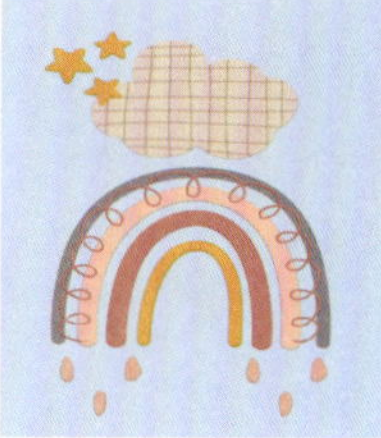

narrowest

1 Circle the widest object.

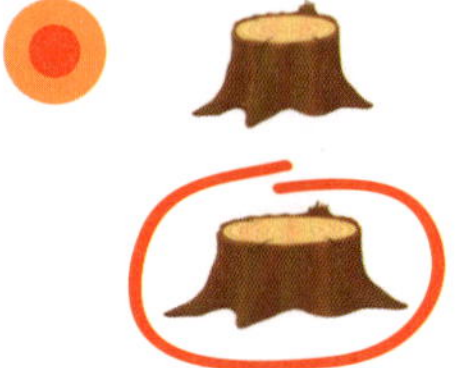

a 

c  

b  

d  

Narrow means skinny. It is the opposite of *wide*.

SELF CHECK Mark how you feel

Got it!	Need help...	I don't get it

1 Circle the narrowest object.

2 Write how wide each object is.

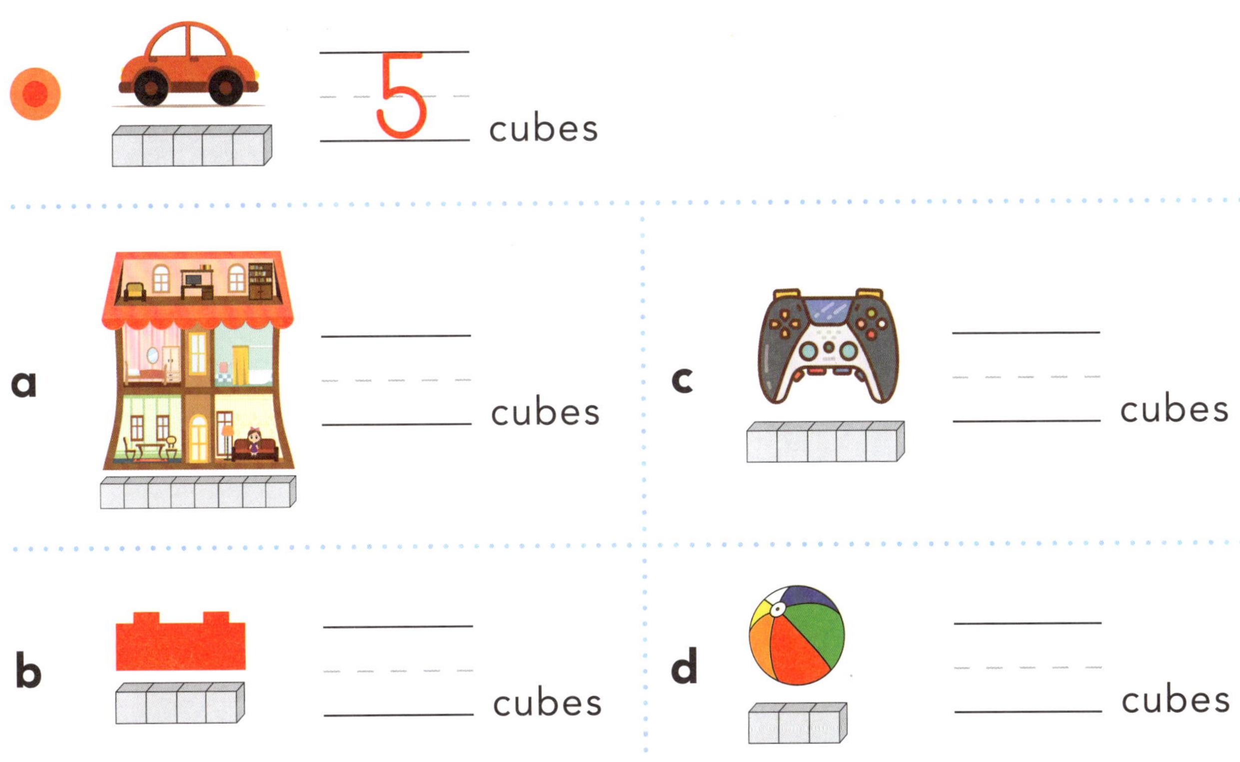

3 Circle the two objects that are the same width.

a 

c 

b 

d 

4 Compare the widths of the objects. Write 1, 2, and 3 to order them from widest to narrowest. The widest is 1. The narrowest is 3.

a 

c 

b 

d 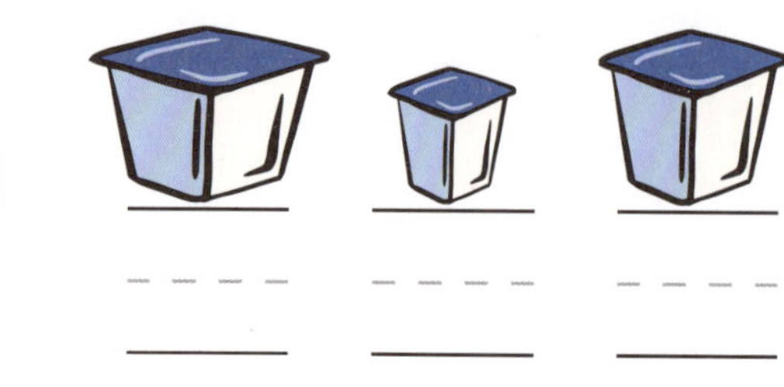

Weight

You can measure and compare the weights of objects.

Weight is how heavy or light something is.

An elephant is heavy. A mouse is light.

You can use a scale to measure weight. A scale shows how much something pushes down on it.

1 Circle the object that is heavier.

a  

c  

b  

d  

Bigger does not always mean heavier. A stapler weighs more than a balloon!

SELF CHECK	Mark how you feel	
Got it!	Need help...	I don't get it
 ☐	 ☐	 ☐

Practice

1 Circle the object that is lighter.

2 Look at the cubes on each scale. Circle the side that weighs more.

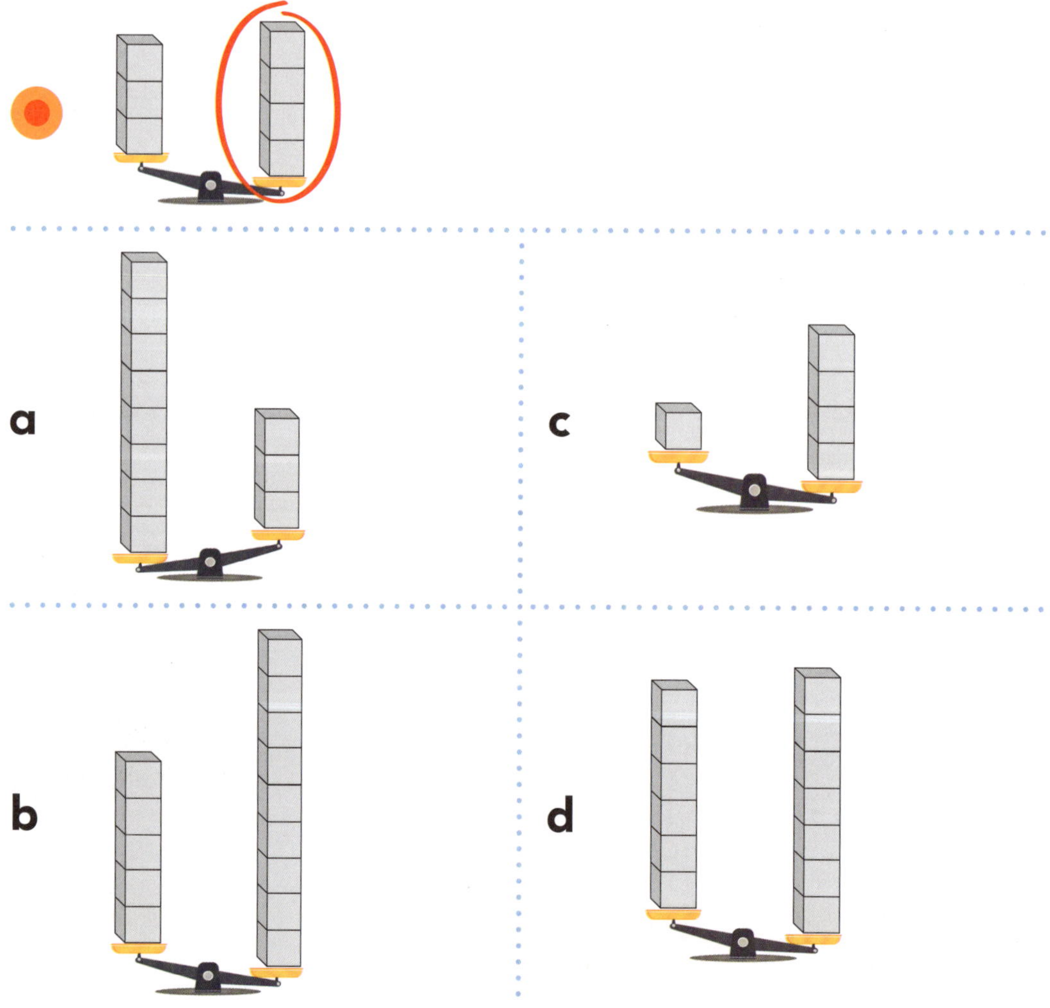

3 Write how many cubes each object weighs.

● 7 cubes

a ______ cubes

c ______ cubes

b ______ cubes

d ______ cubes

4 Circle the heavier object. Underline the lighter object.

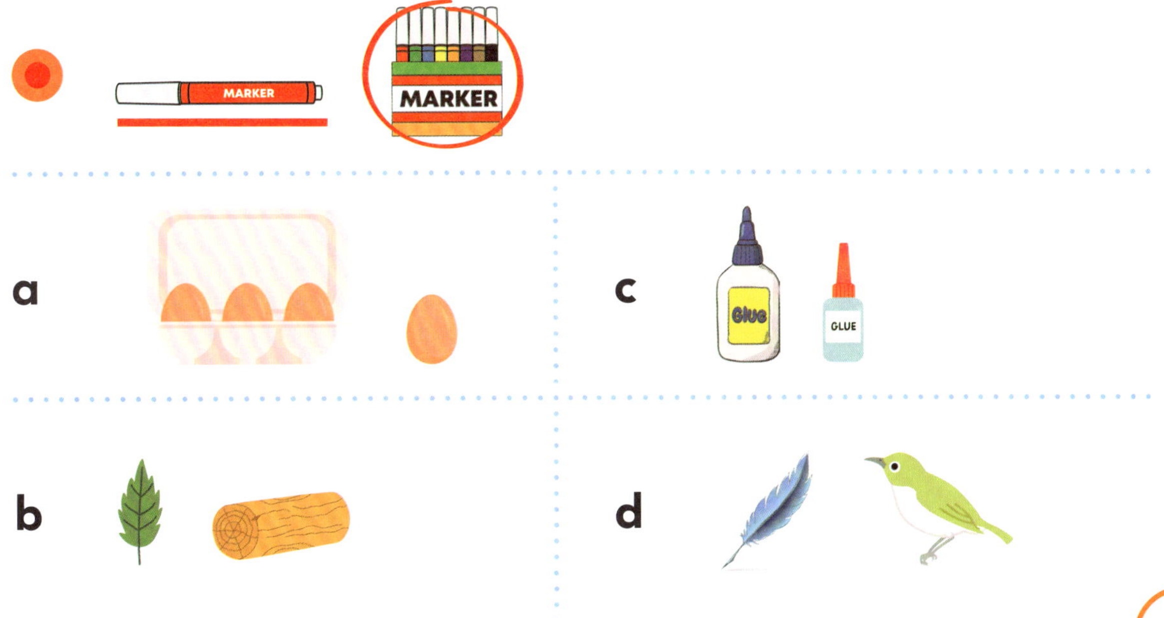

●

a

c

b

d

Capacity

You can measure and compare the capacities of objects.

Capacity tells you how much something can hold.

The pitcher has a greater capacity than the cup. It can hold more water.

The mug has less capacity than the bucket. It can hold less water.

1 Circle the objects that have greater capacity than a fishbowl.

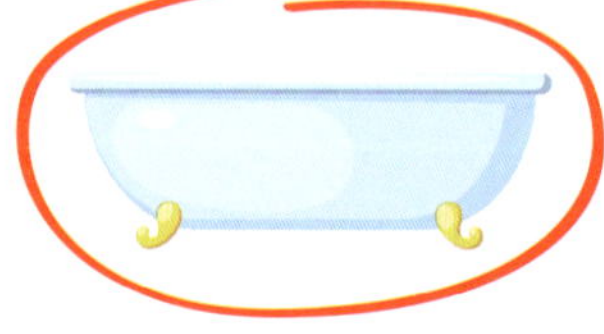

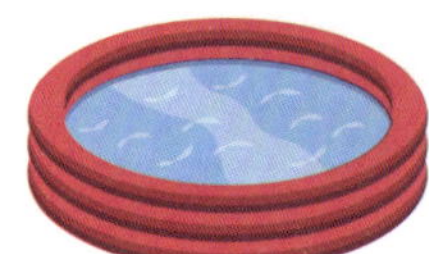

SELF CHECK Mark how you feel		
Got it!	Need help...	I don't get it
 ☐	 ☐	☐

Practice

1 Circle the objects that have less capacity than a popcorn bucket.

2 Compare the capacity of the objects. Write 1, 2, and 3 to order them from greatest to least. The greatest capacity is 1. The least is 3.

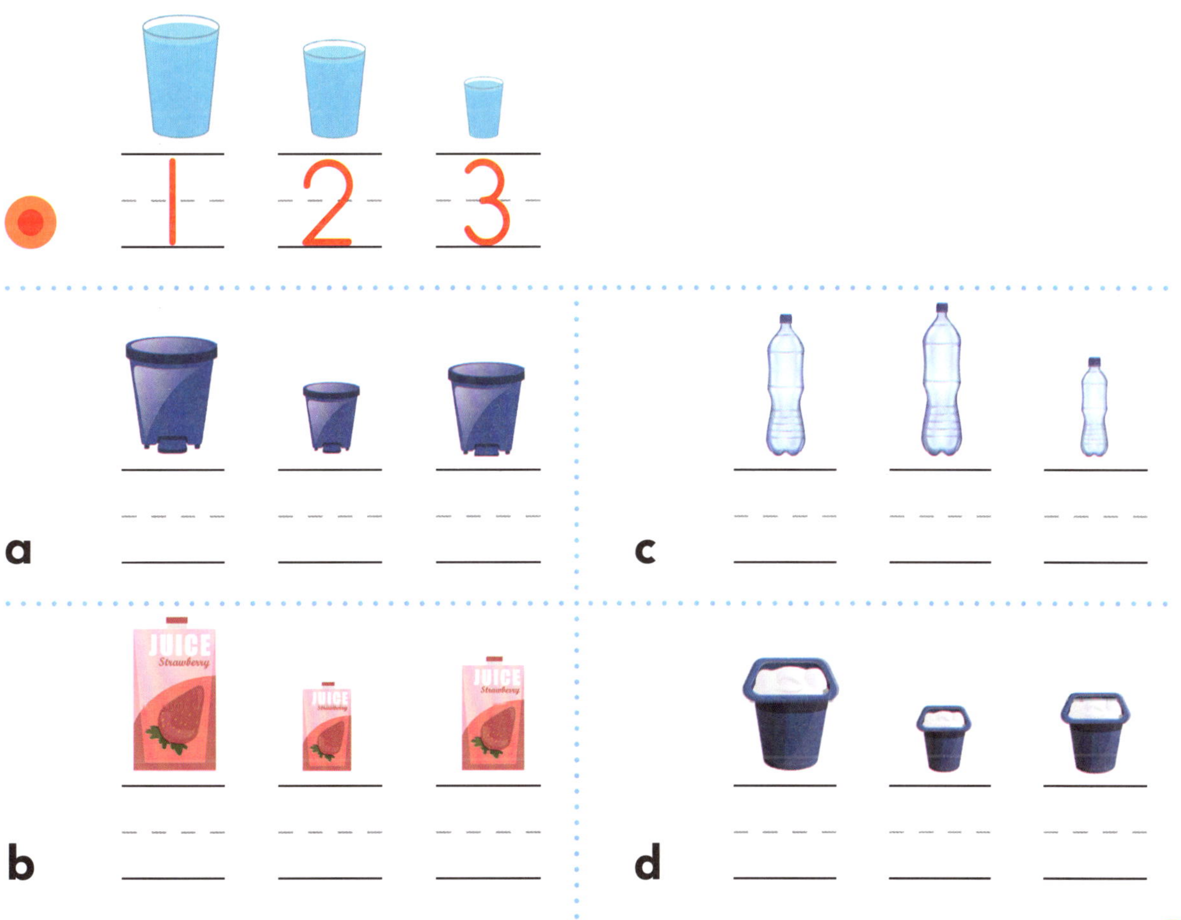

3 Can each item hold more or less than a milk jug? Circle the answer.

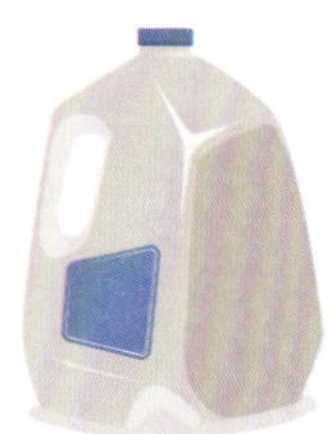

  more

less

a  more / less

c  more / less

b  more / less

d  more / less

4 Can each item hold more or less than a paper shopping bag? Circle the answer.

more

less

a  more / less

c  more / less

b  more / less

d  more / less

Measurement Review

1 Circle the tallest object.

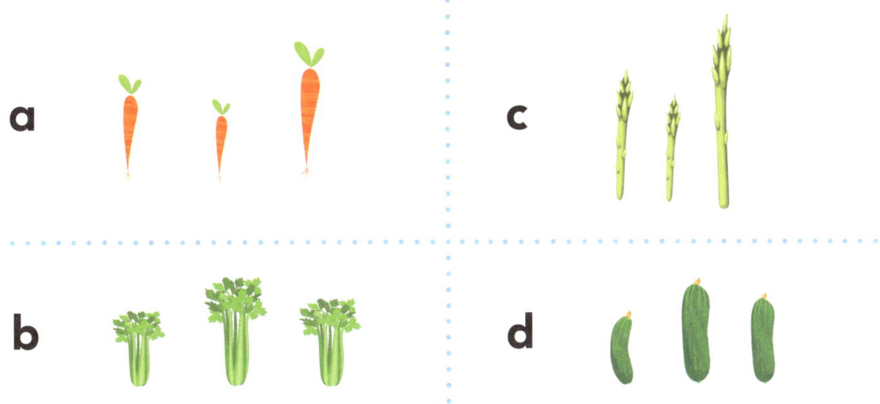

a

b

c

d

2 Write how wide each object is.

a

________ cubes

c

________ cubes

b

________ cubes

d

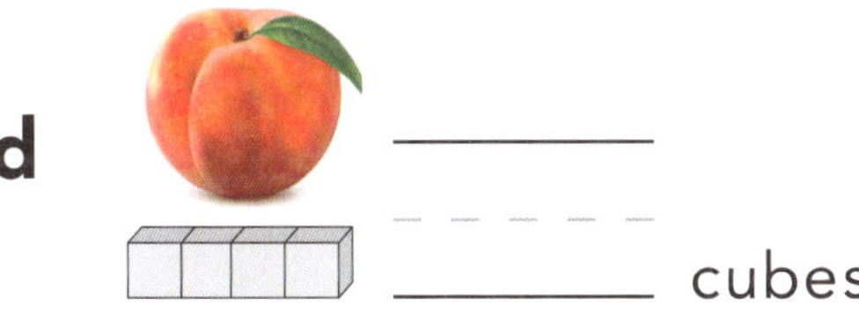

________ cubes

3 Circle the heavier object. Underline the lighter object.

a  

c  

b  

d  

Review

4 Circle the longest object.

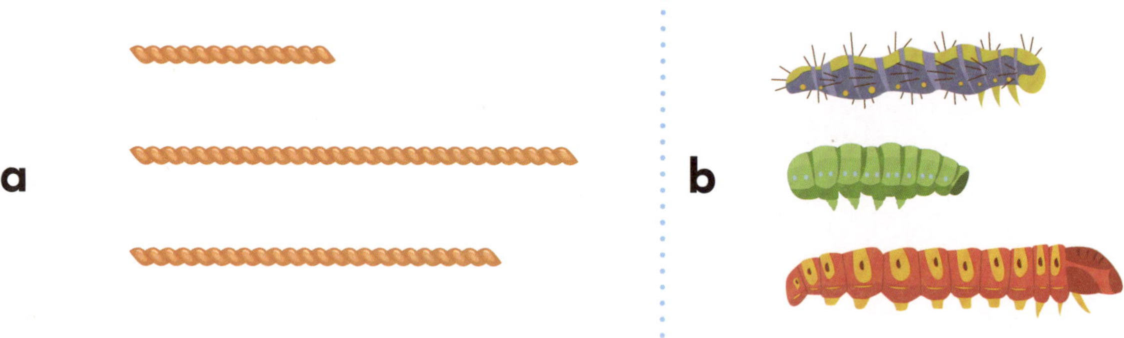

5 Circle the container with the greatest capacity.

6 Write how many cubes each object weighs.

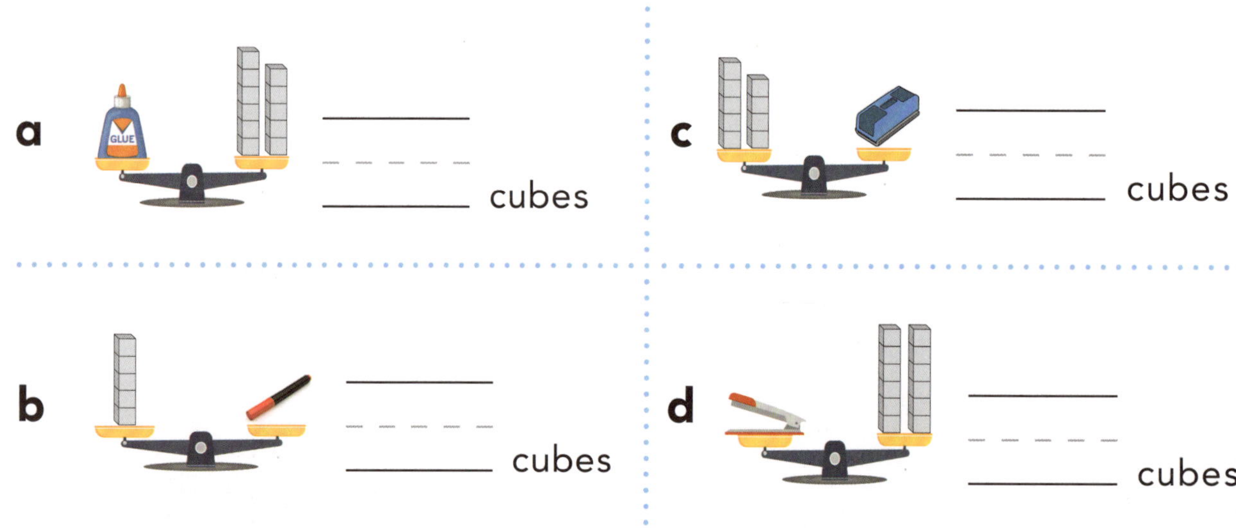

Recognize Patterns

Patterns are sets that repeat. Colors, numbers, or shapes can be used in patterns.

Example 1:

This is an AB pattern.

A B A B A B

A is orange. B is green. It repeats.

Example 2:

This is an ABC pattern.

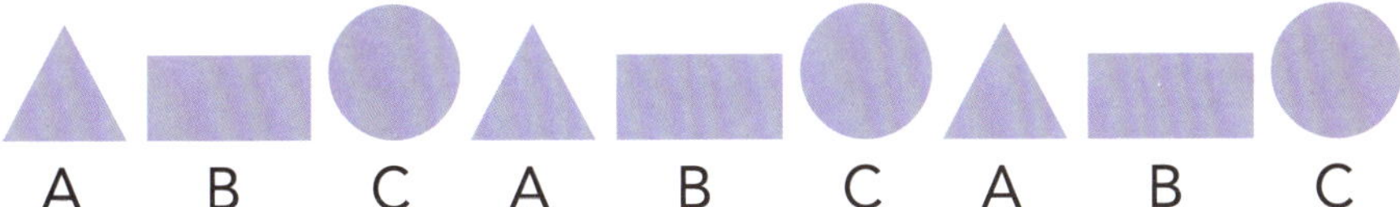

A B C A B C A B C

Example 3:

This is an AAB pattern.

A A B

Example 4:

This is an ABB pattern.

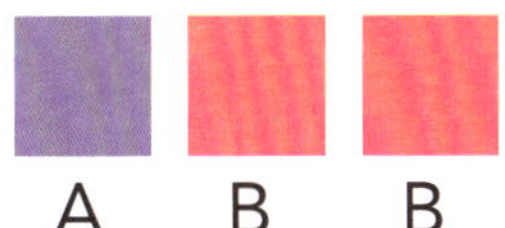

A B B

1 Look at each set below. Circle *yes* if it is a pattern. Circle *no* if it is not.

Practice

1 Look at each set. If it is a pattern, circle it. If not, cross it off.

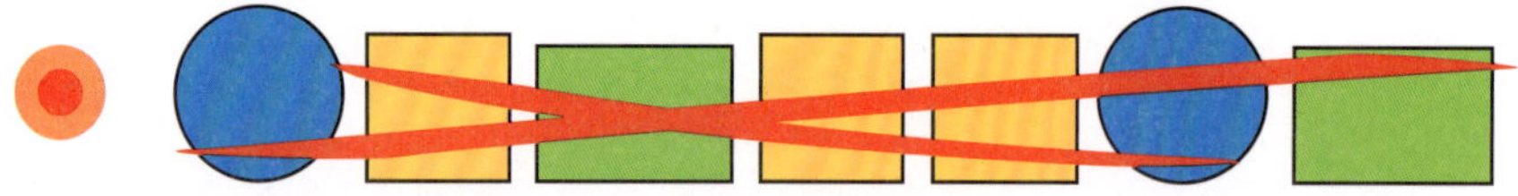

a 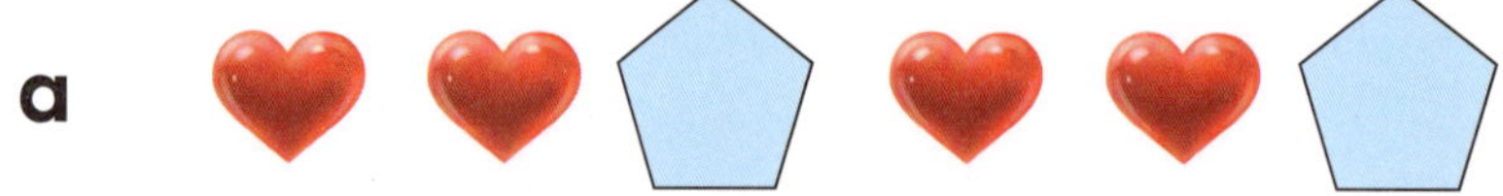

b 

c 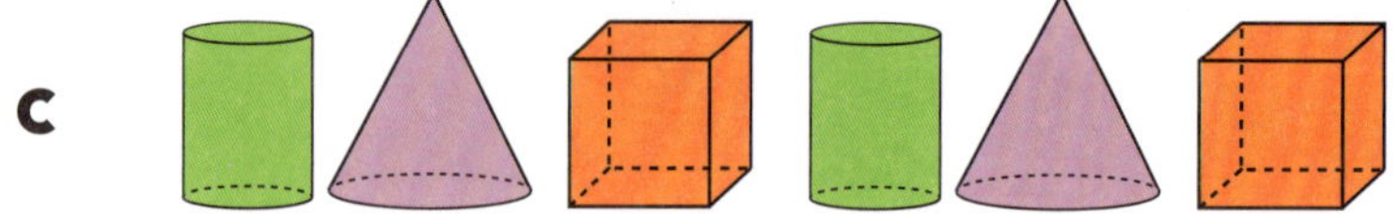

d 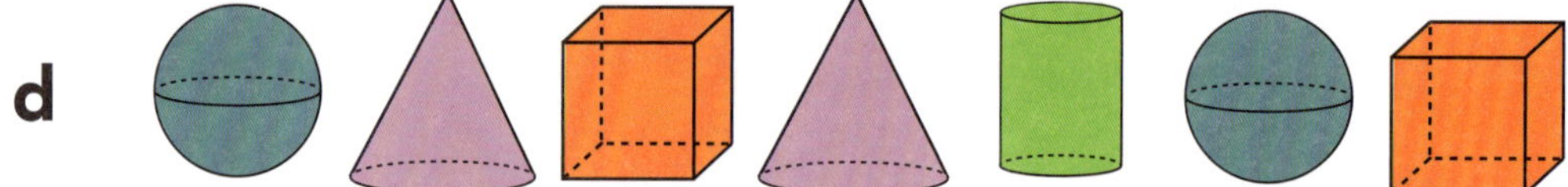

2 Circle the part of each pattern that repeats.

a 

b 

c 

d 

3 Look at each pattern. Write the pattern code.

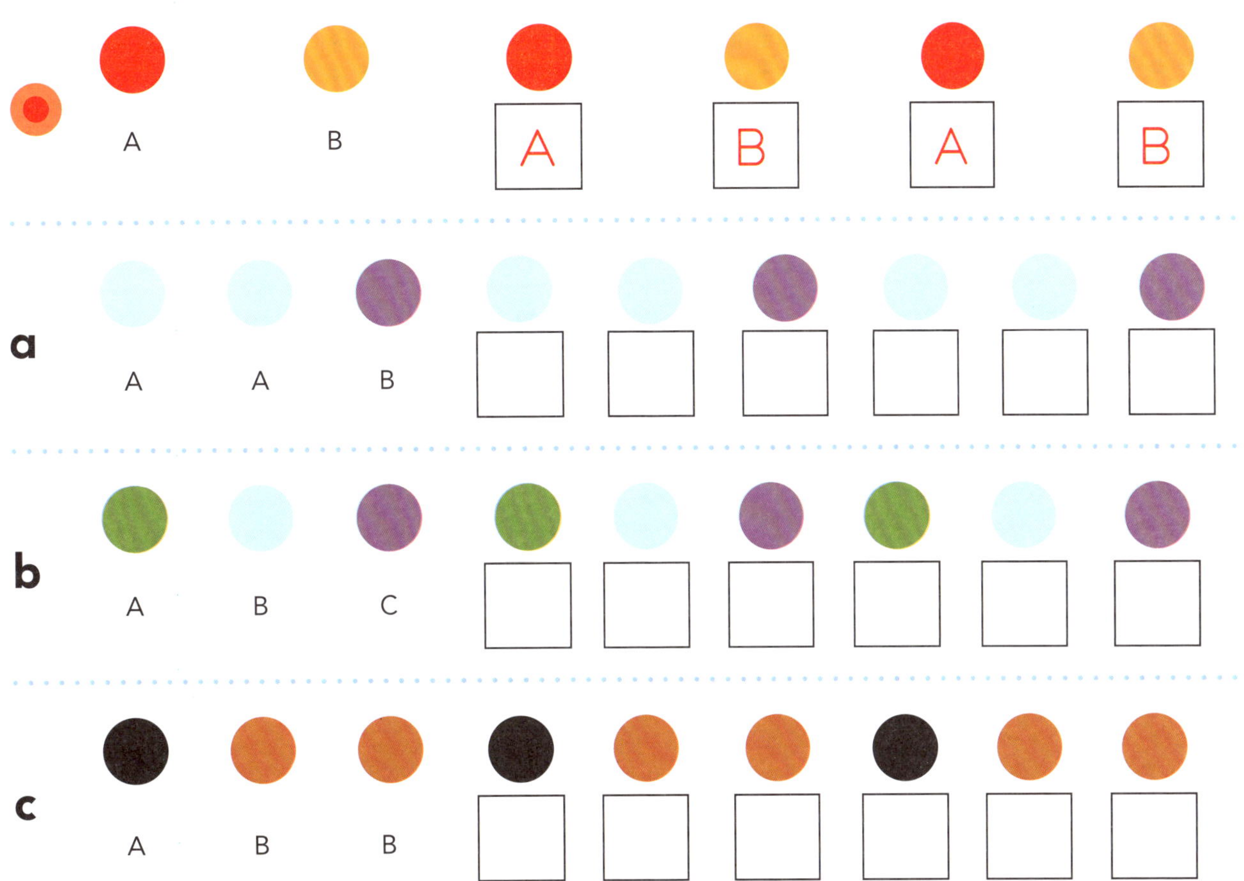

4 Look at each set. Circle *yes* if it is a pattern. Circle *no* if it is not.

●	1	2	2	1	2	2	(yes)	no
a	6	8	8	6	8	8	yes	no
b	1	2	3	1	2	3	yes	no
c	12	8	5	3	9	7	yes	no

Duplicate Patterns

You can duplicate a pattern.

Duplicate means make a copy of something.

The second row is a copy of the first row. The blue and purple triangles follow the same order.

Your turn

1 Duplicate each pattern.

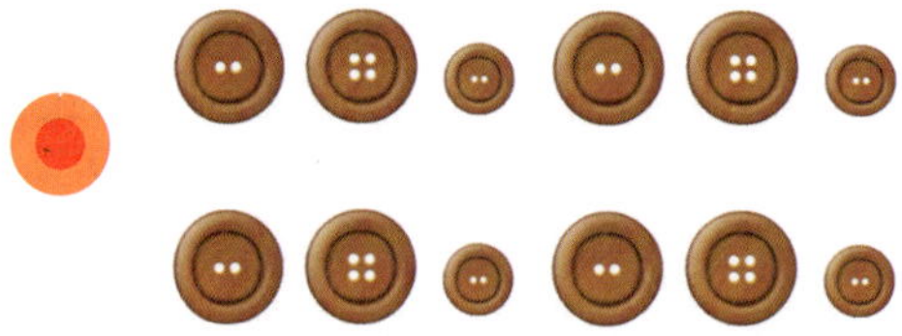

a

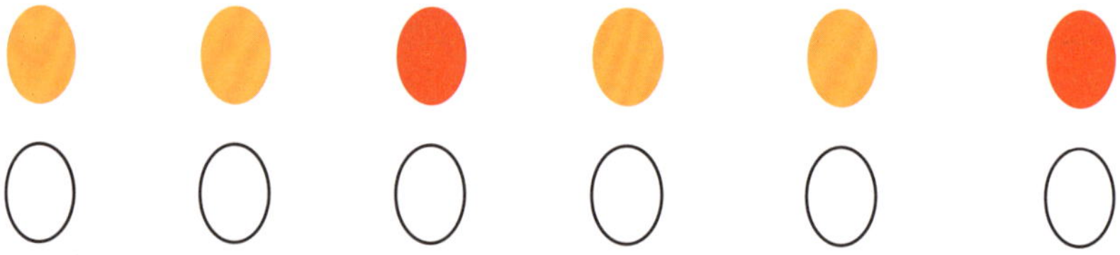

b

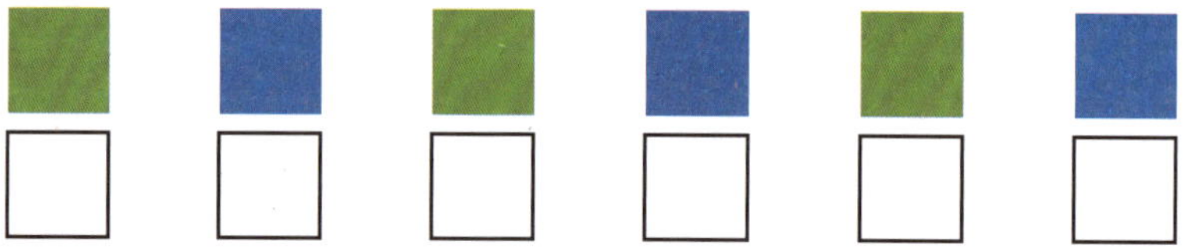

c

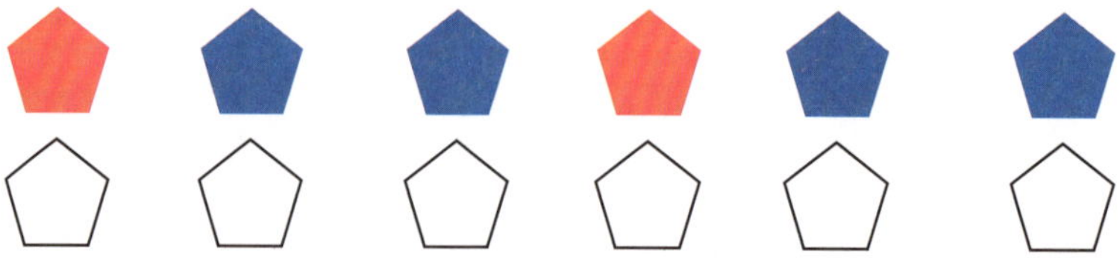

You can duplicate colors, shapes, numbers, blocks, and more.

SELF CHECK Mark how you feel

Got it! | Need help... | I don't get it

Practice

1 Duplicate each number pattern.

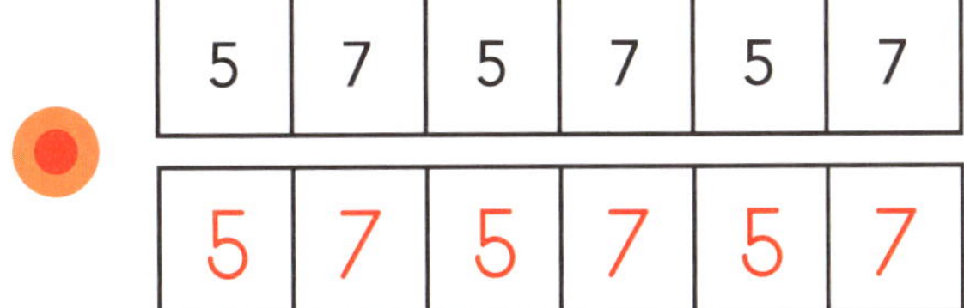

5	7	5	7	5	7
5	7	5	7	5	7

b

8	2	8	2	8	2

a

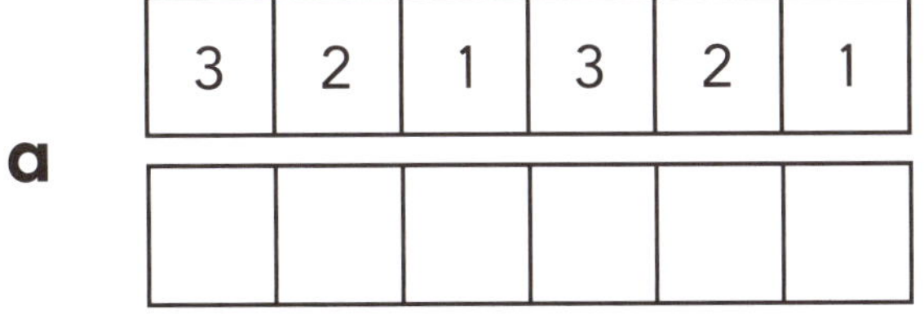

3	2	1	3	2	1

c

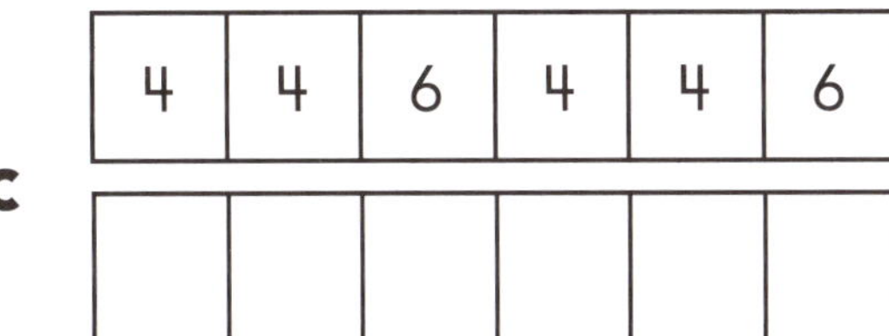

4	4	6	4	4	6

2 Duplicate each pattern.

a

b

c

3 Duplicate each color pattern.

a

b

c

4 Duplicate each color pattern.

b

a

c

Extend Patterns

You can extend a pattern.

To **extend** a pattern means to make it longer by adding to it.

Add another tennis ball to extend the pattern. That is what comes next in the pattern.

1 Color the cubes to extend each pattern.

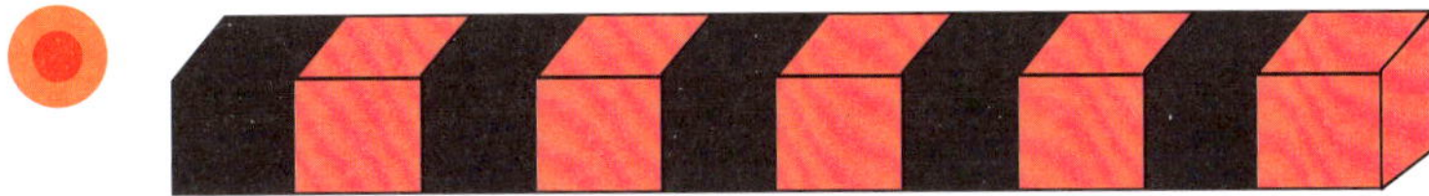

a 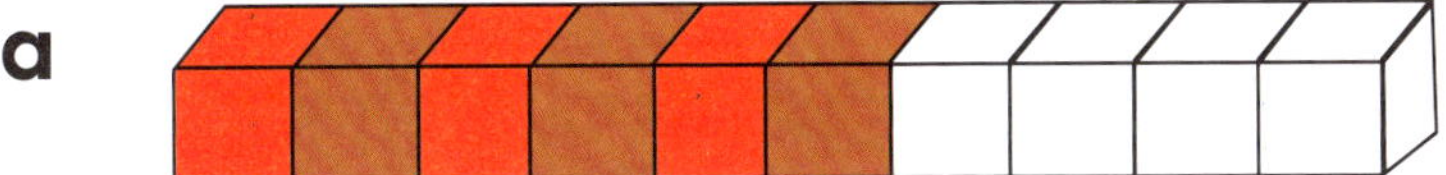

b 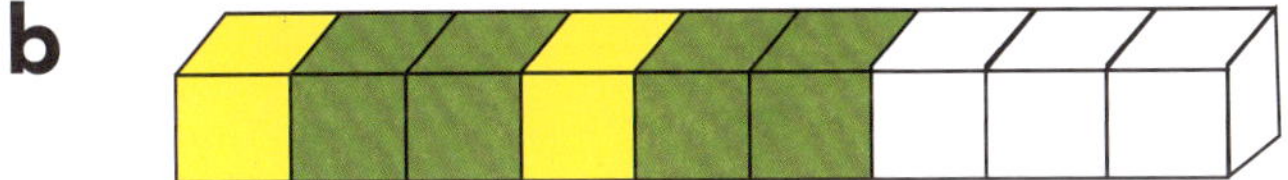

c 

d 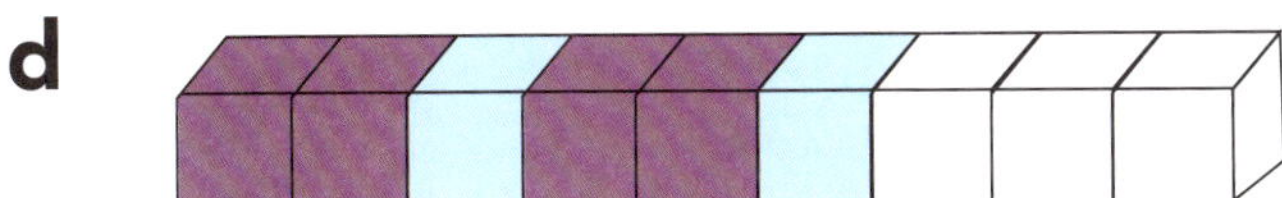

Extending a pattern is like solving a puzzle!

SELF CHECK Mark how you feel

Got it!	Need help...	I don't get it

Practice

1. Trace and extend each pattern.

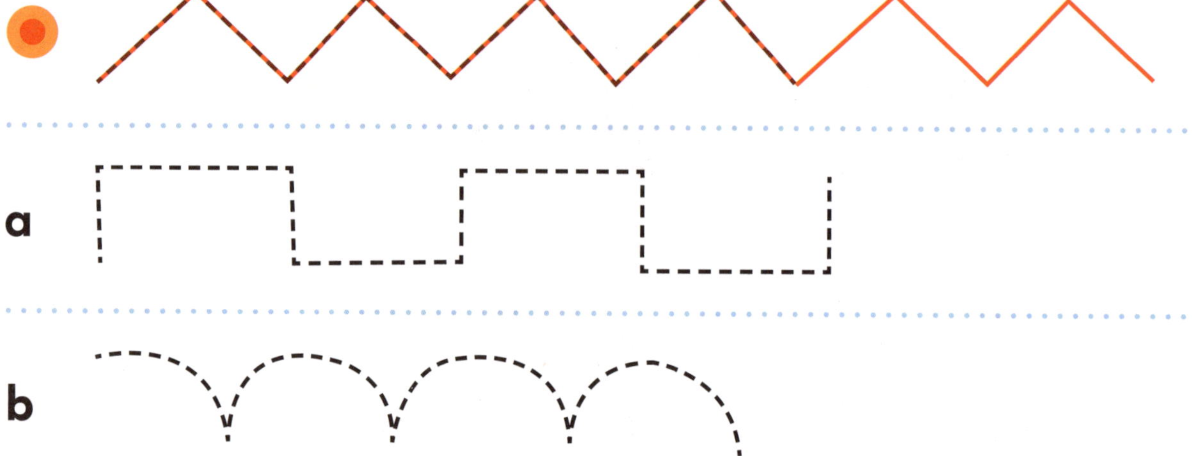

a

b

c

2. Look at each pattern. Draw what comes next.

a

b

c

3 Look at each pattern. Draw what comes next.

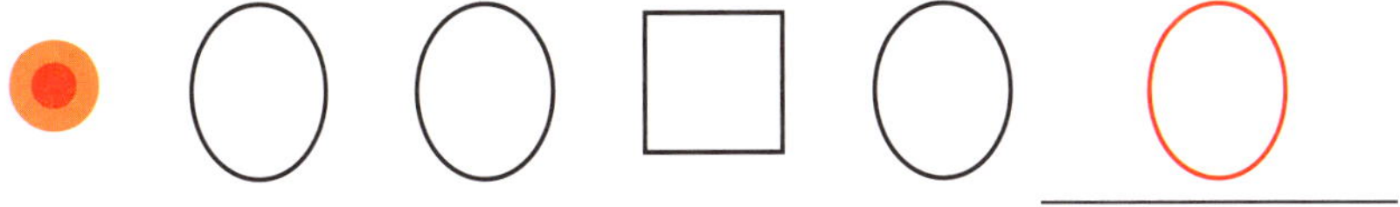

a

b

c

d

4 Look at each number pattern. Write what comes next.

2	3	4	2	3	4	2

a

8	7	8	7	8	7	

b

5	9	10	5	9	10	

c

2	5	5	2	5	5	

d

12	12	18	12	12	18	

Create Patterns

You can create your own patterns.

Example 1:

To **create** means to make something new. You can make a pattern with the colors red and blue.

You could start with a red block. Then, you could add a blue block. Then, you could add another red one. This would make an AB pattern.

Example 2:

You could also create an AAB pattern. It would go red, red, blue.

1 Create AB patterns using the colors shown.

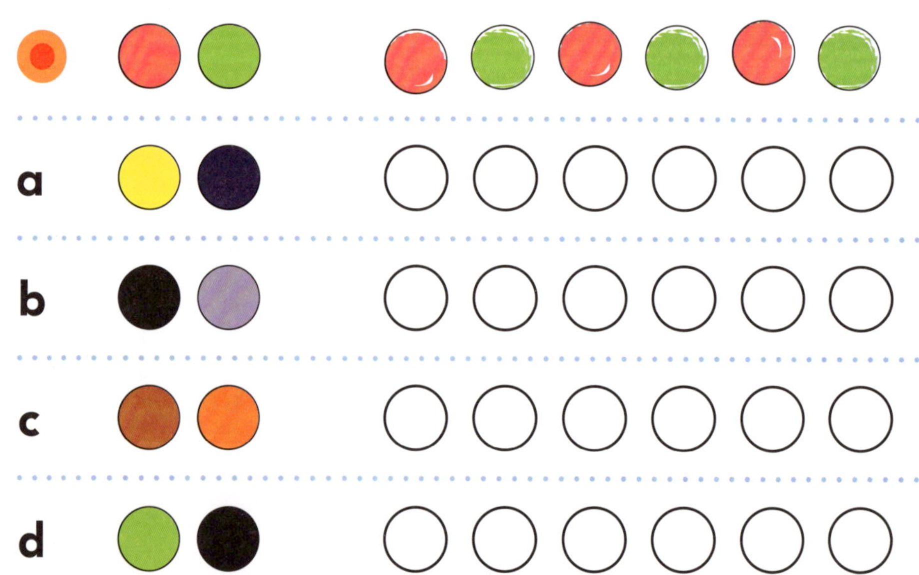

SELF CHECK Mark how you feel

Got it!	Need help...	I don't get it
☐	☐	☐

Practice

1 Color the fish to create ABC patterns.

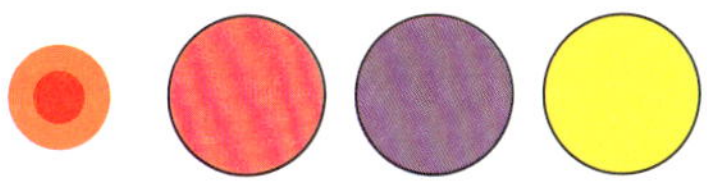

a

b
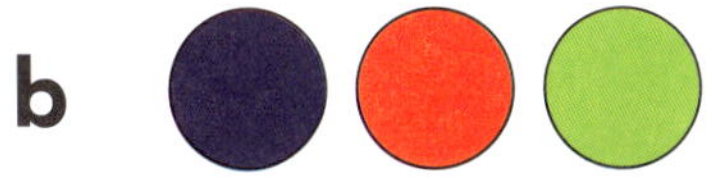

c
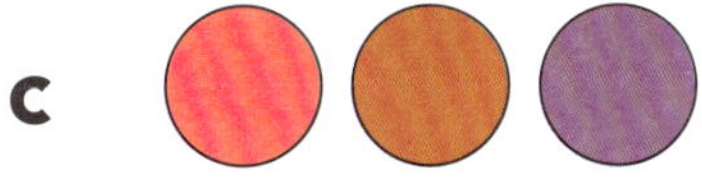

d
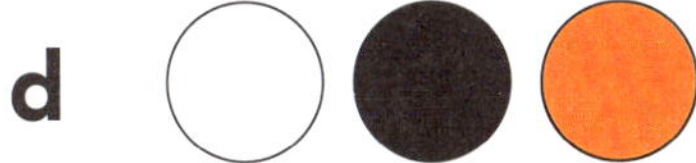

2 Create AB patterns with the shapes.

a

b

c

d
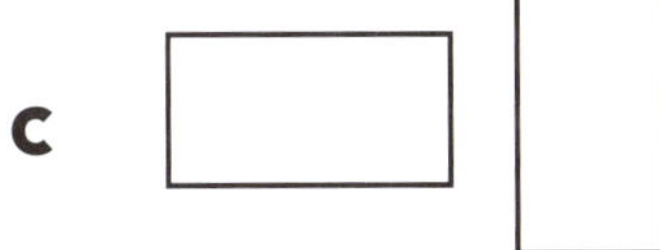

3 Create AAB patterns with the letters.

- M Q — M M Q M M Q M M Q

a P B

b G F

c T A

d K X

4 Create ABC patterns with the numbers.

- 2 3 10 — 2 3 10 2 3 10 2 3 10

a 9 6 3

b 3 7 8

c 1 4 7

d 5 0 6

Patterns Review

1 Duplicate each pattern.

a

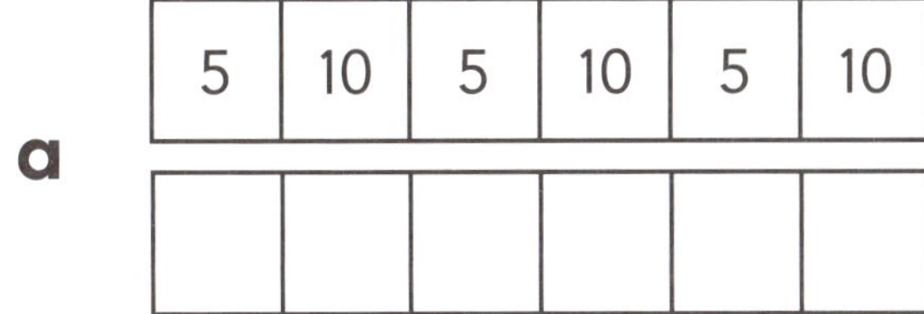

5	10	5	10	5	10

b

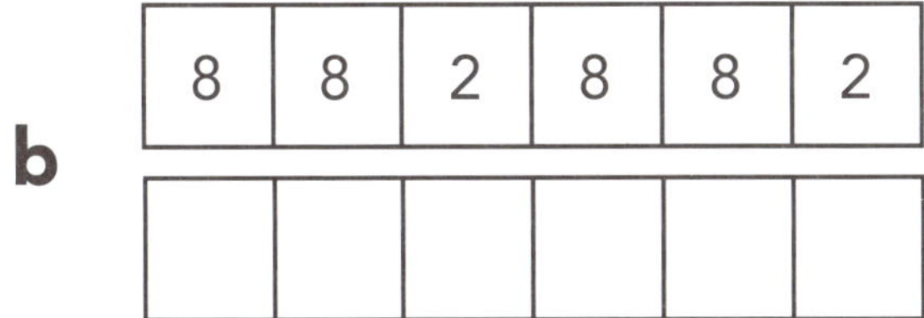

8	8	2	8	8	2

c

7	6	6	7	6	6

2 Look at each set. Circle *yes* if it is a pattern. Circle *no* if it is not.

a

yes

no

b

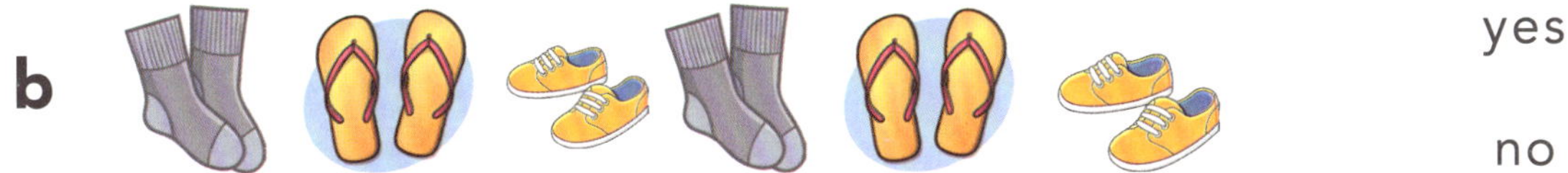

yes

no

c

yes

no

Review

3 Extend each pattern. Draw what comes next.

a

b

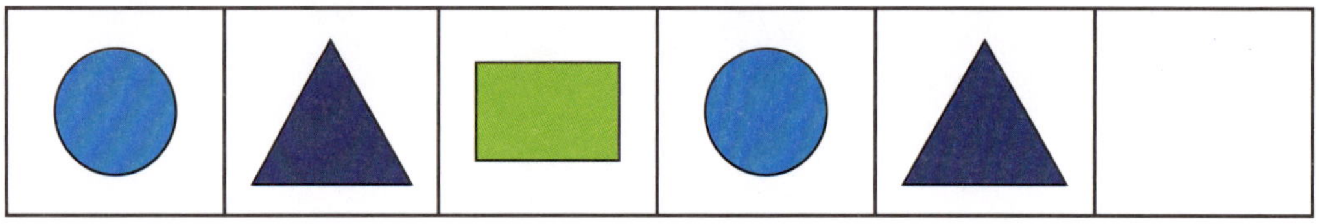

c

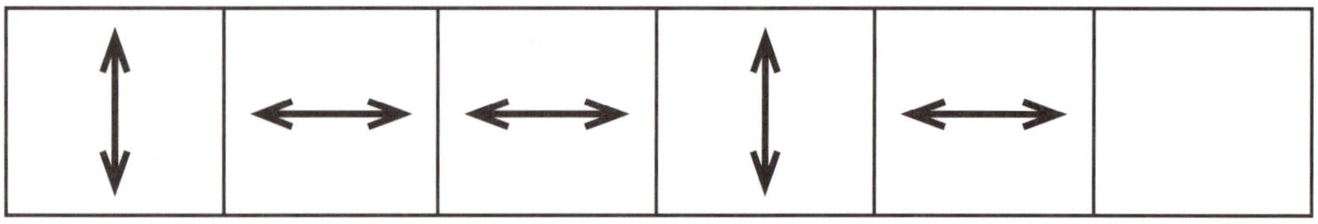

4 Look at each pattern. Write the pattern code.

a

A A B A A B

b

A B B A B B

c

A B C A B C

Review

5 Color the objects to create patterns.

Create an AB pattern.

a

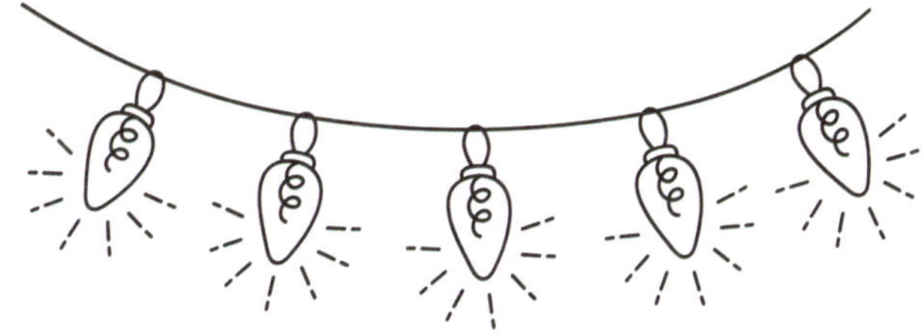

Create an ABB pattern.

b

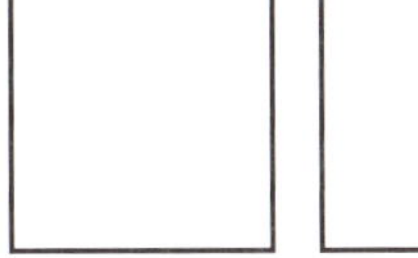

Create an ABC pattern.

c

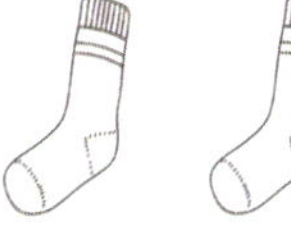

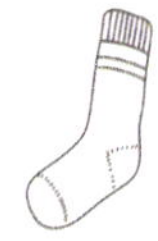
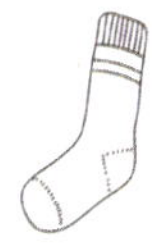
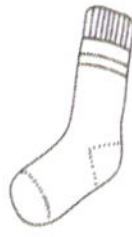

6 Duplicate each pattern.

a

b

c

Yesterday, Today, and Tomorrow

You can tell about yesterday, today, and tomorrow.

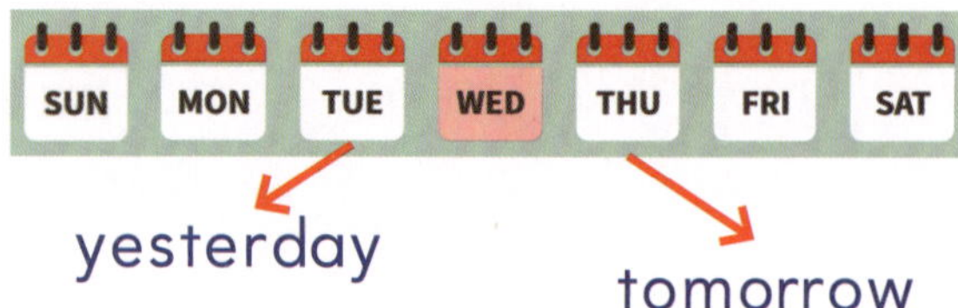

We use special words to talk about time. **Today** is the day you are living in right now.

Yesterday is the day before today. It has already happened. If today is Wednesday, then yesterday was Tuesday.

Tomorrow is the day after today. It has not happened yet. If today is Wednesday, tomorrow will be Thursday.

1 Think about what you have done today. Answer the questions.

- What did you do today when you woke up?

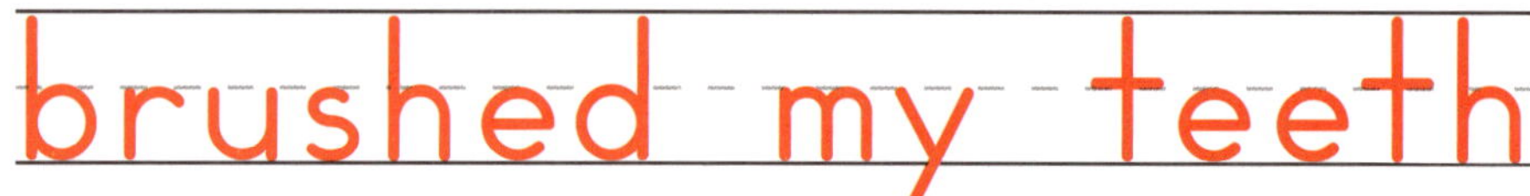

a What day is today?

b What did you eat for breakfast today? Draw a picture.

c What did you wear today? Draw a picture.

Practice

1. Think about what you did yesterday. Answer the questions.

a What day was yesterday? ______________________

b What did you do yesterday? Draw a picture.

2. Imagine today is Wednesday. Look at Maya's weekly calendar. Use it to answer the questions.

Sunday	Monday	Tuesday	Wednesday	Thursday	Friday	Saturday
play on computer	read a book	soccer practice	walk the dog	go to the park	music lesson	go to the beach

a What will Maya do today? ______________________

b What day was yesterday? ______________________

c What did Maya do yesterday? ______________________

d What day will it be tomorrow? ______________________

e What will Maya do tomorrow? ______________________

3 Think about what you might do tomorrow. Answer the questions.

a What would you like to do tomorrow? Draw a picture.

b What day will it be tomorrow?

c What would you like to eat for lunch tomorrow? Draw a picture.

d What toy do you want to play with tomorrow? Draw a picture.

e What is something else you would like to do tomorrow? Draw a picture.

Days and Months

We measure time in days, weeks, and months.

A **day** is one way we measure time. There are names for each day of the week.

- Sunday
- Monday
- Tuesday
- Wednesday
- Thursday
- Friday
- Saturday

We use days to help us plan. There are 7 days in a week.

Months are longer than days and weeks. There are 12 months in a year. These are the names of the months:

- January
- February
- March
- April
- May
- June
- July
- August
- September
- October
- November
- December

1 Answer the questions.

● How many days are in a week? 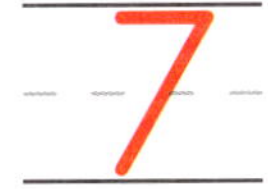

a What day of the week is it today? ______________

b What month is it? ______________

c How many months are in a year? ______________

Practice

1. Write the days of the week in order.

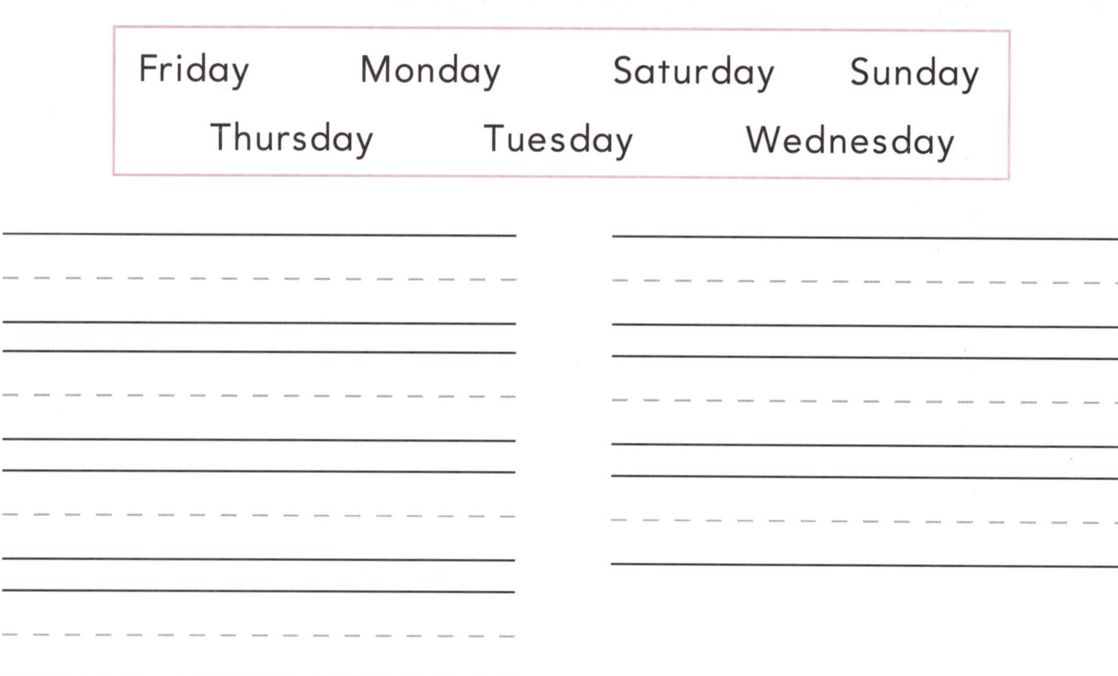

2. Write the months of the year in order.

April August December February
January July June March May
November October September

3 Draw something you do at each of these times.

a in one day

c in July

b on Wednesdays

d in October

4 Write the units of time in order from shortest to longest.

year	day	month	week

Shortest

Longest

Time of Day

You can tell the parts of the day.

Morning is the start of the day.

Afternoon is the middle of the day.

Evening is the end of the day. It lasts until night.

My School Day Timeline

1. Circle when each thing happens.

morning
afternoon (circled)
evening

b

morning
afternoon
evening

a

morning
afternoon
evening

c

morning
afternoon
evening

SELF CHECK Mark how you feel

Got it!	Need help...	I don't get it
 ☐	 ☐	☐

Practice

1 Draw a line to match when each thing happens. Answers may be used more than once.

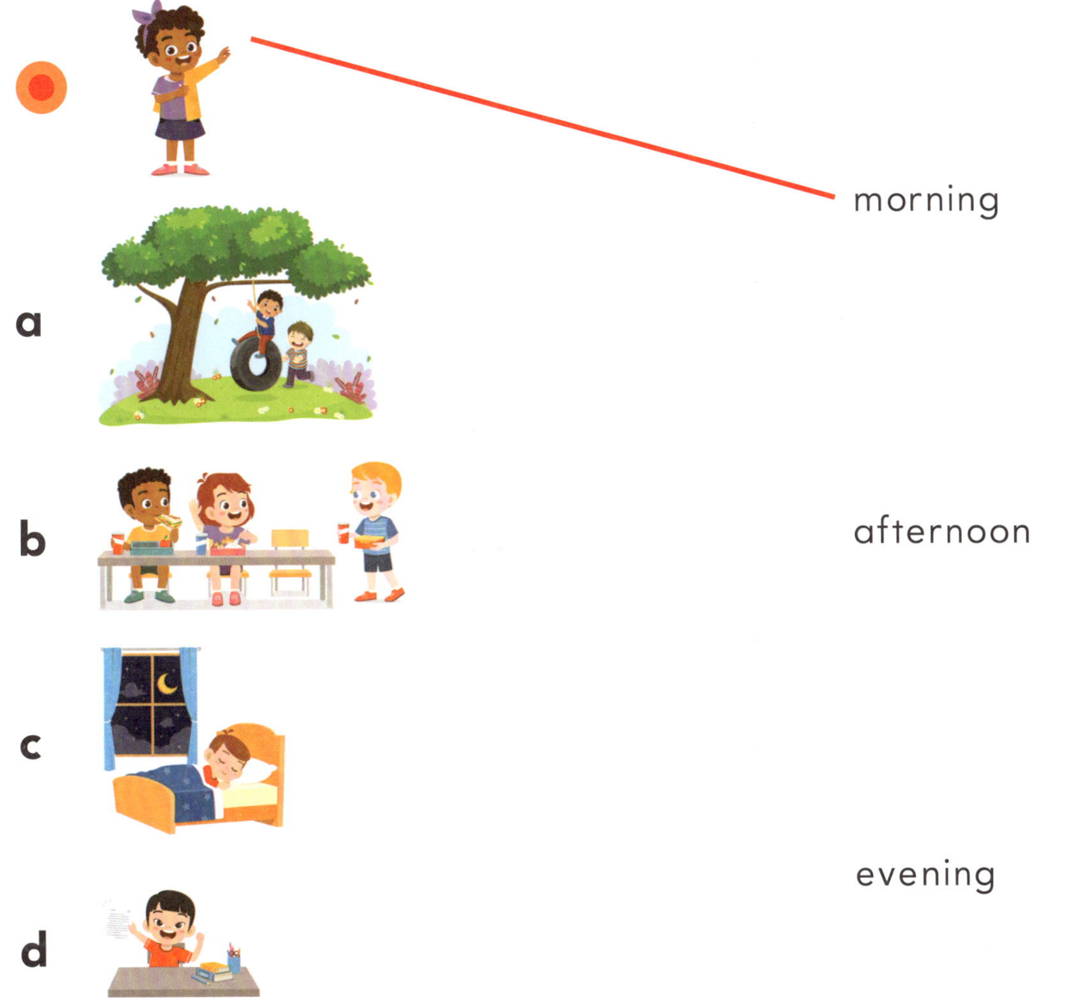

2 Complete the sentences with words or pictures.

a In the morning, I like to

b In the evening, I like to

3. Look around your house. Find objects you use during each time of the day. Draw them in the chart.

Morning	Afternoon	Evening

4. Draw what you do in the morning, afternoon, and evening.

Morning	
Afternoon	
Evening	

Standard Units of Time

You can measure time in seconds, minutes, and hours.

1 second

5 minutes

1 hour

SCAN to watch video

Seconds are tiny moments that pass quickly, such as a snap.

Minutes are longer than seconds. They still pass by quickly, such as a song.

Hours are longer than minutes. They measure things like the time you are at school.

1 Circle how long each activity would take.

● eating a meal  seconds / minutes (circled)

a eating ice cream  seconds / minutes

b turning on a light  seconds / minutes

c baking a pie  seconds / minutes

d putting on your socks  seconds / minutes

SELF CHECK Mark how you feel

Got it!	Need help...	I don't get it
 ☐	 ☐	 ☐

Practice

1 Draw 2 things you can do in each amount of time.

a Seconds

b Minutes

c Hours

2 Circle how long each activity would take.

● writing your name

seconds (circled)
minutes
hours

a taking out the trash

seconds
minutes
hours

b throwing a ball

seconds
minutes
hours

c sleeping at night

seconds
minutes
hours

Time Review

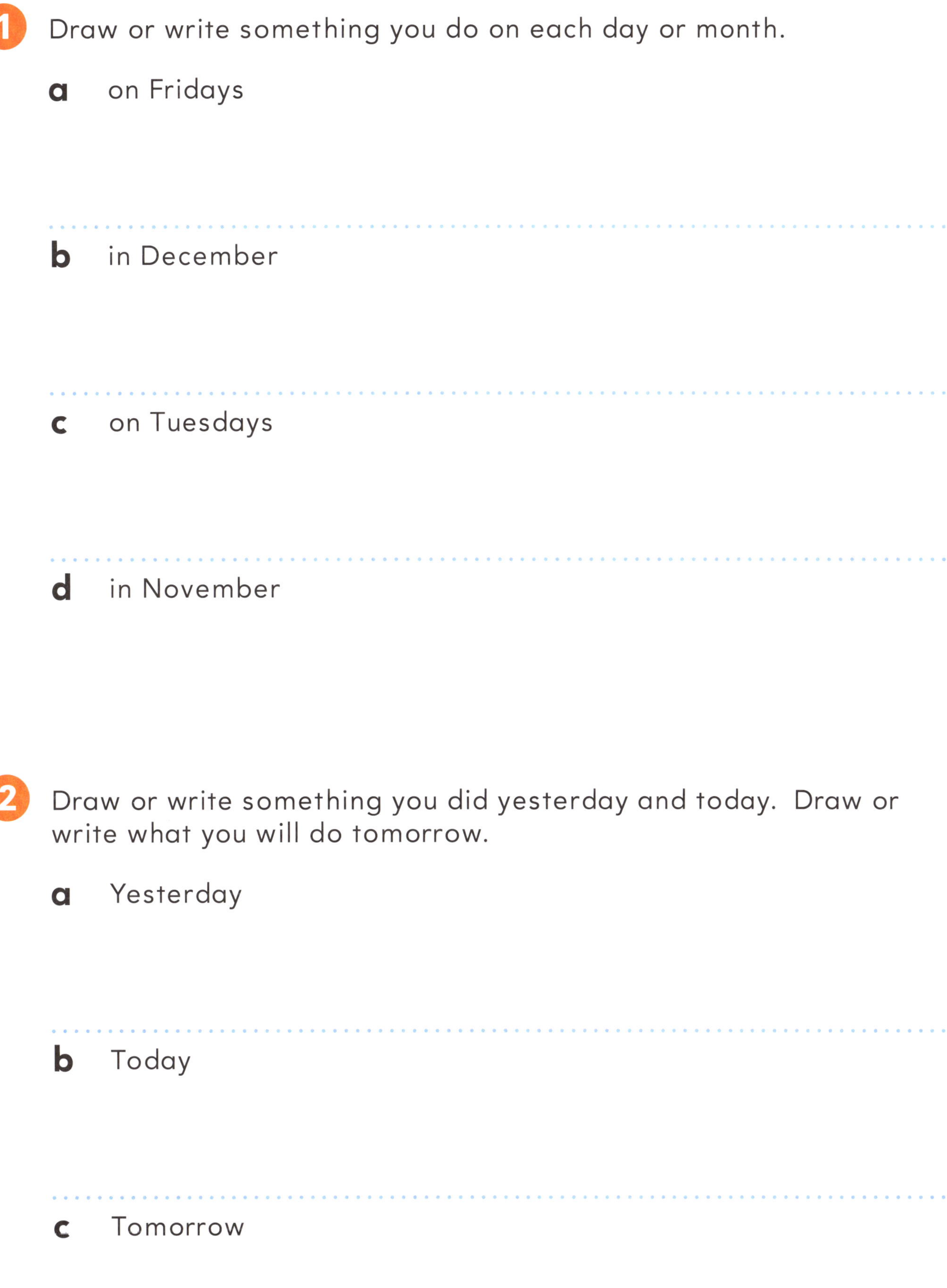

1. Draw or write something you do on each day or month.

   a on Fridays

   b in December

   c on Tuesdays

   d in November

2. Draw or write something you did yesterday and today. Draw or write what you will do tomorrow.

   a Yesterday

   b Today

   c Tomorrow

Review

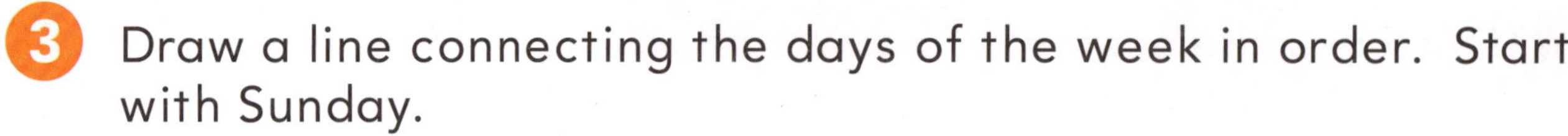

3 Draw a line connecting the days of the week in order. Start with Sunday.

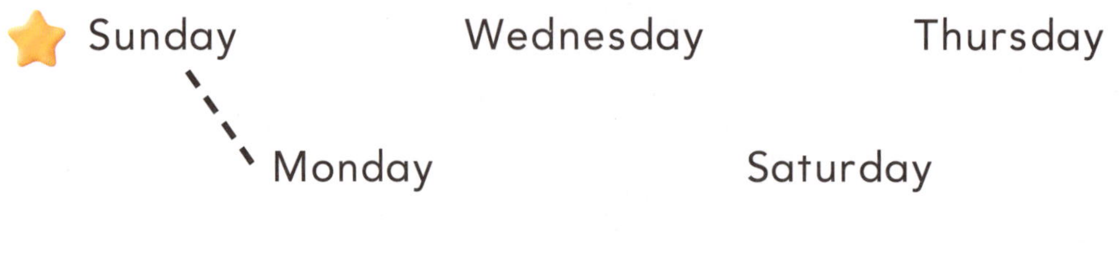

4 Draw something you can do in each amount of time.

a seconds

b minutes

c hours

d days

Review

5 Circle when each activity happens.

a go to school

morning
afternoon
evening

b eat dinner

morning
afternoon
evening

c watch the sunrise

morning
afternoon
evening

6 Circle how long each activity would take.

a watch a TV show

seconds
minutes
hours

b listen to a song

seconds
minutes
hours

c clap your hands

seconds
minutes
hours

d sleep at night

seconds
minutes
hours

Collect, Sort, and Organize Data

You use data. It helps you learn about things around you.

Data is the information we collect about the world. For this data, people were asked which color they like best.

Favorite Color	
blue	~~||||~~
orange	||
pink	|
red	||

We can **sort** the data into groups. Each line is called a **tally**. One tally is written for each person who said they like that color.

You can see that 5 people like blue and 2 people like orange.

How many people like red? Count the tally marks.
2 people liked red.

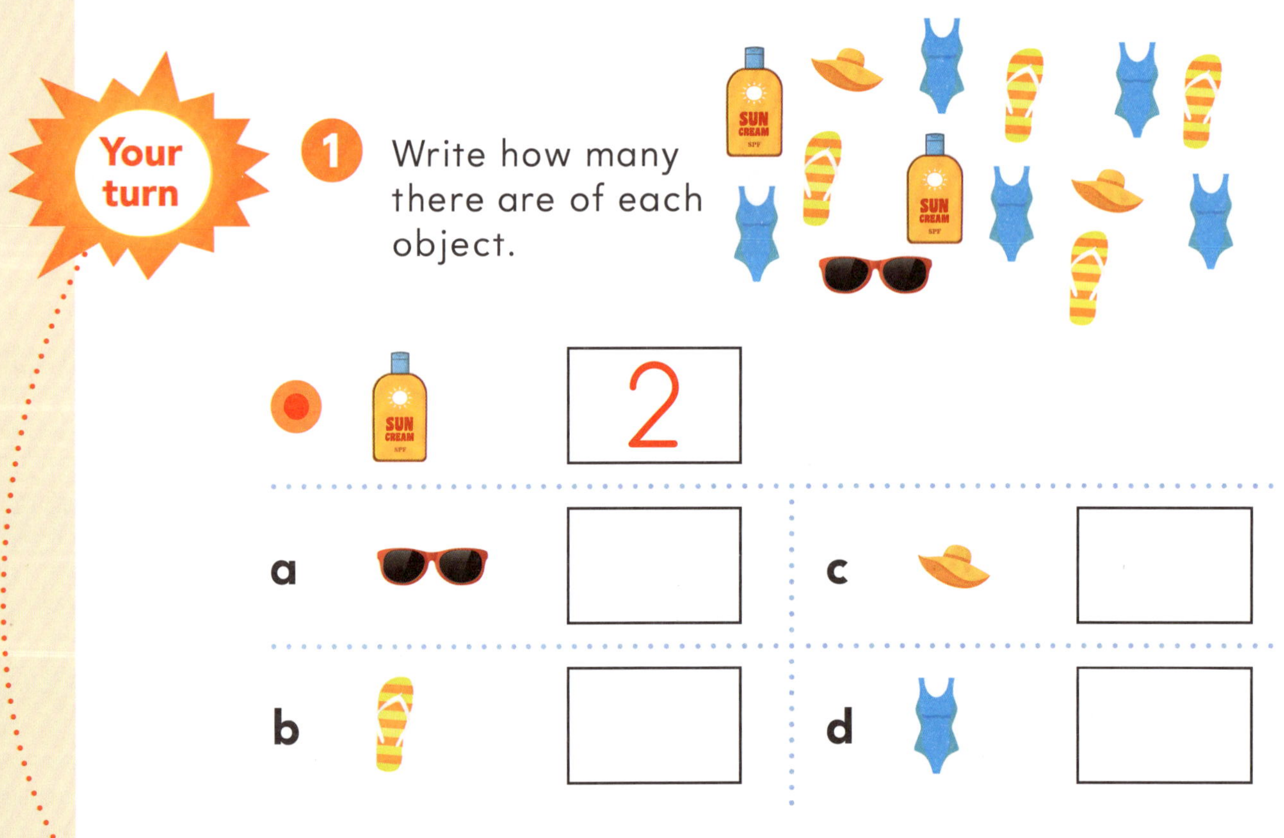

SELF CHECK Mark how you feel

Got it!	Need help...	I don't get it
☐	☐	☐

Practice

1 Zara picked some vegetables from her garden. Complete the table to sort what she collected.

	Type of Vegetable	Tallies	Number
●	red pepper	卌 III	8
a	zucchini		
b	broccoli		
c	potato		
d	beet		

2 Use the table to answer the questions.

a How many zucchinis did Zara collect? ______________

b Which vegetable did she collect the most of? ______________

c Which vegetable did she collect the least of? ______________

3 Rohan asked his friends about their favorite ice cream flavors. Use the data below to complete the table.

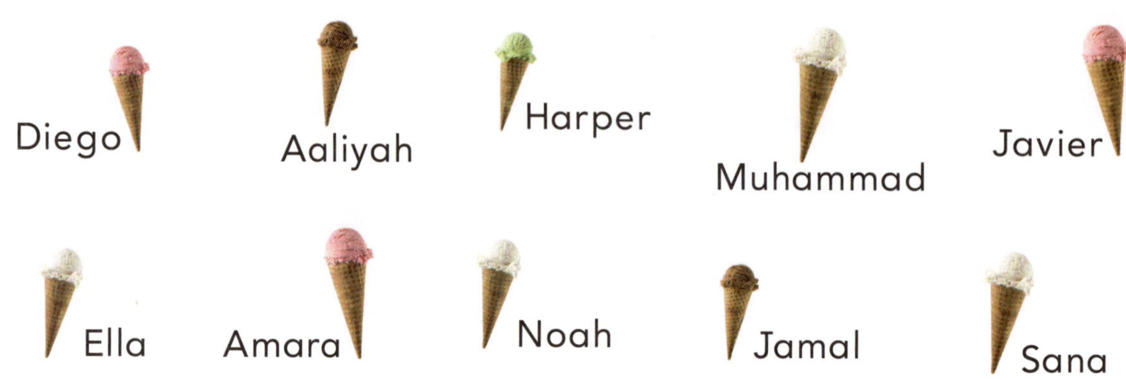

	Flavor	Tallies	Number
●	chocolate	||	2
a	vanilla		
b	strawberry		
c	mint chip		

4 Answer the questions. Use the table above.

a How many friends liked chocolate the best? ____________

b Which flavor was liked the most? ____________

c Which flavor was liked the least? ____________

Picture Graphs

Picture graphs use pictures to show data.

This is a picture graph. It shows the animals Fatima saw at the zoo. Each picture stands for 1 animal she saw. She saw 9 monkeys. But she only saw 1 panda.

Animals I Saw at the Zoo	
zebras	
monkeys	
pandas	
tigers	
toucans	

1 Use the table to color in the picture graph.

How We Get to School	
walk	5
car	6
bike	3

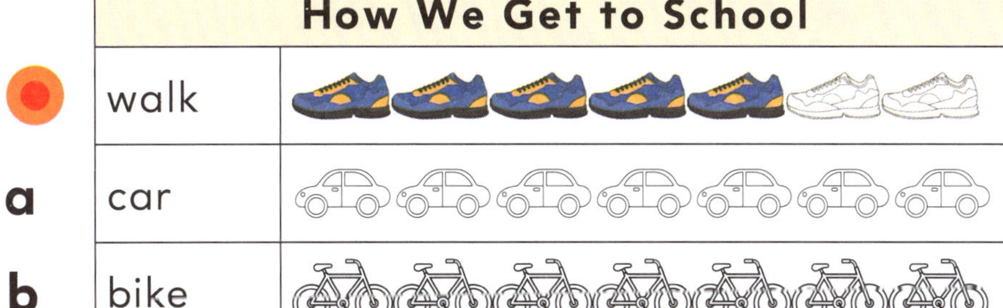

	How We Get to School	
●	walk	
a	car	
b	bike	

SELF CHECK	Mark how you feel	
Got it! ☐	Need help... ☐	I don't get it ☐

Practice

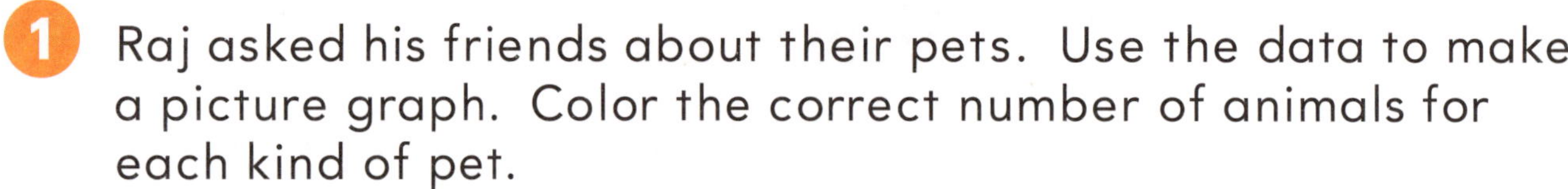

1 Raj asked his friends about their pets. Use the data to make a picture graph. Color the correct number of animals for each kind of pet.

Our Pets	
turtle	||||
cat	卌 ||
dog	卌 卌
bird		
fish	||||

Our Pets

10					
9					
8					
7					
6					
5					
4					
3					
2					
1					
Number of Pets	turtle	cat	dog	bird	fish

2 Ada collected data about peoples' favorite sports. Complete the chart to sort her data.

	Favorite Sport	Tallies	Number
●	soccer	𝍸	5
a	basketball		
b	football		
c	tennis		
d	volleyball		

3 Make a picture graph. Use data from the chart above.

Favorite Sport	
soccer	
basketball	
football	
tennis	
volleyball	

Read and Use Graphs

You can read and use data from a picture graph.

This picture graph tells you about the weather for 1 week. You can see there were more rainy days than sunny days.

Weather This Week	
Rainy Days	💧💧💧💧 ← 4 rainy days
Cloudy Days	☁☁
Sunny Days	☀ ← 1 sunny day

1 Use the picture graph to answer the questions.

Part of Cupcake You Eat First	
icing	(6 icing pictures)
cake	(5 cake pictures)
both	(8 cupcake pictures)

● How many people eat the icing first? 6

a How many people eat the cake first? _____

b How many people eat both first? _____

Practice

1 Use the picture graph to answer the questions.

Favorite Fruits

bananas	apples	oranges	avocados	pears

● How many people like pears best? 1

a How many people like avocados best? ______

b How many people like apples best? ______

c How many people like bananas best? ______

d How many people like oranges best? ______

2 The picture graph shows how many snowballs each child made. Use the graph to answer the questions.

Snowballs Made	
Aisha	
Tyler	
Leia	
Priya	
Omar	
Mateo	

● How many snowballs did Leia make? 3

a Who made fewer snowballs than Leia? ____________

b Who made the same number of snowballs as Priya? ____________

c Who made more snowballs than Tyler? ____________

d How many snowballs did the kids make in all? ____________

3 The picture graph shows the number of candies sold at the snack bar. Use the graph to answer the questions.

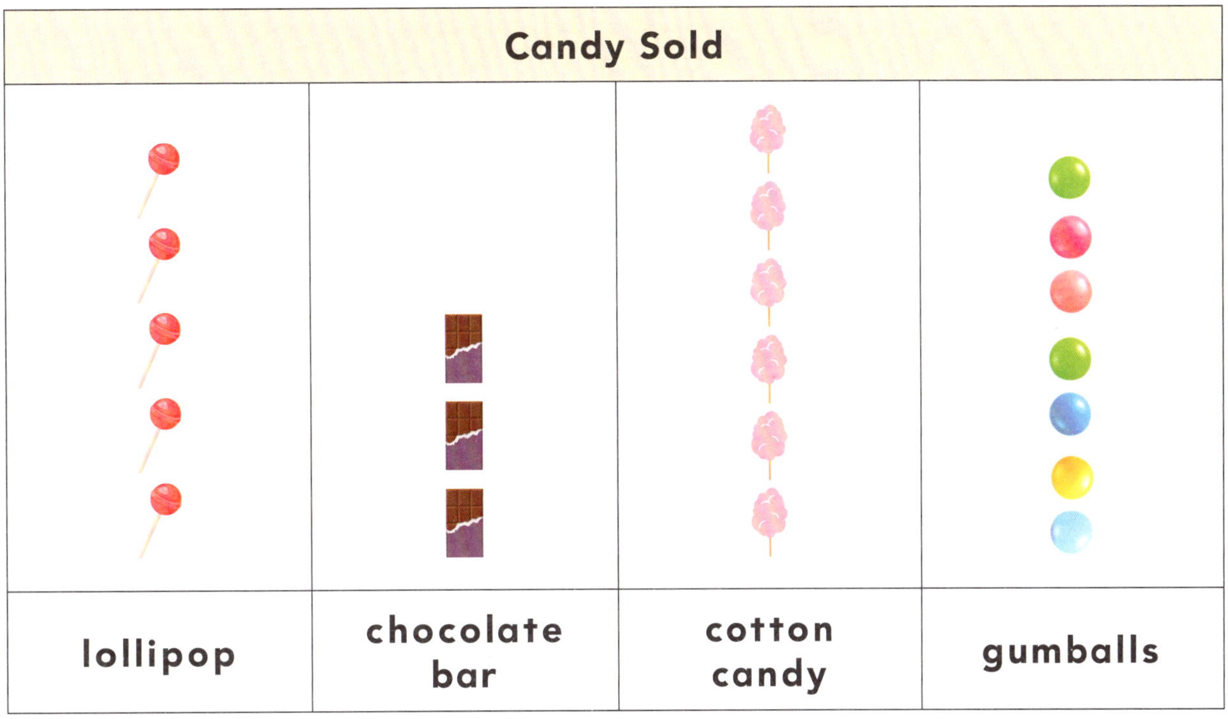

Candy Sold

lollipop	chocolate bar	cotton candy	gumballs

● How many pieces of candy were sold at the snack bar? 21

a How many chocolate bars were sold at the snack bar? ____________

b Which sold more, gumballs or lollipops? ____________

c Which sold less, gumballs or chocolate bars? ____________

d How many lollipops and chocolate bars were sold? ____________

4 The picture graph shows the books Room 4 borrowed from the library. Use the graph to answer the questions.

Books Borrowed from the Library	
Monday	📕📕📕📕📕📕
Tuesday	📕📕📕
Wednesday	📕📕📕📕
Thursday	📕📕📕📕📕
Friday	📕📕📕📕

● How many books were borrowed on Friday? 4

a On which day were the most books borrowed? ____________

b How many books were borrowed from the library in total? ____________

c On which 2 days were the same number of books borrowed?

____

d On which day were the fewest books borrowed? ____________

Data Review

1 Rick asked his friends about their favorite part of the school day. Color the stars to show how the kids voted.

Favorite Part of School	
library	𝍸 |
art	| |
reading	| | | |
math	𝍸 |
lunch	𝍸 | |

Favorite Part of School	
library	☆ ☆ ☆ ☆ ☆ ☆ ☆ ☆
art	☆ ☆ ☆ ☆ ☆ ☆ ☆ ☆
reading	☆ ☆ ☆ ☆ ☆ ☆ ☆ ☆
math	☆ ☆ ☆ ☆ ☆ ☆ ☆ ☆
lunch	☆ ☆ ☆ ☆ ☆ ☆ ☆ ☆

2 Use the graph above to answer the questions.

a How many people total were asked about their favorite part of the school day? ____________

b Which two parts of the school day have the same number of votes? ____________

c Which part of the school day is liked the least? ____________

d Which part of the school day is liked the most? ____________

Review

3 Sort the data into the table.

	Favorite Ocean Animal	Tallies	Number
a	shark		
b	octopus		
c	dolphin		
d	fish		

Review

4 Use the graph to answer the questions.

Favorite Food at a BBQ	
hamburger	 🍔 🍔 🍔 🍔 🍔 🍔 🍔
watermelon	 🍉 🍉 🍉 🍉 🍉
chips	 chips chips chips
corn	 🌽 🌽 🌽 🌽 🌽 🌽

a How many people like corn best? ______

b Which food do most people like best? ______

c Which food do the fewest people like best? ______

d How many people like watermelon best? ______

In, On, and Under

You can use the words *in*, *on*, and *under* to tell where things are.

Words can help us understand where something is.

This bear is **in** the box.

This bear is **on** the box.

This bear is **under** the box.

1 Circle the correct picture to answer each question.

Which letter is **in** the mailbox?

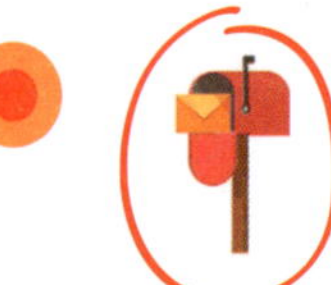

a Which dog is **on** the doghouse?

b Which lunchbox is **under** the table?

c Which bird is **in** the nest?

SELF CHECK Mark how you feel

Got it!	Need help...	I don't get it
 ☐	 ☐	 ☐

Practice

1 Match each picture to the correct sentence.

2 Draw each picture.

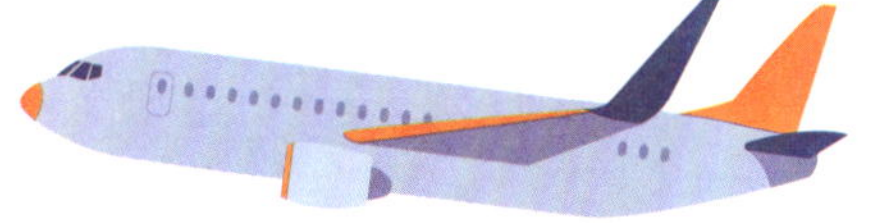

a	Draw a bird under the plane.	**c**	The plane is under a cloud. Draw the cloud.
b	Draw a tree under the plane.	**d**	Draw a kite on the ground.

3 Look at the picture. Circle where each of the objects are.

● The grapes are ____ the bowl. (in) under

a The orange is ____ the bowl. in under

b The table is ____ the bowl. in under

c The lemon is ____ the table. in on

d The strawberry is ____ the table. under on

4 Write the words to complete the sentences. Use each word once.

in	on	under

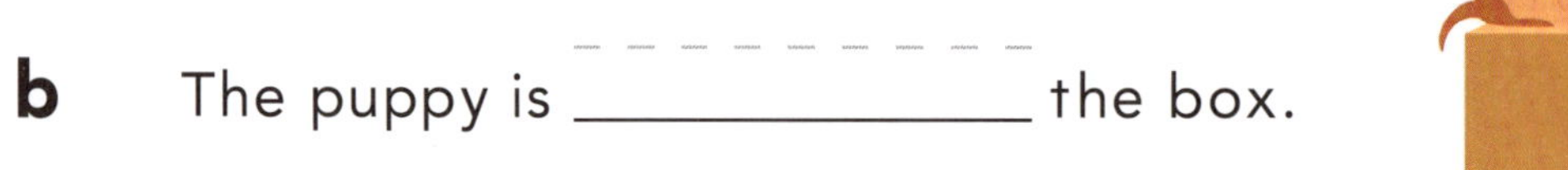

a The puppy is ______________ the box.

b The puppy is ______________ the box.

c The box is ______________ the puppy.

Up and Down

You can use the words *up* and *down* to tell about where things are.

Example 1: People and things move around. The rocket will go **up**.

Example 2: This child will go **down**.

Up and down are opposites!

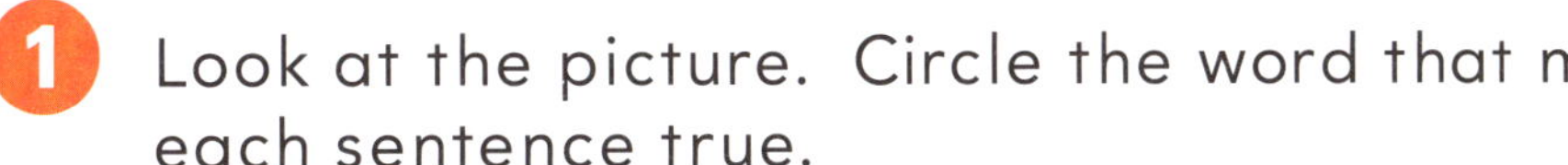

Your turn

1 Look at the picture. Circle the word that makes each sentence true.

The cat is going up / down.

a

The car is going up / down.

b

The boy is walking up / down the stairs.

c

The ball is going up / down.

SELF CHECK	Mark how you feel	
Got it!	Need help...	I don't get it

Practice

1 Which way must the dog go to get the bone? Circle *up* or *down*.

 up  down

b  up down

a  up down

c  up down

2 Look at the pictures. Circle the *up* pictures. Put an X on the *down* pictures.

b  

a 

c  

3 Color the animals that are up.

4 Read the directions. Draw each picture.

a Draw a bike going down.

b Draw a spaceship going up.

c Draw an airplane going up.

d Draw a ball going down.

Inside and Outside

You can use the words *inside* and *outside* to tell about where things are.

These coins are **inside** the purse.

These coins are **outside** the purse.

1 Circle the pictures that show something **inside**.

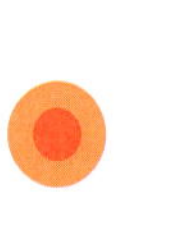  

a  

b  

c  

SELF CHECK	Mark how you feel	
Got it!	Need help...	I don't get it

Practice

1. Circle the pictures that show something **outside**.

a 

c 

b  

d  

2. Look at each picture. Write *inside* or *outside* to tell where the animal is.

a 

____

c 

____

b 

____

d 

____

3 Circle the word that best describes each picture.

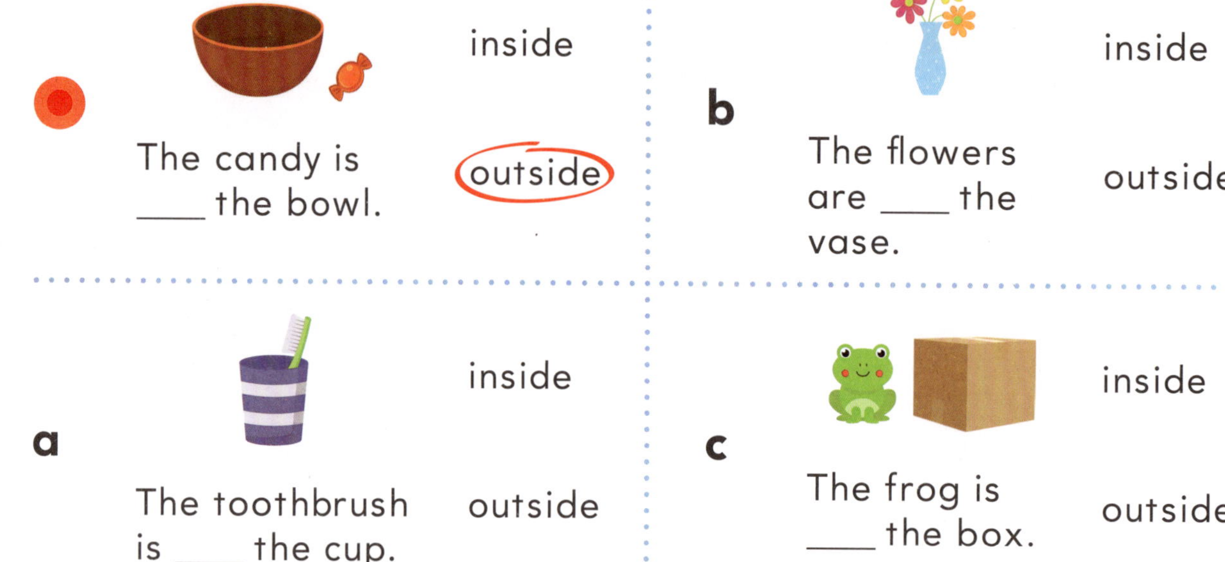

●	The candy is ____ the bowl.	inside / outside
b	The flowers are ____ the vase.	inside / outside
a	The toothbrush is ____ the cup.	inside / outside
c	The frog is ____ the box.	inside / outside

4 Draw a line to match each picture to the correct sentence.

●

a

b

c

d

The bed is **inside** the room.

The children are **inside** the bus.

The girl is **outside** the house.

The boy is **inside** the bed.

The children are **outside** the bus.

Beside and Between

You can use the words *beside* and *between* to tell about where things are.

This dog is **beside** the girl. Beside means next to.

This bird is **between** the eggs. Between means in the middle of.

Your turn

1 Circle the word that best describes each picture.

The butterfly is between / beside the flowers.

a 

The apple is between / beside the bananas.

b 

The carrot is between / beside the bunny.

c 

The alien is between / beside the spaceships.

d 

The ball is between / beside the boxes.

Practice

1. Draw a line to match each picture to the correct sentence.

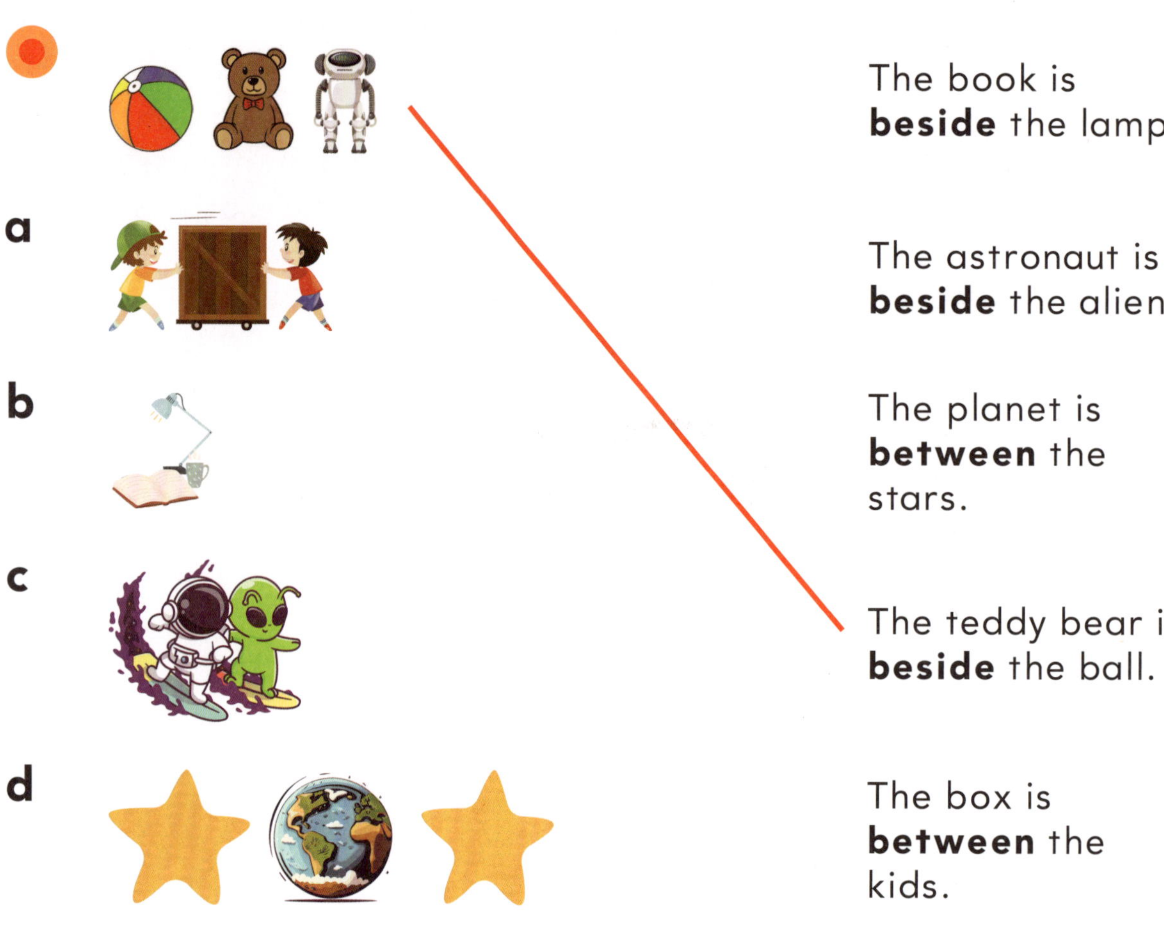

The book is **beside** the lamp.

The astronaut is **beside** the alien.

The planet is **between** the stars.

The teddy bear is **beside** the ball.

The box is **between** the kids.

2. Circle the picture that is **between** two objects.

a   

c   

b 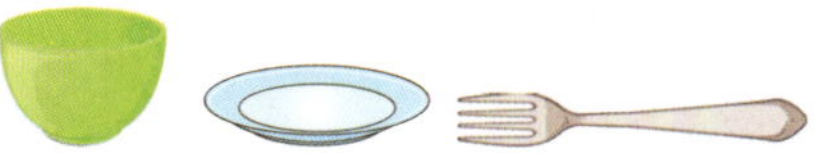

d  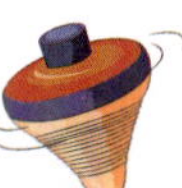 

3 Look at each picture. Circle the word that makes the sentence true.

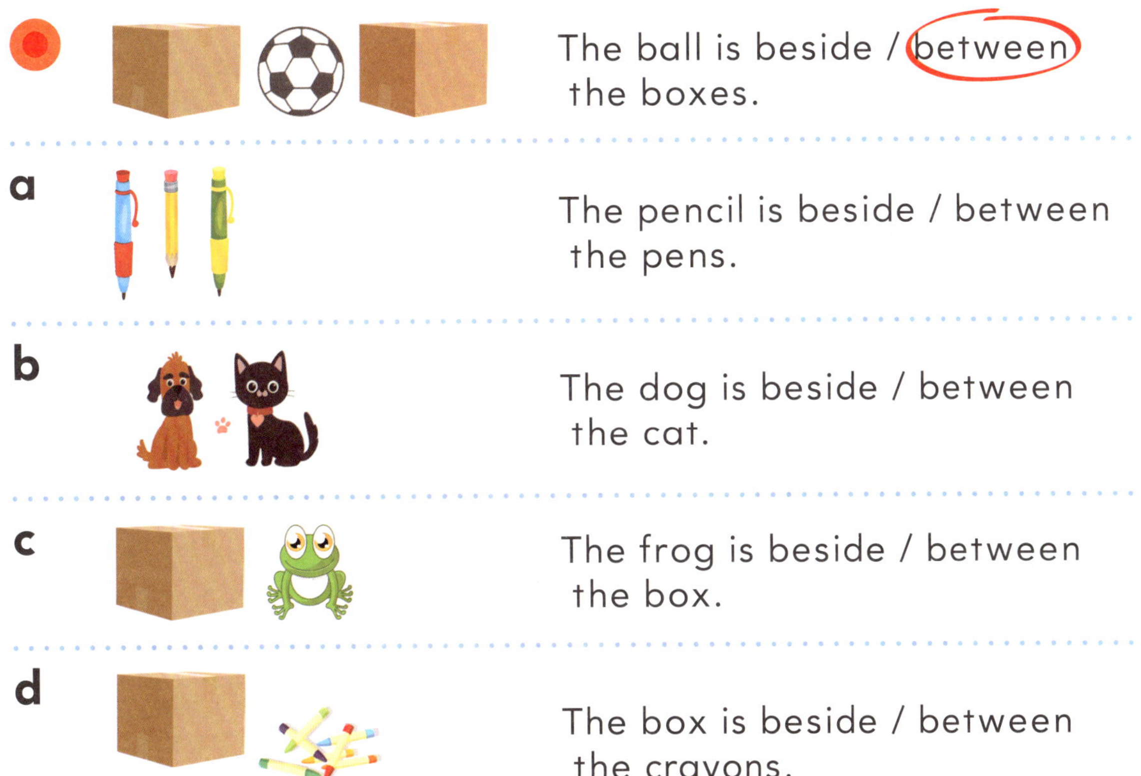

● The ball is beside / between the boxes.

a The pencil is beside / between the pens.

b The dog is beside / between the cat.

c The frog is beside / between the box.

d The box is beside / between the crayons.

4 Write **beside** or **between** to best describe the circled object.

● between

a ____________________

b ____________________

c ____________________

d ____________________

In Front and Behind

You can use the words *in front* and *behind* to tell where things are.

The ball is **in front** of the box.

The ball is **behind** the box.

In front and ***behind*** are opposites!

1 Look at each picture. Circle whether the dog is **in front** of or **behind** each object.

in front behind

a

in front behind

c

in front behind

b

in front behind

d

in front behind

SELF CHECK Mark how you feel		
Got it!  ☐	Need help...  ☐	I don't get it  ☐

Practice

1 Look at each picture. Circle whether the bird is **in front** of or **behind** each object.

in front behind

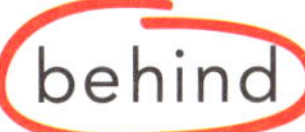

a 

in front behind

c 

in front behind

b 

in front behind

d 

in front behind

2 Write an X over each picture where the mouse is **in front**. Circle each picture where the mouse is **behind**.

a 

c 

b 

d 

3 Put an X over each picture where the cat is **behind**. Circle each picture where the cat is **in front**.

a 

c 

b 

d 

4 Draw a line to match each sentence to the correct picture.

- The car is **in front** of the tree.
- a The car is **behind** the dog.
- b The car is **in front** of the gate.
- c The man is **in front** of the car.
- d The car is **in front** of the man.

Spatial Reasoning Review

1 Look at each picture. Circle the word that best describes the ball.

a beside behind

c in front under

b in front inside

d beside under

2 Complete the tasks.

a Draw a bird on the scarecrow.

b Draw a cat inside the tractor.

c Draw a bee between the flowers.

d Draw a farmer on the hill.

Review

3 Circle the word that tells about the squirrel.

a

The squirrel is ____ the table.

above below

c

The squirrel is ____ the house.

in front of behind

b

The squirrel is ____ the acorn.

above beside

d

The squirrel is ____ the table.

above below

4 Finish each sentence to tell where the bee is.

a  The bee is ______________ the flower.

b  The bee is ______________ the flower.

c  The bee is ______________ the flower.

d  The bee is ______________ the flower.

Review

5 Write an X on the things going **up**. Circle the things going **down**.

a 

c

b 

d

6 Complete the tasks.

a Draw a toy **inside** the box.

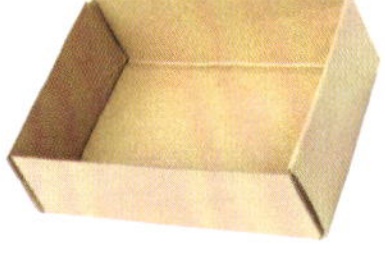

b Draw a toy **beside** the box.

c Draw a toy **under** the box.

d Draw a toy **between** the boxes.

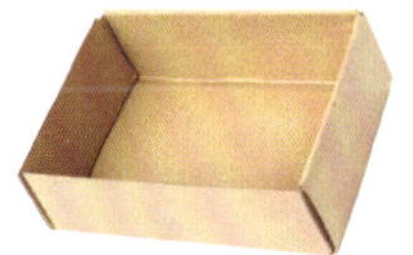

Pennies

Pennies are a kind of coin. They are worth 1¢.

This is a penny.

front

back

Pennies are a copper color.

Pennies have a smooth edge.

Pennies are smaller than nickels and quarters.

Pennies are larger than dimes.

1

2

3

4

5

There are 5 pennies. Together, they are worth 5¢.

You count by 1s when counting the value of pennies.

1 Circle the pennies.

SELF CHECK	Mark how you feel	
Got it! ☐	Need help... ☐	I don't get it ☐

Practice

1 Count and write each amount.

●      5 ¢

a     ______ ¢

b ______ ¢

c        ______ ¢

2 Circle the correct number of pennies.

● 3¢      

a 5¢     

b 4¢     

c 1¢     

d 2¢     

3 Circle the pennies.

Nickels

Nickels are a kind of coin. They are worth 5¢.

This is a nickel.

front

back

Nickels are a silver color.

Nickels have a smooth edge.

Nickels are bigger than pennies and dimes.

Nickels are smaller than quarters.

You count by 5s when counting the value of nickels.

5 10 15 20 25

There are 5 nickels. Together, they are worth 25¢.

1 Circle the nickels.

SELF CHECK Mark how you feel		
Got it! ☐	Need help... ☐	I don't get it ☐

Practice

1 Circle the correct number of nickels.

● 10¢

a 25¢

b 15¢

c 20¢

2 Count and write each amount.

● 25 ¢

a ____ ¢

b ____ ¢

c ____ ¢

d ____ ¢

3 Circle the nickels.

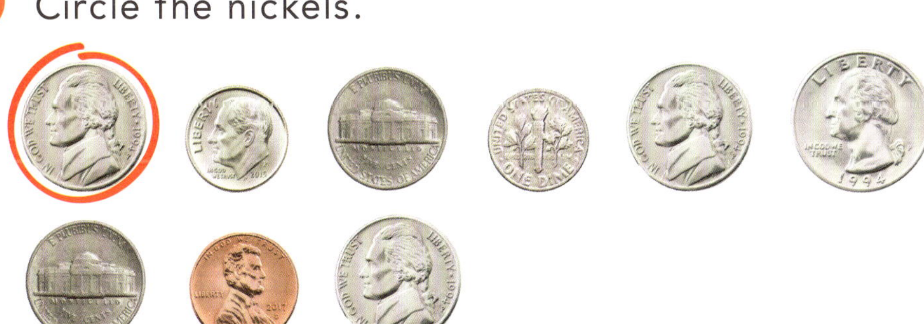

Dimes

Dimes are a kind of coin. They are worth 10¢.

This is a dime.

front

back

Dimes are a silver color.

Dimes have a ridged edge.

Dimes are the smallest coin in size.

10 20 30 40 50

There are 5 dimes. Together, they are worth 50¢.

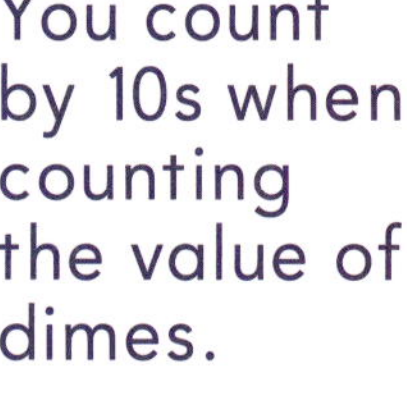

You count by 10s when counting the value of dimes.

1 Circle the dimes.

SELF CHECK	Mark how you feel	
Got it! ☐	Need help... ☐	I don't get it ☐

Practice

1 Count and write each amount.

●  40 ¢

a   ______ ¢

b  ______ ¢

c  ______ ¢

2 Circle the correct number of dimes.

● 30¢     

a 20¢     

b 40¢     

c 10¢     

d 50¢     

3 Circle the dimes.

Quarters

Quarters are a kind of coin. They are worth 25¢.

This is a quarter.

front

back

Quarters are a silver color.

Quarters have a ridged edge.

Quarters are bigger than pennies, nickels, and dimes.

25

50

75

100

There are 4 quarters. They are worth 100¢. That is the same as 1 dollar.

You count by 25s when counting the value of quarters.

1 Circle the quarters.

SELF CHECK Mark how you feel

Got it!	Need help...	I don't get it
 ☐	  ☐	 ☐

Practice

1 Circle the correct number of quarters.

● 50¢

a 25¢

b 75¢

c 100¢

2 Count and write each amount.

● 75 ¢

a ______ ¢

b ______ ¢

d ______ ¢

3 Circle the quarters.

Money Review

1 Complete the chart.

	Picture of Coin	Name of Coin	Value
a			
b			
c			
d			

2 Write the value of each set of coins.

a    

______ ¢

b  

______ ¢

c  

______ ¢

d   

______ ¢

e     

______ ¢

Review

3 Circle the coins to make the correct amount.

a 10¢      

b 4¢     

c 40¢     

d 50¢     

4 Draw a line from each coin to its value.

a  10¢

b  1¢

c  5¢

d  25¢

Review

5 Circle the coin with the greater value.

a  

c  

b  

d  

6 Draw a line from each coin to its name.

a  quarter

b  nickel

c  dime

d  penny

Answers

1. COUNTING

Count to 5

Page 15 — Your Turn

1. a 3 coins b 2 frogs

Page 16 — Practice

1. a 2 pigs c 1 bus
   b 5 crayons d 4 hearts
2. a 4 b 2 c 3

Count to 10

Page 17 — Your Turn

1. a 7 balls b 6 hats

Page 18 — Practice

1. a 9 bears c 8 flowers
   b 6 boats d 4 diamonds

2. a 5 b 7 c 9

3.

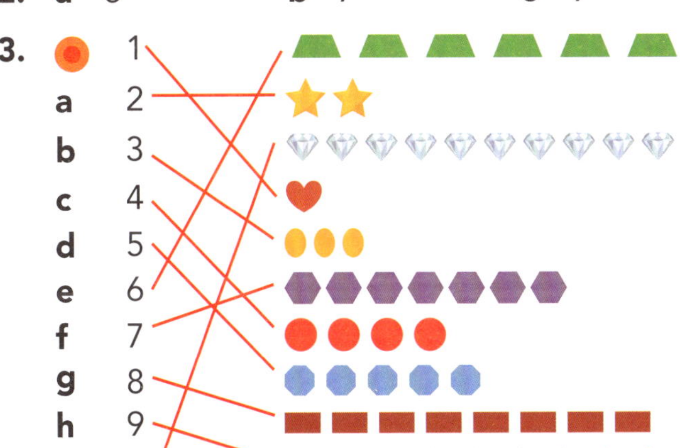

Count to 20

Page 20 — Your Turn

1. a 12 hats

Page 21 — Practice

1. a 16 pumpkins c 15 suns
   b 17 bugs
2. a 19 b 14 c 20

3.

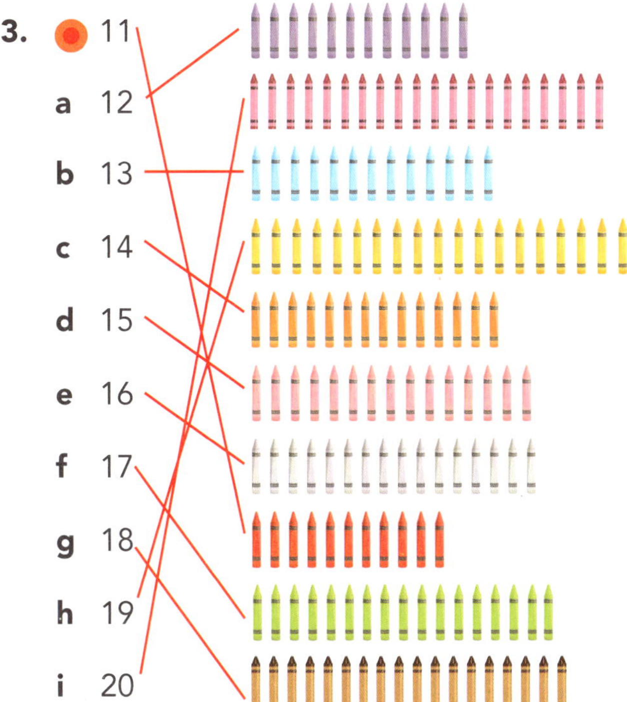

Count to 100

Page 23 — Your Turn

1. a 60 pennies

Page 24 — Practice

1. a 80 bees

2. a 92 oranges b 86 hats

Skip Count by 10s

Page 26 — Your Turn

1. a 30 cars

Page 27 — Practice

1. a 60 jellybeans c 20 spoons
   b 100 basketballs d 80 tractors
2. a 40 b 50 c 90 d 70

Counting On

Page 29 — Your Turn

1. a 15 paper clips b 17 rocks

Answers

Page 30 — Practice

1. **a** 40 books   **b** 27 hearts   **c** 6 shapes   **d** 8 bows
2. **a** 13   **b** 22   **c** 15   **d** 18   **e** 20

Counting Backward

Page 32 — Your Turn

1. **a** 3, 2, 1
   b 8, 7, 6, 5, 4, 3, 2, 1

Page 33 — Practice

1. **a** 6, 5, 4, 3, 2, 1
   b 10, 9, 8, 7, 6, 5, 4, 3, 2, 1
2. **a** 8, 7, 6, 5, 4, 3, 2, 1
   b 10, 9, 8, 7, 6, 5, 4, 3
   c 12, 11, 10, 9, 8, 7, 6, 5
3. **a** 10, 9, 8, 7, 6, 5, 4
   b 20, 19, 18, 17, 16, 15
   c 7, 6, 5, 4, 3, 2, 1
   d 18, 17, 16, 15, 14, 13
4. 

Ordinal Numbers

Page 35 — Your Turn

1. **a** 
   b 
   c     

Page 36 — Practice

1. **a**   
   b
   c
2. **a** 
   b 
   c 
   d   
3. **a** 
   b 
   c 
4. 

Counting Review — Page 38

1. **a** 8 cats   **b** 6 snakes   **c** 20 cookies
2. **a** 35   **b** 55   **c** 23
3. **a** 100 crayons   **b** 40 marbles   **c** 60 cookies
4. **a** 14 ducks   **b** 62 buttons   **c** 30 stars
5. **a** 8 mugs   **b** 5 lanterns   **c** 25 coins

Answers

6. a 8, 7, 6, 5, 4, 3
   b 6, 5, 4, 3, 2, 1
   c 17, 16, 15, 14, 13, 12

7. a 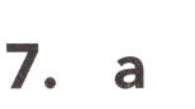     
   b 
   c 
   d 

8. a     
   b   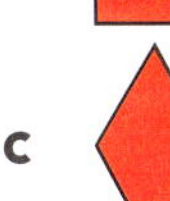
   c 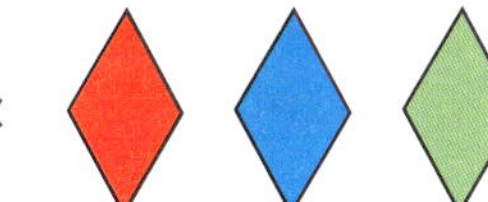
   d 

2. NUMBER SENSE

Subitize

Page 42 — Your Turn

1. a 2 b 1 c 4 d 3

Page 43 — Practice

1. a 3 b 4 c 1 d 2
2. a 2 b 4 c 1 d 3
3. a 4 c 1 e 2
   b 2 d 3 f 5

Generate Numbers

Page 45 — Your Turn

Check that the correct number of circles have been drawn.

Page 46 — Practice

1. a 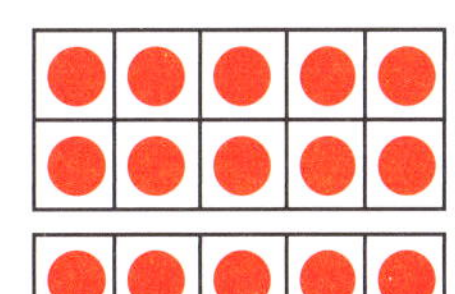 c 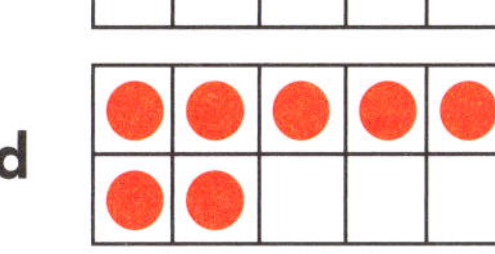
   b 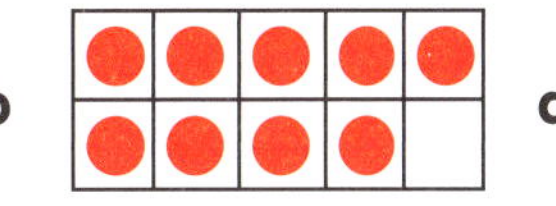 d
2. Check that the correct number of objects have been drawn.
3. a 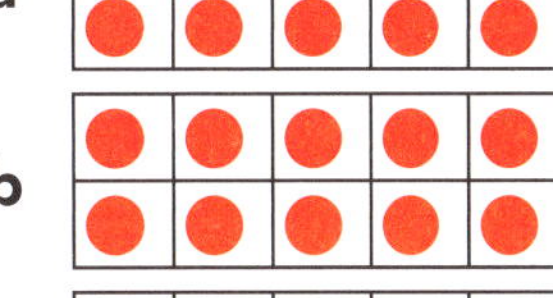 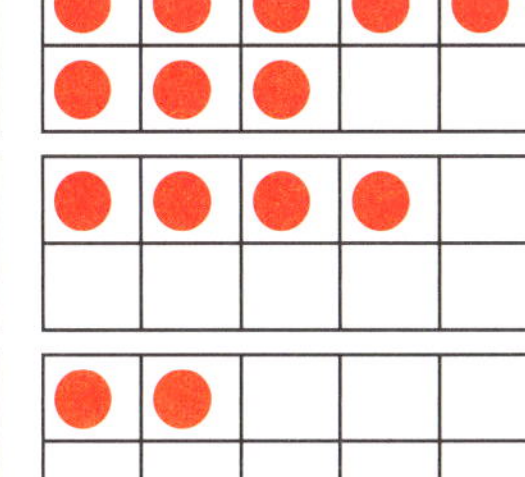
   b
   c
   d 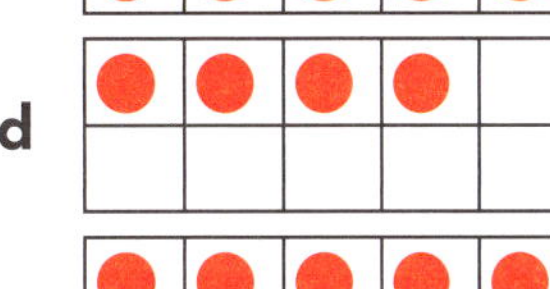
   e
   f 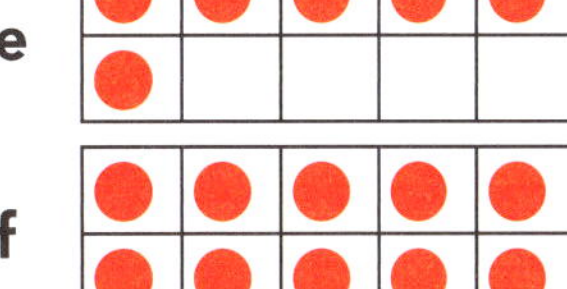 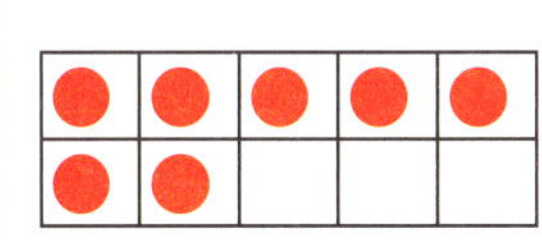

Whole and Part

Page 48 — Your Turn

1. a  c 
   b d

Page 49 — Practice

1. a   c  
   b   d  

Answers

2. a 

b 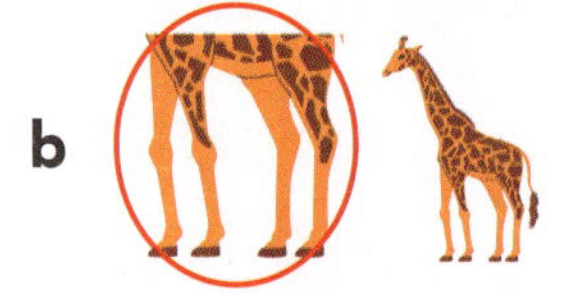

c 

d 

3. a 

c 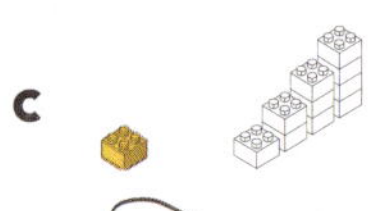

b 

d 

4. a 

c 

b 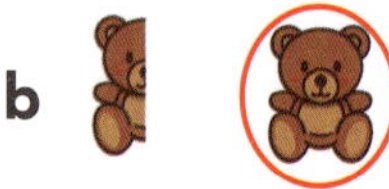

d 

Foundations in Place Value

Page 51 — Your Turn

1. a 11 12 13 14 15

b 11

c 11 12 13 14 15 16 17 18 19

d 11 12 13 14 15 16

Page 52 — Practice

1. 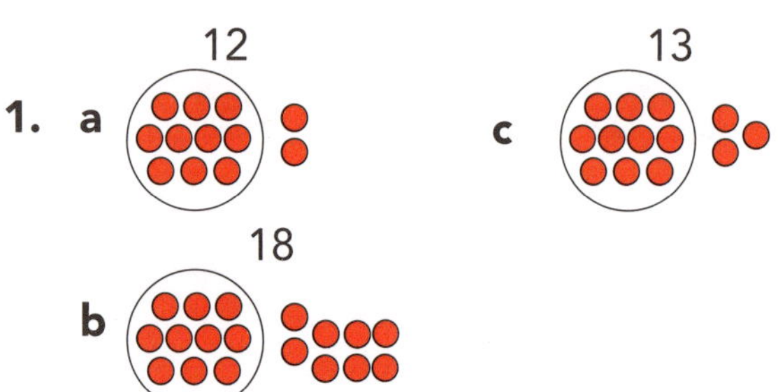

2. 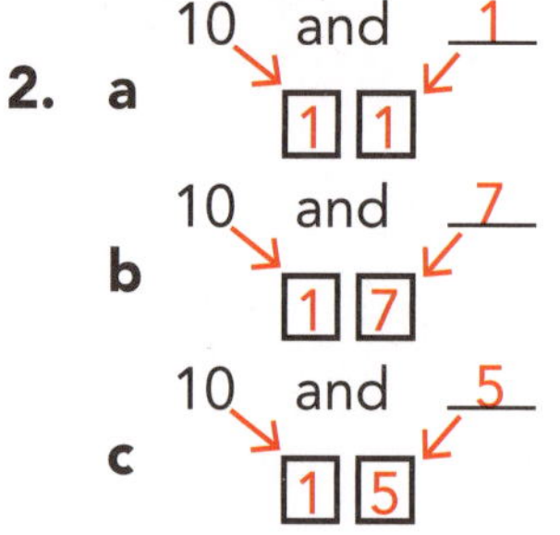

3. a 12 **b** 15 **c** 13 **d** 19

4. a 14 **b** 12 **c** 16 **d** 11

Number Sense Review — Page 54

1. 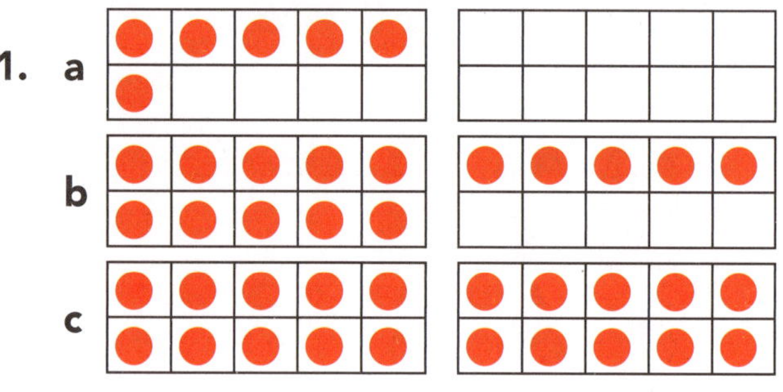

2. 

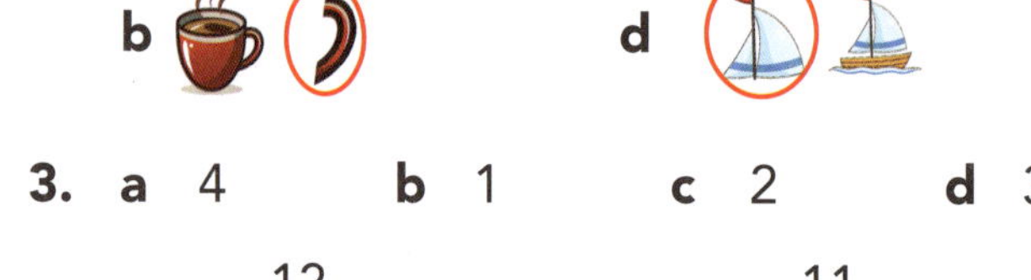

3. a 4 **b** 1 **c** 2 **d** 3

4. 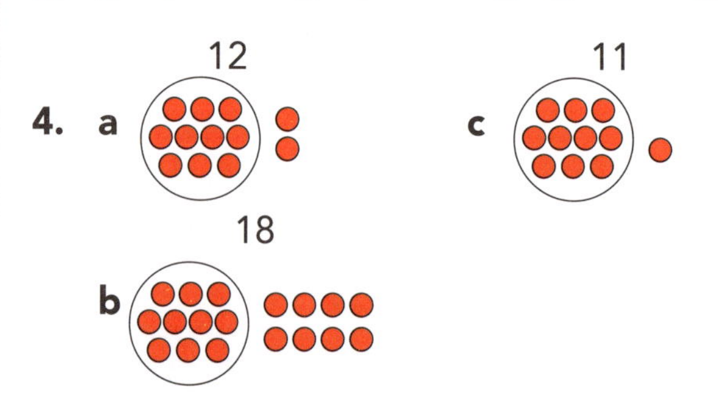

5. Check that students have drawn the correct number of objects.

6. a 18 **b** 14 **c** 15 **d** 20

Answers

3. COMPARE NUMBERS

Greater Than

Page 56 — Your Turn

1. a

b

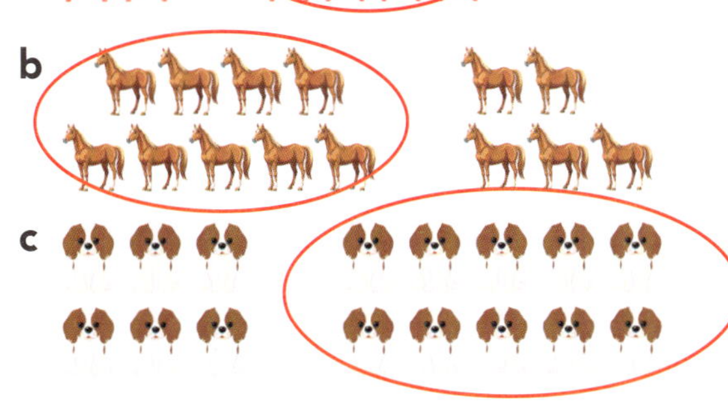

c

Page 57 — Practice

1. a

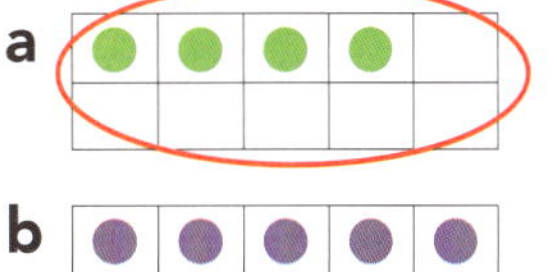

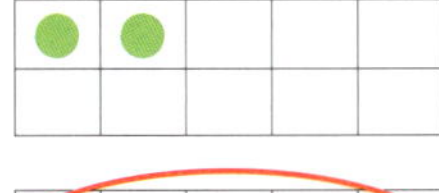

b

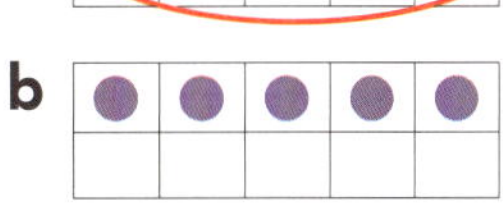

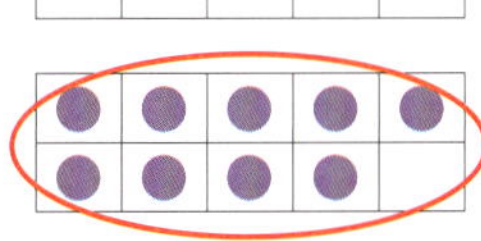

c

d

e

f

2. Sets should be greater than the sets shown.

Less Than

Page 59 — Your Turn

1 a

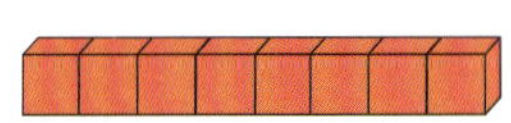

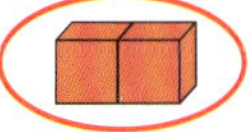

b

c

d

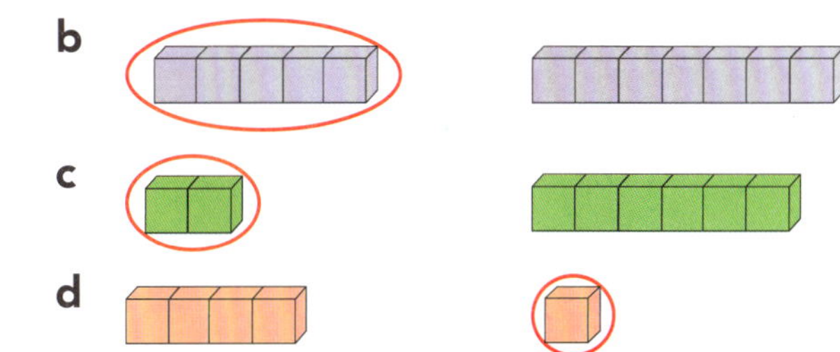

Page 60 — Practice

1. a

b

c

d

e

f

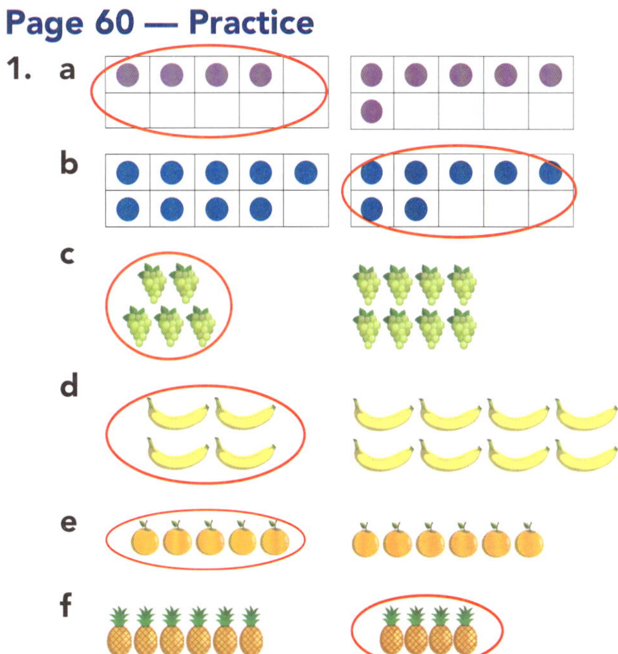

2. Sets should be less than the set shown.

Equal To

Page 62 — Your Turn

1.

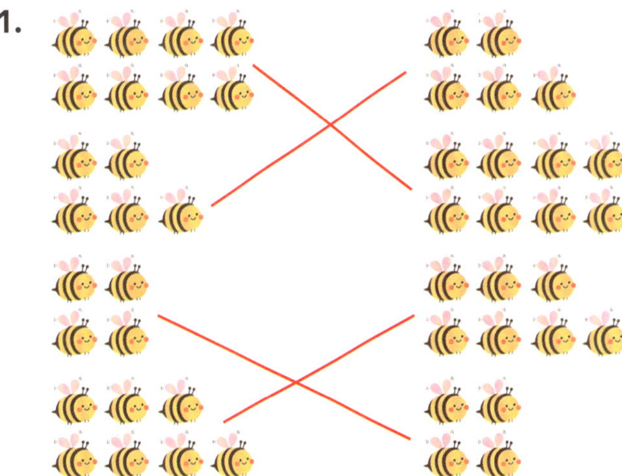

Answers

Page 63 — Practice

1. a b c d

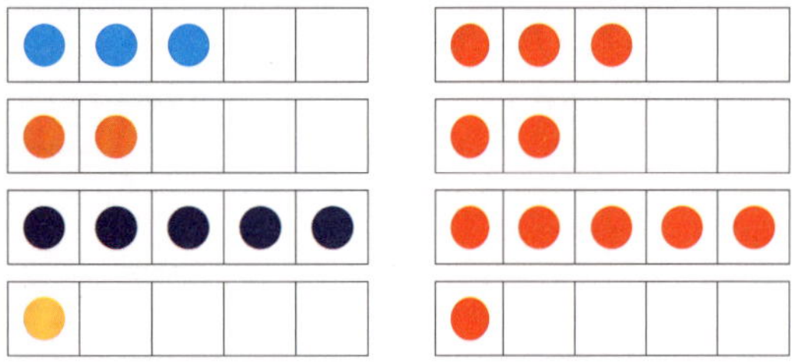

2. a b c d

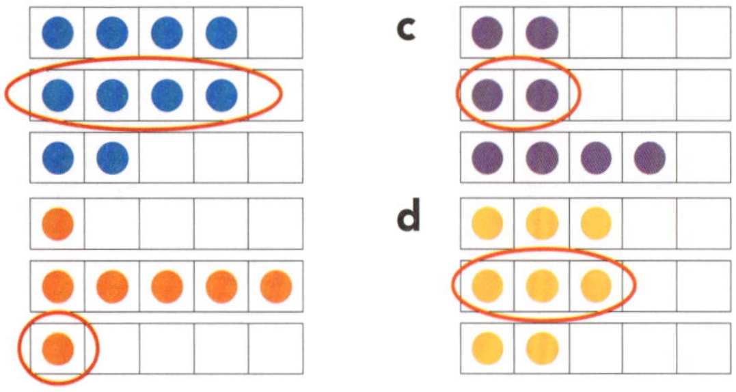

3. Check that equal sets have been drawn.

4. a b c

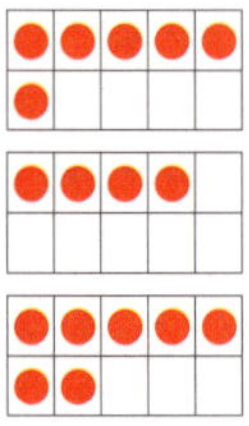

Written Numerals

Page 65 — Your Turn

1. a 2; 9 b 5; 3 c 6; 2

Page 66 — Practice

1. a 18; 12 b 11; 5 c 6; 9
2. a 8 and 9 c 7 and 4
   b 5 and 1 d 9 and 2
3. a 15 and 18 c 4 and 15
   b 12 and 17 d 19 and 14
4. a ~~16 and 14~~ c ~~18 and 15~~
   b 15 and 15 d 19 and 19
5. a less than
   b equal to
   c less than
   d more than

Compare Numbers Review — Page 68

1. Sets should be greater than the sets shown.
2. a b c

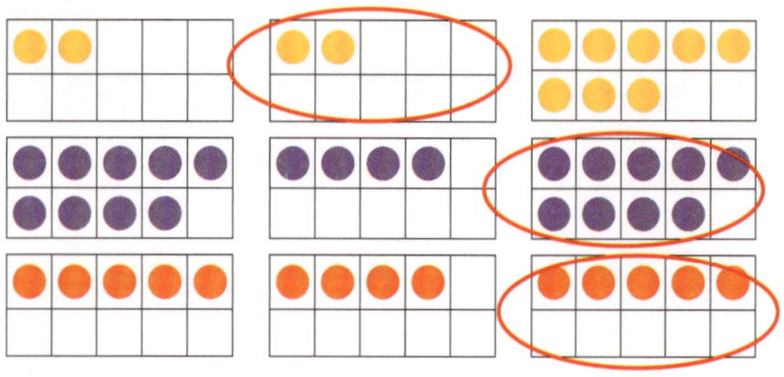

3. a

b

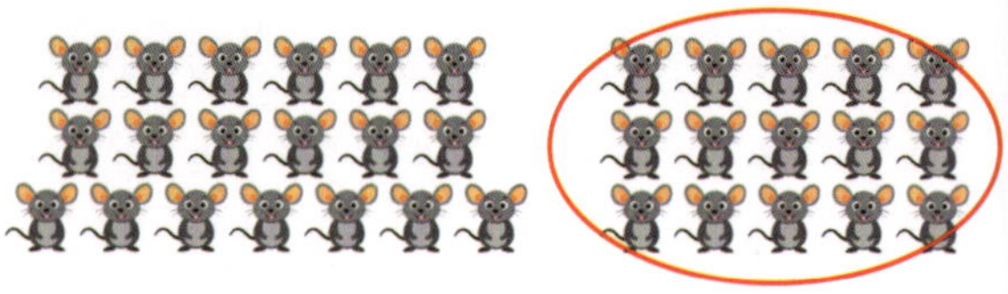

4. a more than
   b less than
   c equal to
   d more than
5. Sets should be less than the sets shown.
6. a 1; 9 b 8; 10 c 4; 9

4. ADDITION

Add 1

Page 70 — Your Turn

1. a–d Check that 1 more has been drawn and written.

Page 71 — Practice

1. a 3

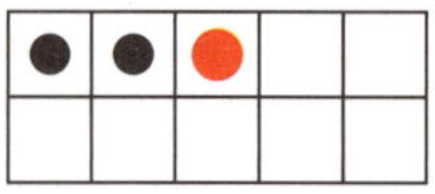

c 9

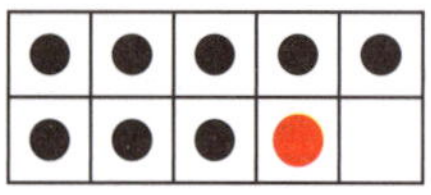

b 7

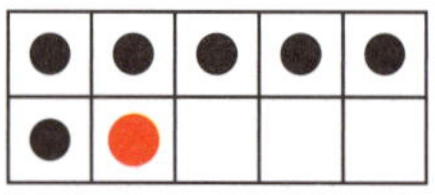

d 4

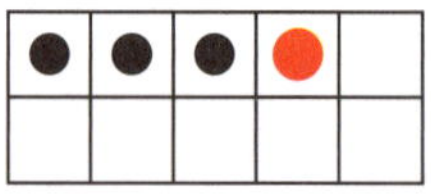

2. Check that 1 more than the given numbers have been written and drawn.

Answers

3. **a** 8

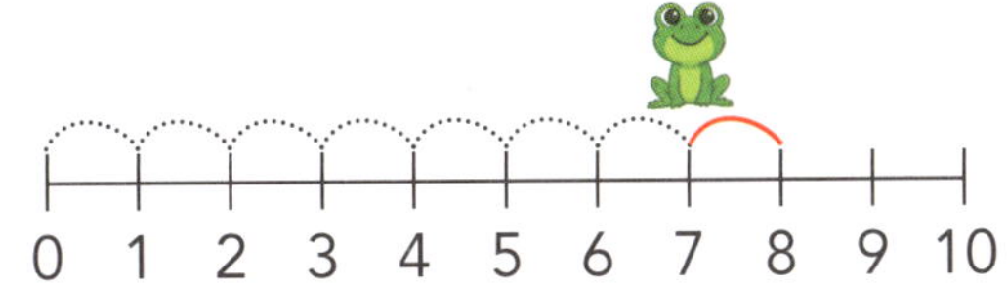

b 6

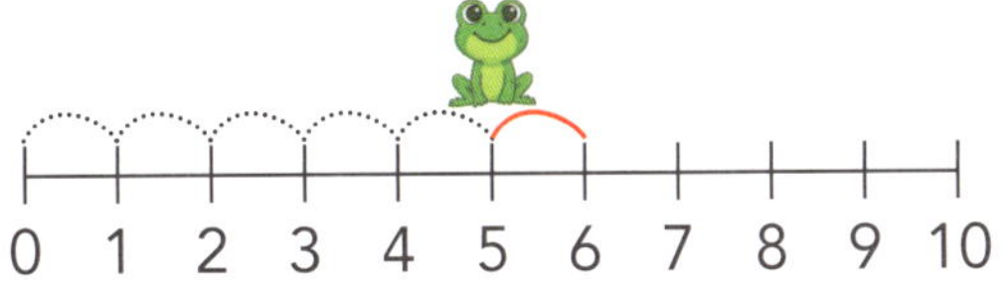

c 7

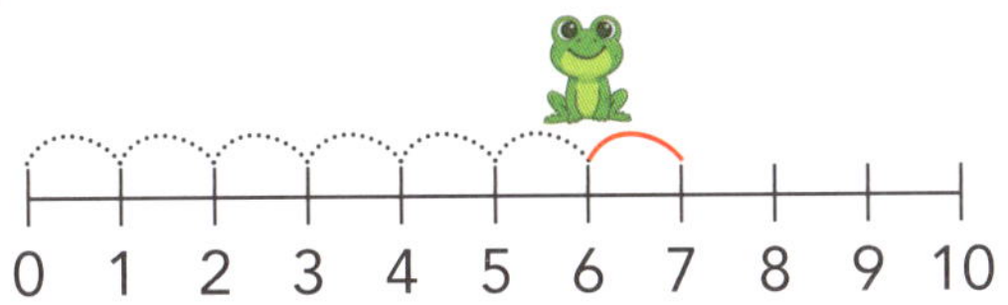

4. **a** 17 **b** 14 **c** 8

Add 2 Groups

Page 73 — Your Turn

1. **a**
   b
   c
   d

Page 74 — Practice

1. **a**

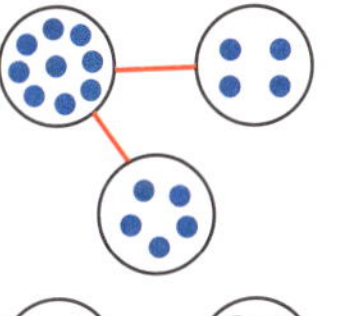

c

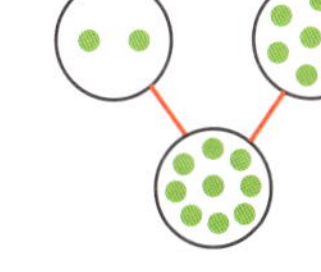

b

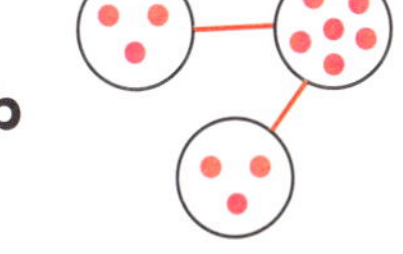

2. **a**

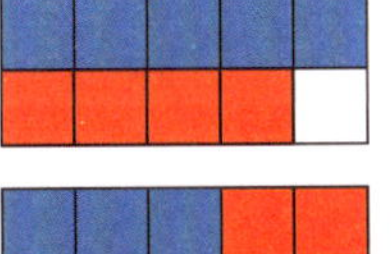

b

d

e

c

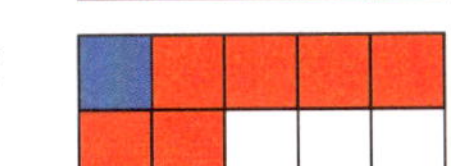

3. **a**

b

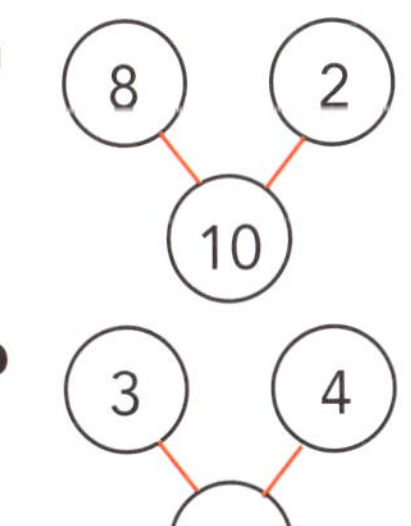

c

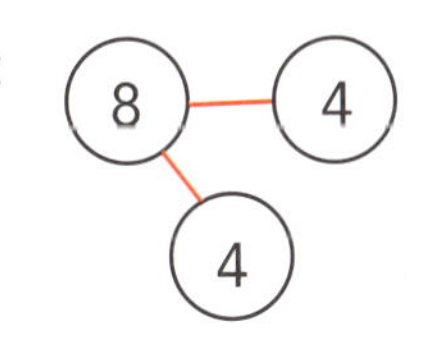

4. Check that drawings match the number sentences.
   a 6 **b** 7 **c** 10 **d** 9

Make 10

Page 76 — Your Turn

1. **a** 6 and 4 make 10.
   c 10 and 0 make 10.
   b 9 and 1 make 10.

Page 77 — Practice

1. **a** 6 **b** 9 **c** 3 **d** 8 **e** 7 **f** 7 **g** 5 **h** 4 **i** 8
2. **a** 8 and 2 make 10.
   c 4 and 6 make 10.

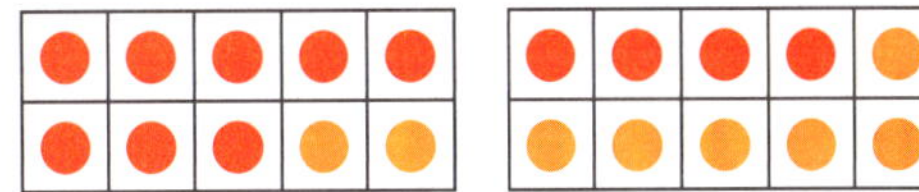

b 1 and 9 make 10.

3. **a** 9 **b** 0 **c** 5 **d** 6 **e** 8 **f** 1 **g** 4 **h** 2 **i** 3

Fluency Within 5

Page 79 — Your Turn

1. **a**
   b

c
d

Page 80 — Practice

1. **a** 1 and 3 make 4.

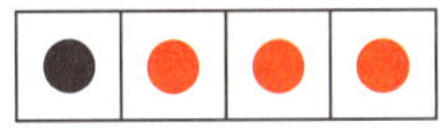

c 0 and 2 make 2.

b 2 and 1 make 3.

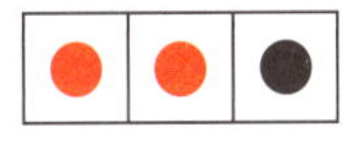

d 3 and 1 make 4.

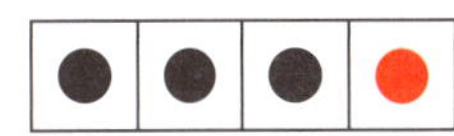

Answers

2. a 4 c 2 e 0
   b 3 d 1
3. a 1 + 3 c 3 + 0
   b 3 + 1 d 1 + 4
4. a 5 d 0 g 2
   b 4 e 4 h 2
   c 3 f 4 i 3

10 and Some More

Page 82 — Your Turn

1. a 10 and 8 make 18.
   b 10 and 5 make 15.

Page 83 — Practice

1. a 15

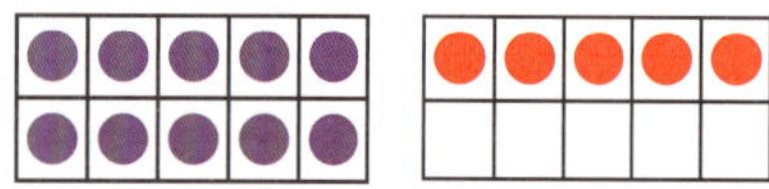

   b 18

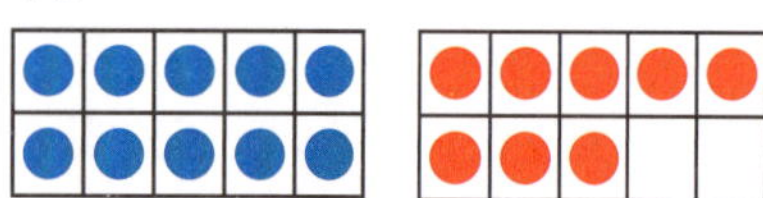

   c 19

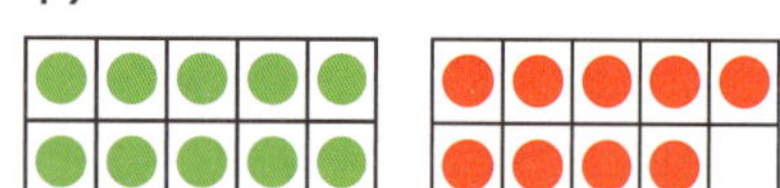

   d 11

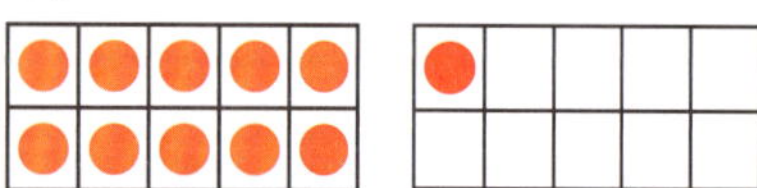

2. a 10 + 2 = 10 c 10 + 6 = 16
   b 10 + 7 = 17 d 10 + 3 = 13
3. a 10 2 7 c 10 6 9
   b 6 2 10 d 10 1 5
4. a 18 c 17
   b 12 d 11

Addition Review — Page 85

1. a

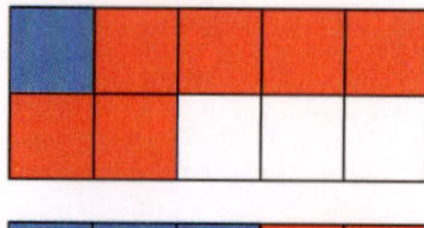

   c

   b

   d

2. a 8

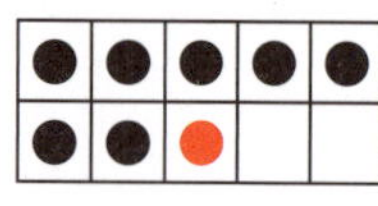

   c 10

   b 2

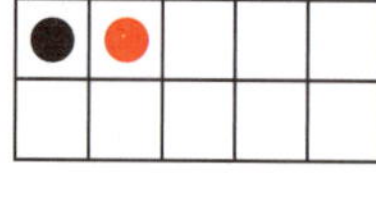

   d 5

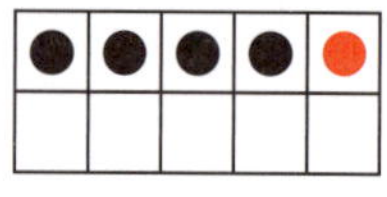

3. a 2 c 0
   b 5 d 3
4. a 5 and 5 make 10.

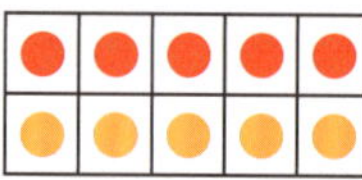

   c 2 and 8 make 10.
   b 6 and 4 make 10.
   d 7 and 3 make 10.
5. a 9 b 10 c 8 d 8
6. a 3 c 4
   b 4 d 2
7. a 8 c 9
   b 3 d 4
8. a 10 + 4 = 14 d 10 + 6 = 16
   b 10 + 8 = 18 e 10 + 3 = 13
   c 10 + 1 = 11

5. SUBTRACTION

Subtract 1

Page 88 — Your Turn

1. Check that one picture has been crossed out.
   a 6 c 4
   b 2 d 9

Answers

Page 89 — Practice

1. Check that one dot has been crossed out.
   a 3 b 7 c 8 d 0

2. a 5 b 3 c 1 d 7

3. Check that a matching picture has been drawn and that 1 has been crossed off.
   a 15 b 10 c 12 d 9

4. Check that 1 dot has been crossed off.
   a 17 b 13 c 16 d 8

Subtract 1 Group

Page 91 — Your Turn

1. a b c d

Page 92 — Practice

1. a

b

c

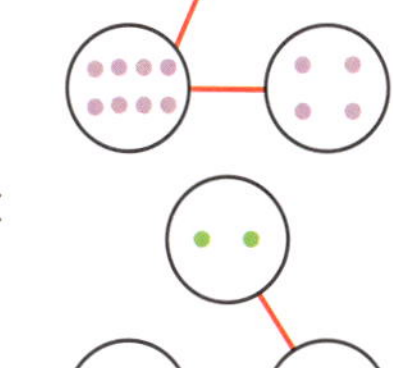

d

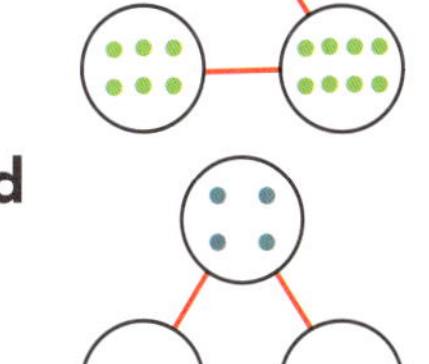

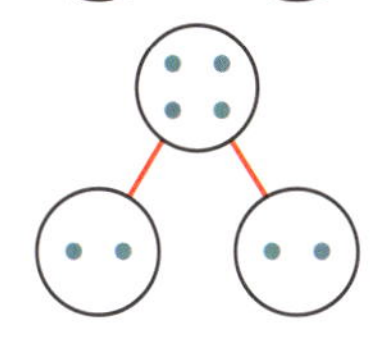

e

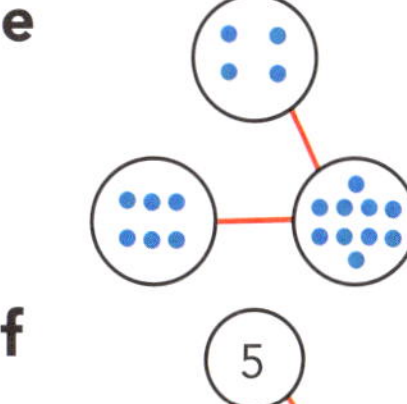

f 5, 2, 3

g 2, 4, 2

h

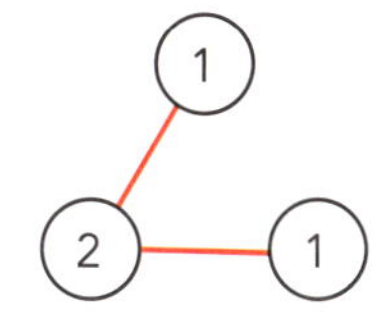

2. a b c d

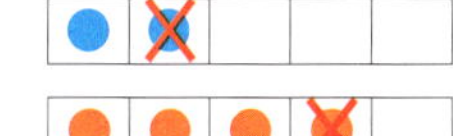

3. a 1

b 0

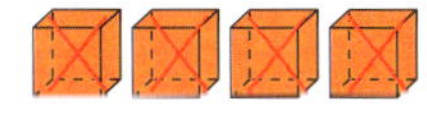

c 1

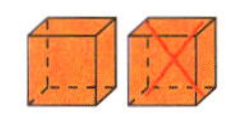

d 0

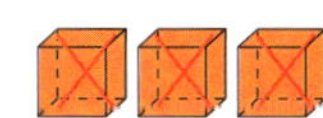

Subtract Within 10

Page 94 — Your Turn

1. a $7 - 2 = 5$ b $3 - 3 = 0$ c $10 - 8 = 2$ d $8 - 4 = 4$

Page 95 — Practice

1. a 2 b 0 c 1 d 3

2. Check that the correct number of dots have been crossed out.
   a 8 b 4 c 7 d 1

3. a $5 - 1 = 4$ b $4 - 2 = 2$ c $7 - 5 = 2$

4. Check that drawings match the equations.
   a $10 - 2 = 8$ b $7 - 1 = 6$ c $5 - 2 = 3$

Fluency Within 5

Page 97 — Your Turn

1. Check that the correct number of circles have been crossed out.
   a $5 - 4 = 1$ b $5 - 2 = 3$ c $5 - 3 = 2$

Page 98 — Practice

1. a 3 minus 1 is 2.
   b 2 minus 0 is 2.
   c 1 minus 1 is 0.
   d 4 minus 3 is 1.

2. a $5 - 1$ b $3 - 1$ c $5 - 0$ d $5 - 2$

3. a $5 - 1$ b $2 - 1$ c $2 - 0$ d $4 - 3$

4. a 0 b 1 c 0 d 4 e 1 f 1 g 2

Answers

Subtract 10

Page 100 — Your Turn

1. **a** 16 minus 10 is 6.
b 12 minus 10 is 2.
c 17 minus 10 is 7.
d 14 minus 10 is 4.

Page 101 — Practice

1. **a** 8
b 3
c 1

2. **a** 14 – 10 = 4 **c** 17 – 10 = 7
b 13 – 10 = 3 **d** 19 – 10 = 9

3. **a** 8 **c** 7 **e** 5 **g** 3
b 2 **d** 1 **f** 6

Subtraction Review — Page 103

1. **a**

b
c
d

2. **a** 7
b 2
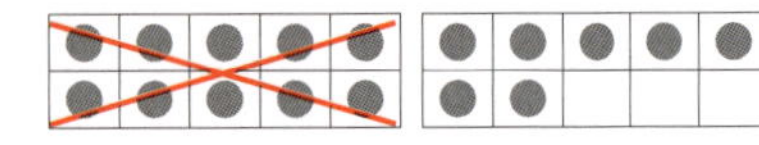
c 3
d 6

3. **a** 5 **b** 3 **c** 1 **d** 2

4. Check that drawings match the equations.
a 5 **c** 3
b 5 **d** 2

5. **a** 7
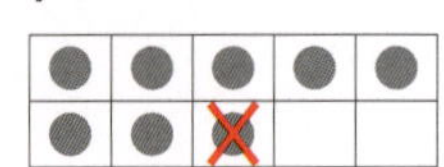
c 1
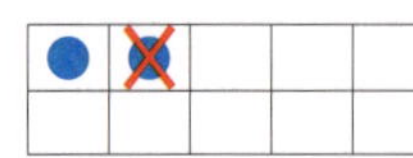
b 2
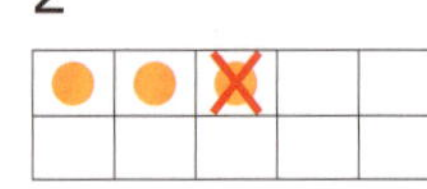
d 5
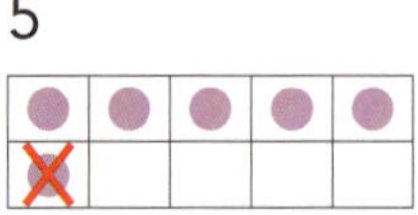

6. Check that the correct number of blocks have been crossed off.
a 1 **b** 3 **c** 1 **d** 3

6. 2D SHAPES

Squares

Page 106 — Your Turn

1.
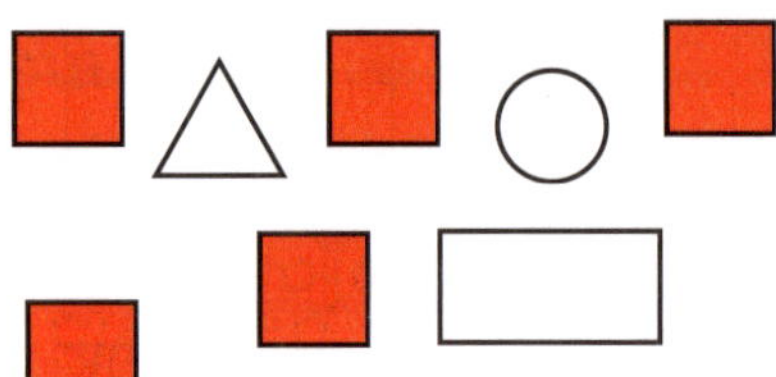

Page 107 — Practice

1.
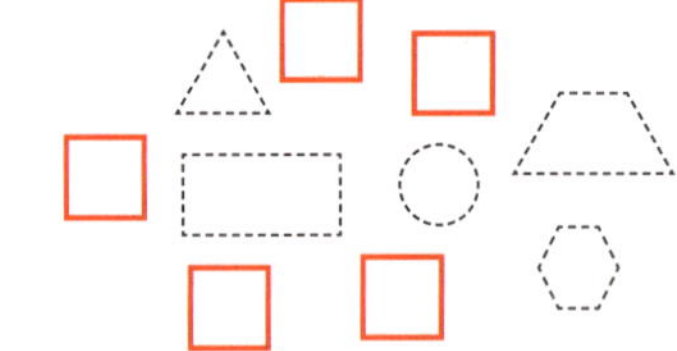

2.
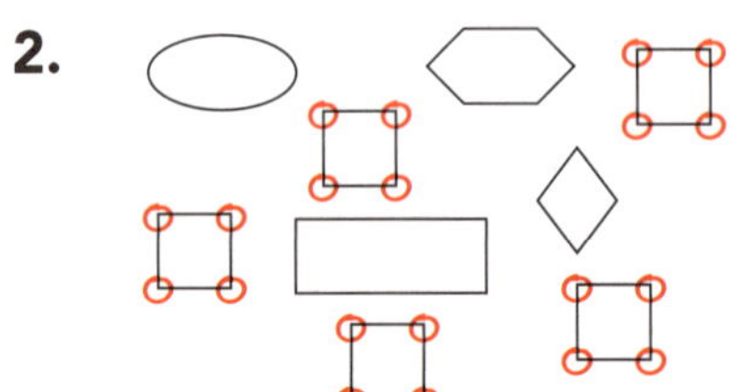

3.

Answers

4. a 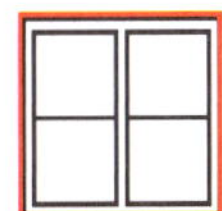

b 

c 

d 

e 

Circles

Page 109 — Your Turn

1. 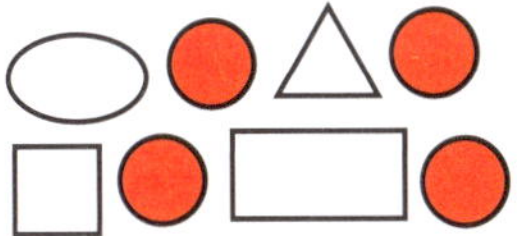

Page 110 — Practice

1. 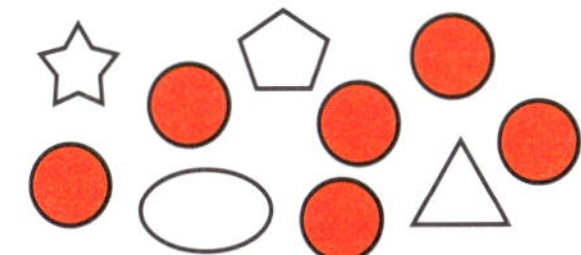

2. 

3. 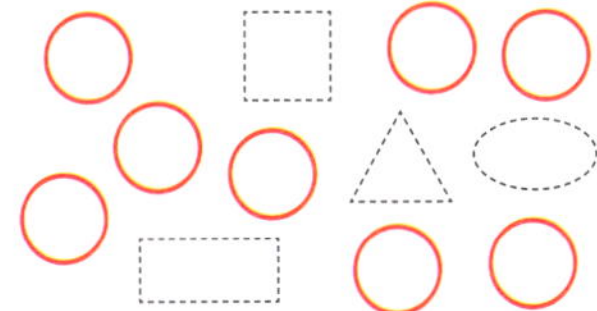

4. 

Triangles

Page 112 — Your Turn

1. 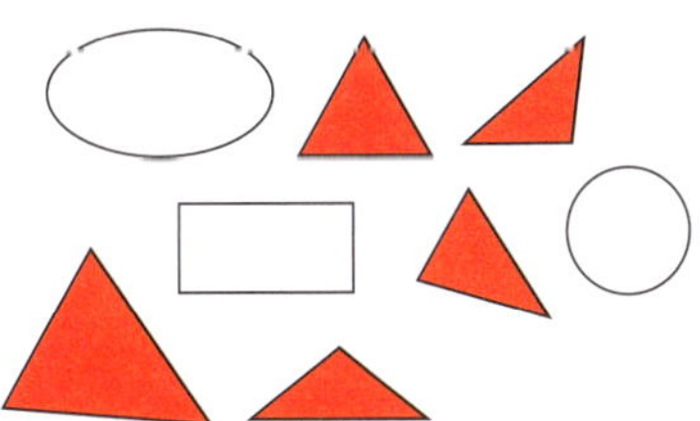

Page 113 — Practice

1. 

2. a 

c 

b 

d 

3. 

4. 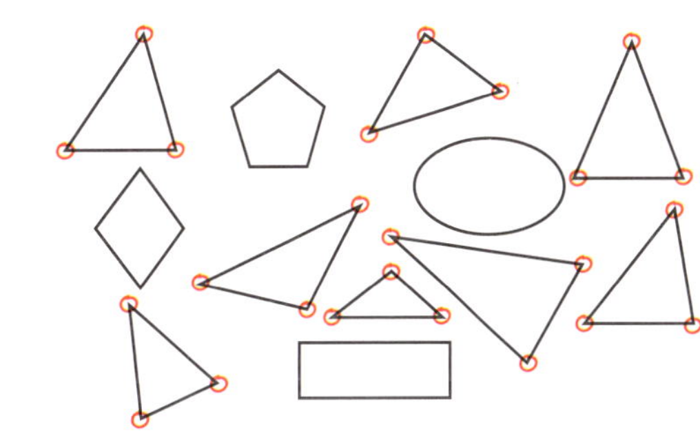

Rectangles

Page 115 — Your Turn

1. 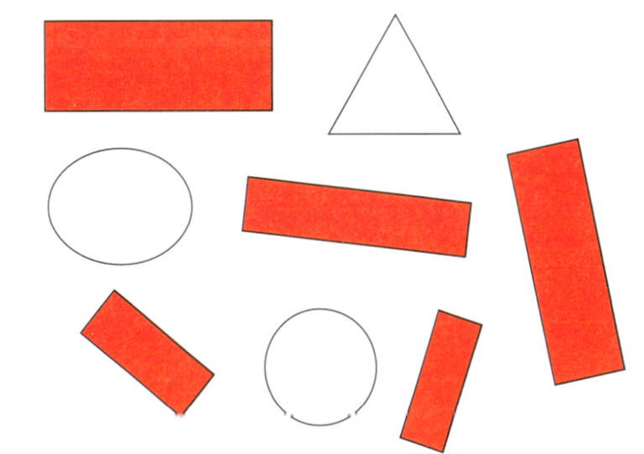

Answers

Page 116 — Practice

1.

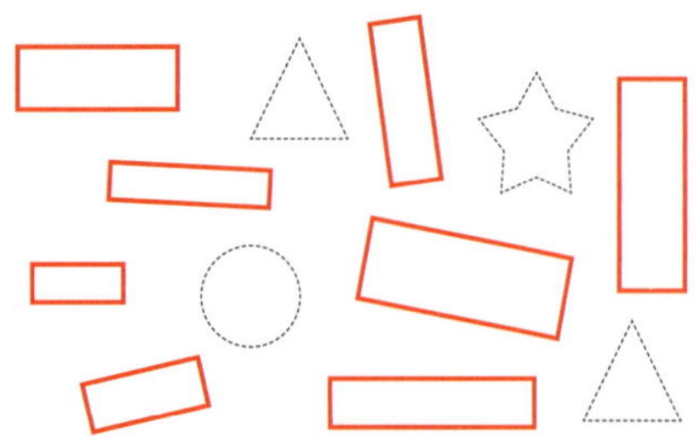

2.

3.

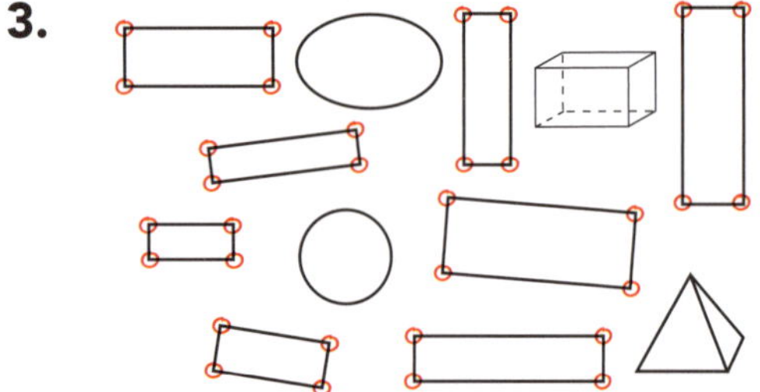

4. a

c

b

d

Hexagons and Pentagons

Page 118 — Your Turn

1.

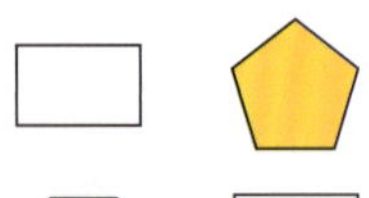
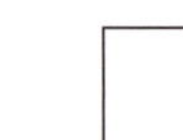

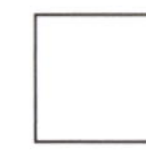

Page 119 — Practice

1.

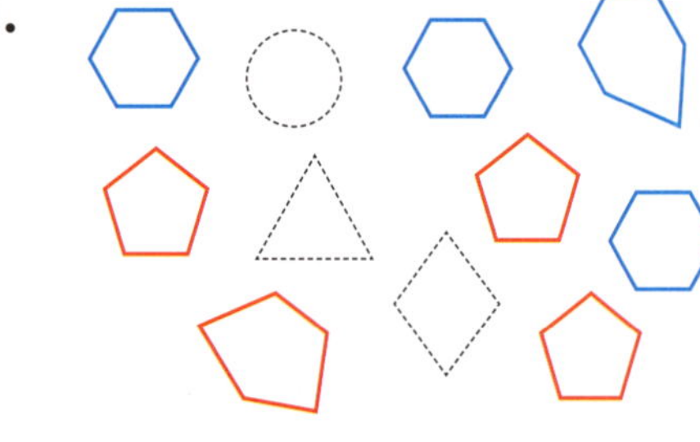

2.

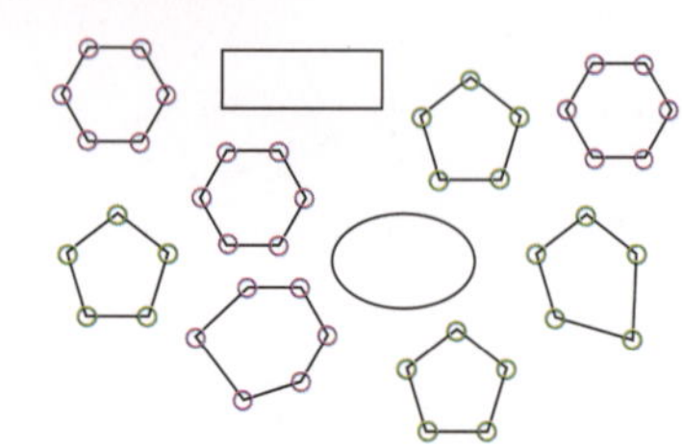

3.

4.

Describe and Make Shapes

Page 121 — Your Turn

1.

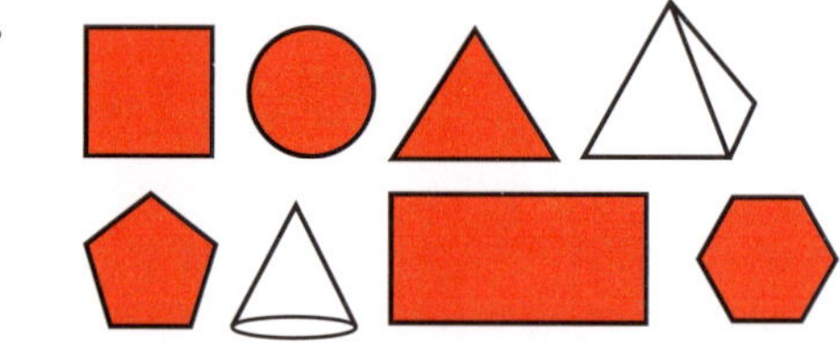

Page 122 — Practice

1. Check that the shapes have been correctly colored, traced, and drawn.
2. a circle

   b triangle

   c rectangle

Answers

3.

Combine Shapes

Page 124 — Your Turn

1. a b c

Page 125 — Practice

1.
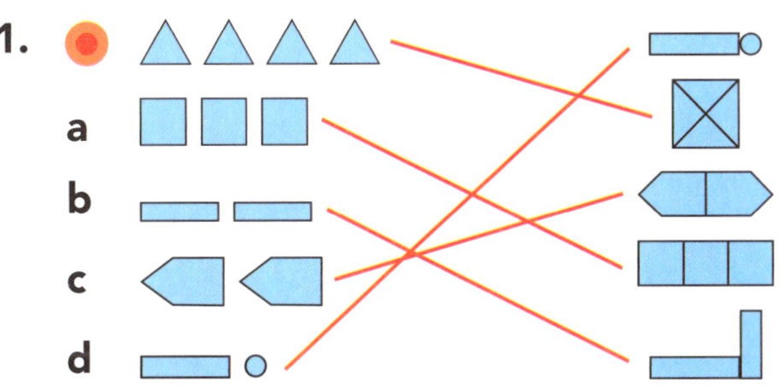

2. Check that answers are reasonable.
3. Check that answers are reasonable.

2D Shapes Review — Page 127

1.
2.
3.

4.
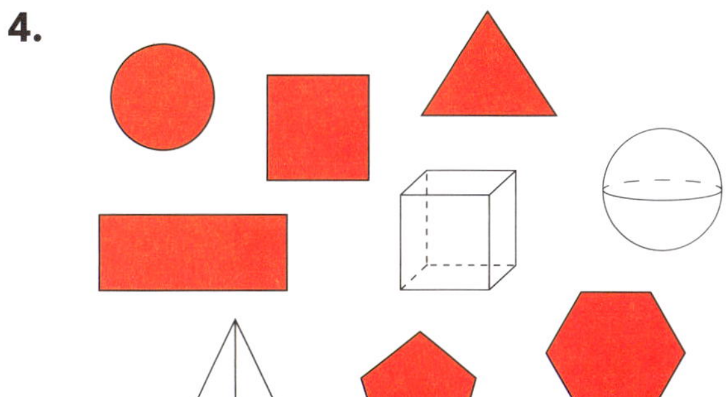

5.
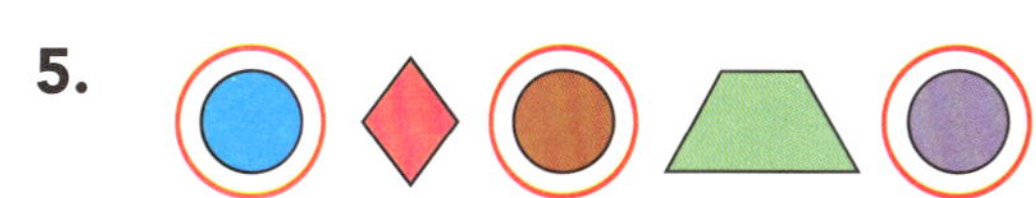

6.

7. Check that answers use the given shapes.
8.

7. 3D SHAPES

Cubes

Page 129 — Your Turn

1.
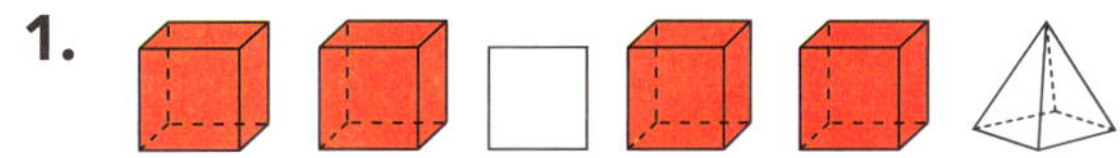

Page 130 — Practice

1.
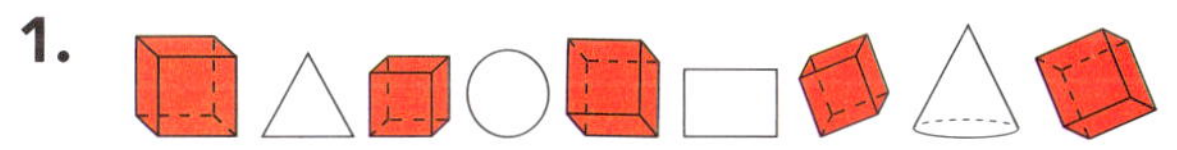

2. a 8 vertices c 12 edges
   b square d solid

3.

4. Accept all reasonable responses. Possible answers include an ice cube, a number cube, and a tissue box.

Answers

Cones

Page 132 — Your Turn

1. 

Page 133 — Practice

1. 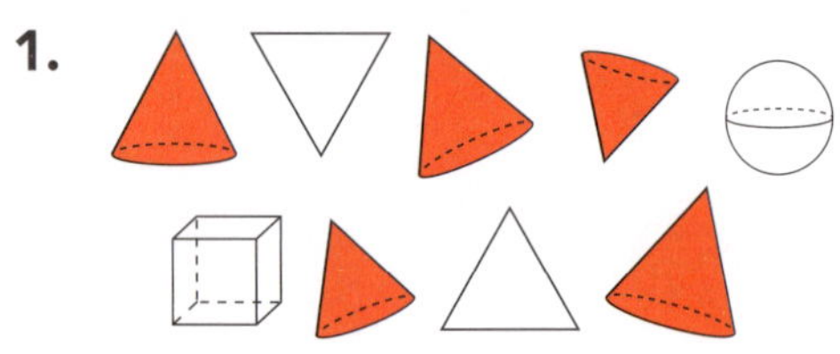

2. **a** 2 faces **c** solid
   b 1 edge

3. 

4. Accept all reasonable responses. Possible answers include a traffic cone, an ice cream cone, and a party hat.

Cylinders

Page 135 — Your Turn

1. 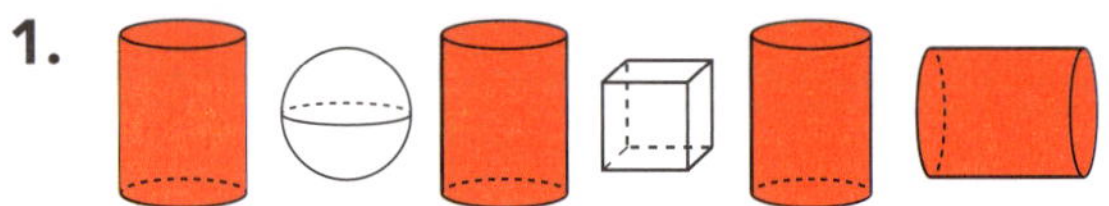

Page 136 — Practice

1. **a** 3 faces **c** 2 edges
   b circle **d** 0 vertices

2. 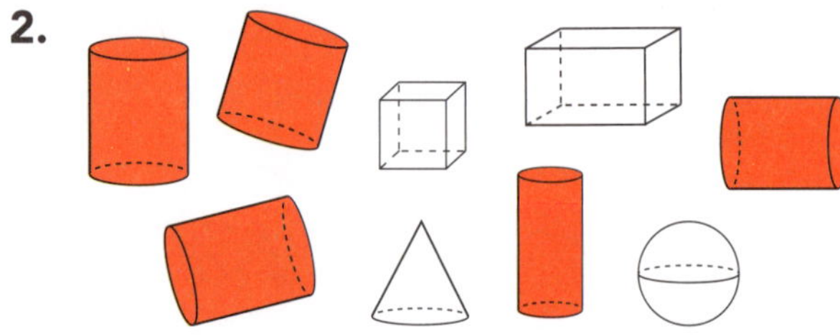

3. 

4. Accept all reasonable responses. Possible answers include a soup can, a glass, a pencil, and a trash can.

Spheres

Page 138 — Your Turn

1. 

Page 139 — Practice

1. **a** 0 vertices **c** 0 edges
   b 0 flat faces **d** solid shape

2. 

3. 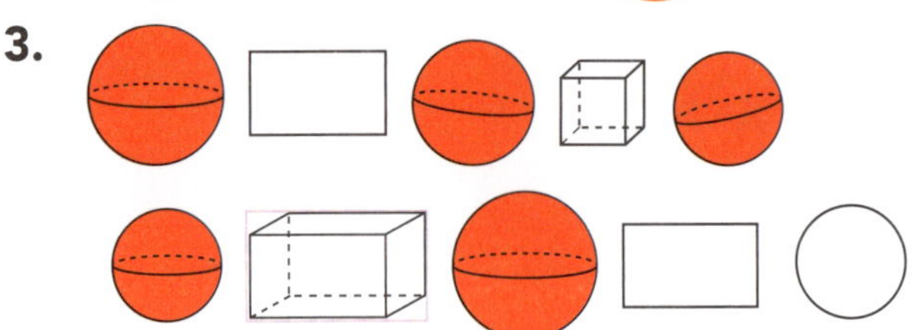

4. Accept all reasonable answers. Possible answers include: a ball, an orange, a blueberry, and a gumball.

Rectangular Prisms

Page 141 — Your Turn

1. 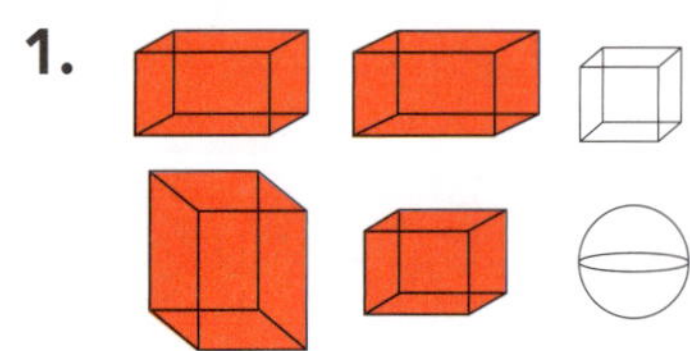

Answers

Page 142 — Practice

1. 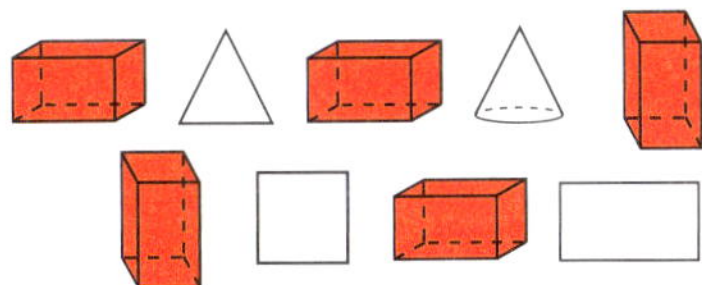

2. a 8 corners
   b rectangles
   c 12 edges
   d 6 faces

3. 

4. Accept all reasonable answers. Possible answers include: a juice box, a cereal box, an eraser, and a fish tank.

Describe 3D Shapes

Page 144 — Your Turn

1. 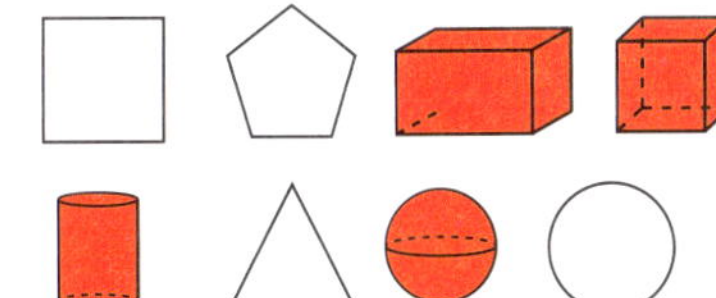

Page 145 — Practice

1. Check that shapes are colored and traced correctly.

2. a 
   b 
   c 
   d 

3. a cone
   b sphere
   c cylinder
   d rectangular prism

4. a, b, c 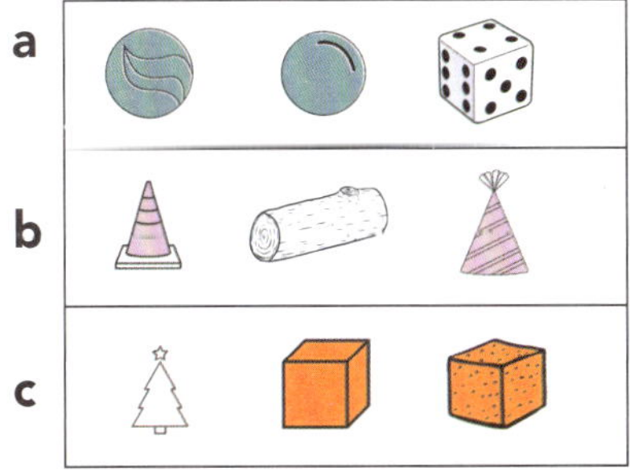

d, e 

3D Shapes Review — Page 147

1. 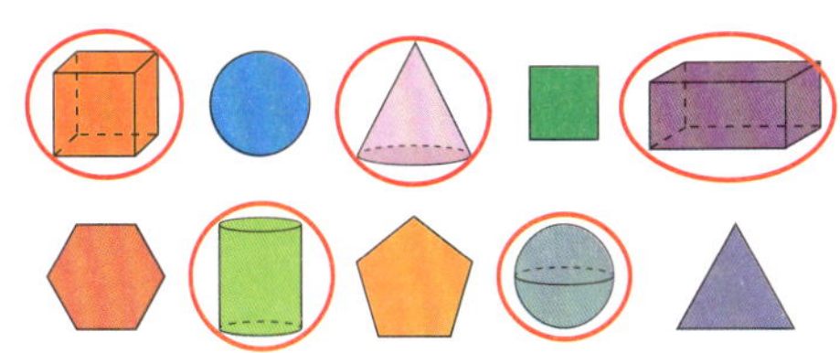

2. a Any of the six faces may be shaded. Example:

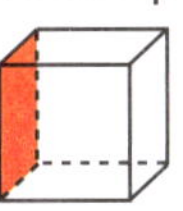

b Either of the two circular bases may be shaded. Example:

c 

d Any of the six faces may be shaded. Example:

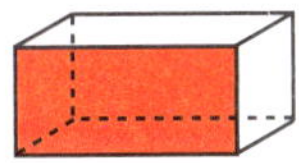

3. 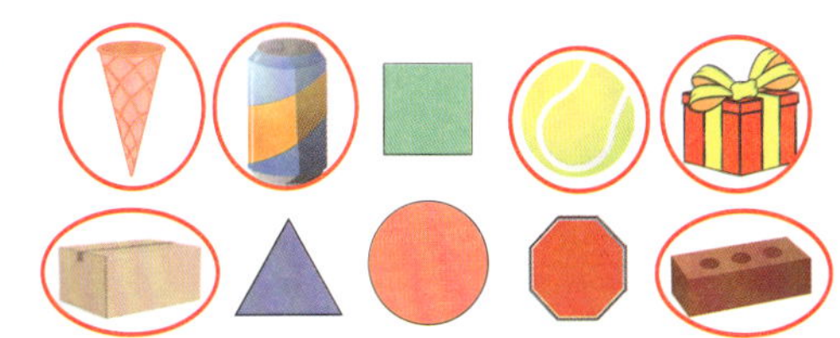

4. a sphere
   b cylinder
   c rectangular prism
   d cube
   e cone

5. a 8 vertices
   b 0 vertices
   c 1 vertex
   d 0 vertices
   e 8 vertices

Answers

8. MEASUREMENT

Length

Page 149 — Your Turn

1. a 

   b 

Page 150 — Practice

1. a 

   c 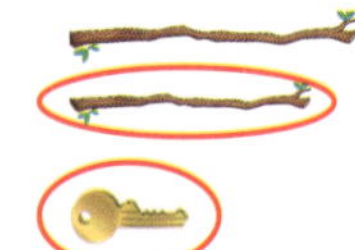

   b

   d

2. a 9 cubes
   c 7 cubes
   b 5 cubes
   d 9 cubes

Height

Page 151 — Your Turn

1. a 

   b  

Page 152 — Practice

1. a 

   c 

   b 

2. a 

   c   

   b

3. a 6 cubes
   c 4 cubes
   b 5 cubes

4. a 1 3 2
   b 1 3 2
   c 3 1 2

Width

Page 154 — Your Turn

1. a  

   c 

   b  

   d 

Page 155 — Practice

1. a 

   c  

   b 

   d 

2. a 8 cubes
   c 5 cubes
   b 4 cubes
   d 3 cubes

3. a 

   c  

   b  

   d  

4. a 1 2 3
   b 3 1 2
   c 1 3 2
   d 1 3 2

Weight

Page 157 — Your Turn

1. a 

   c 

   b  

   d 

Page 158 — Practice

1. a  

   c  

   b  

   d 

Answers

2. a 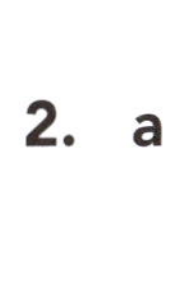  c 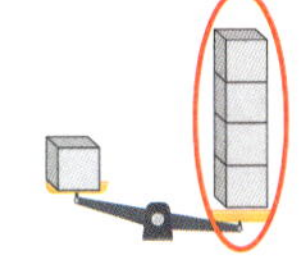
   b 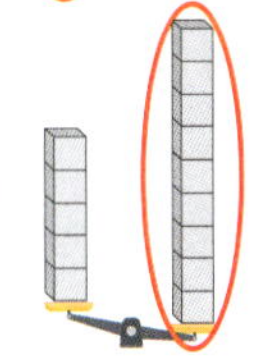 d

3. a 18 cubes c 12 cubes
   b 8 cubes d 2 cubes

4. a 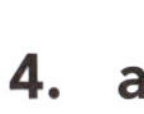 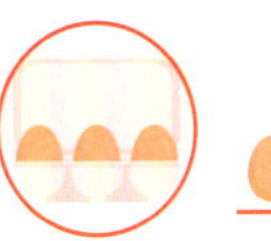  c  
   b   d 

Capacity

Page 160 — Your Turn

1.  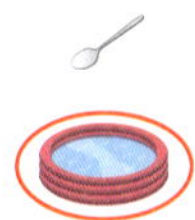   

Page 161 — Practice

1. a          

2. a 1 3 2
   b 1 3 2
   c 2 1 3
   d 1 3 2

3. a more c less
   b more d less

4. a more c more
   b less d less

Measurement Review — Page 163

1. a   c  
   b d

2. a 5 cubes c 3 cubes
   b 10 cubes d 4 cubes

3. a   c  
   b   d  

4. a 
   b

5. a   c 
   b   

6. a 11 cubes c 9 cubes
   b 5 cubes d 12 cubes

9. PATTERNS

Recognize Patterns

Page 165 — Your Turn

1. a yes b no c yes d yes

Page 166 — Practice

1. a c
   b d

2. a 
   b
   c
   d

3. a AAB AAB
   b ABC ABC
   c ABB ABB

Answers

4. **a** yes **b** yes **c** no

Duplicate Patterns

Page 168 — Your Turn

1. Check that patterns have been duplicated correctly.

Page 169 — Practice

1. Check that patterns have been duplicated correctly.
2. Check that patterns have been duplicated correctly.
3. Check that patterns have been duplicated correctly.
4. Check that patterns have been duplicated correctly.

Extend Patterns

Page 171 — Your Turn

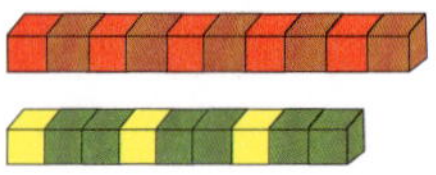

1. **a** **c**
   b **d**

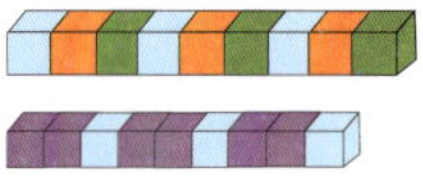

Page 172 — Practice

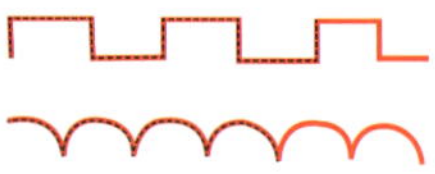

1. **a** **c**
   b
2. **a**
   b
   c 
3. **a** ◊ ○ △ ◊ ○ △
   b □ ⬡ □ ⬡
   c ○ ○ ⬠ ○ ○ ⬠
   d 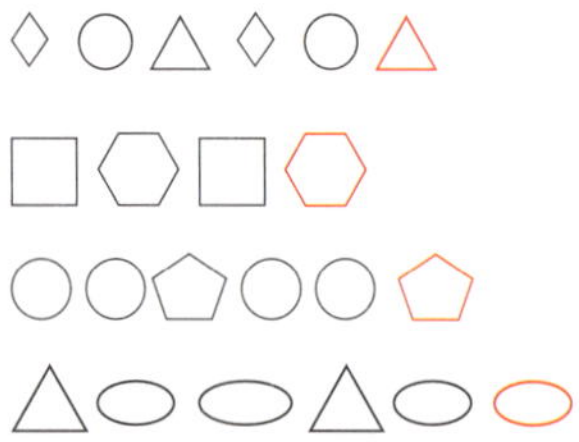
4. **a** 8 **c** 2
   b 5 **d** 12

Create Patterns

Page 174 — Your Turn

1. Patterns may start with either color. Possible answers:
   a **c**
   b **d**

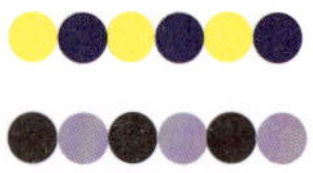

Page 175 — Practice

1. Patterns may go in any order as long as they repeat and use the given colors in ABC patterns. Possible answers:
   a
   b
   c
   d 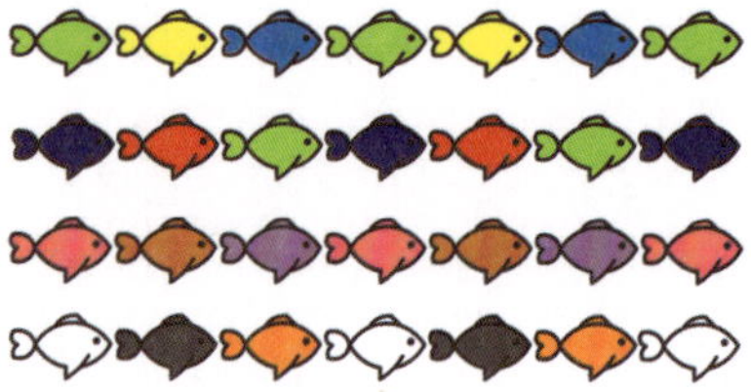
2. Patterns may start with either shape. Possible answers:
   a
   b ◇ △ ◇ △ ◇ △
   c
   c ☆ ♡ ☆ ♡ ☆ ♡ 
3. Patterns may start with either letter. Possible answers:
   a P P B P P B P P B
   b G G F G G F G G F
   c T T A T T A T T A
   d K K X K K X K K X
4. Patterns may go in any order as long as they repeat and use the given numbers in ABC patterns. Possible answers:
   a 9 6 3 9 6 3 9 6 3
   b 3 7 8 3 7 8 3 7 8
   c 1 4 7 1 4 7 1 4 7
   d 5 0 6 5 0 6 5 0 6

Patterns Review — Page 177

1. Check that patterns have been duplicated correctly.
2. **a** yes **b** yes **c** no
3. **a**
   b
   c ⟷ 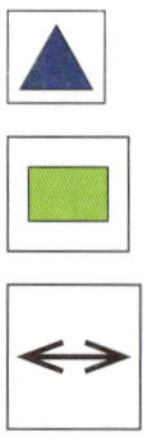
4. **a** AAB
   b ABB
   c ABC

5. Check that objects are colored in the codes given. Possible answers:

   a 

   b 

   c 

6. Check that patterns have been duplicated correctly.

10. TIME

Yesterday, Today, and Tomorrow

Page 180 — Your Turn

1. Check that answers are reasonable.

Page 181 — Practice

1. Check that answers are reasonable.
2. **a** walk the dog **d** Thursday
   b Tuesday **e** go to the park
   c soccer practice
3. Check that answers are reasonable.

Days and Months

Page 183 — Your Turn

1. **a** Check that answer is correct.
   b Check that answer is correct.
   c 12 months

Page 184 — Practice

1. Check that order is correct. Answers may start with Sunday or Monday.
2. January July
   February August
   March September
   April October
   May November
   June December
3. Check that answers are reasonable.
4. day
   week
   month
   year

Time of Day

Page 186 — Your Turn

1. Check that students circled a reasonable time of day.

Page 187 — Practice

1. Check that students matched each activity to a reasonable time of day.
   a afternoon **c** evening
   b morning **d** afternoon
2. Check that answers are reasonable.
3. Check that answers are reasonable. Answers may include a toothbrush, a plate, a book, toys, a table, and a bed.
4. Check that answers are reasonable.

Standard Units of Time

Page 189 — Your Turn

1. **a** minutes **c** minutes
   b seconds **d** seconds

Page 190 — Practice

1. Check that answers are reasonable.
2. **a** minutes **c** hours
   b seconds

Time Review — Page 191

1. Check that answers are reasonable.
2. Check that answers are reasonable.
3. Sunday → Monday → Tuesday → Wednesday → Thursday → Friday → Saturday
4. Check that answers are reasonable.

5. a morning
   b evening
   c morning
6. a minutes
   b minutes
   c seconds
   d hours

11. DATA

Collect, Sort, and Organize Data

Page 194 — Your Turn

1. a 1 b 4 c 2 d 5

Page 195 — Practice

1.

	Type of Vegetable	Tallies	Number
a	zucchini	卌	5
b	broccoli	|||	3
c	potato	卌 ||||	9
d	beet	||||	4

2. a 5
   b potato
   c broccoli

3.

	Flavor	Tallies	Number
a	vanilla	||||	4
b	strawberry	|||	3
c	mint chip			1

4. a 2
   b vanilla
   c mint chip

Picture Graphs

Page 197 — Your Turn

1.

	How We Get to School	
a	car	
b	bike	

Page 198 — Practice

1.

Our Pets					
10					
9					
8					
7					
6					
5					
4					
3					
2					
1					

2.

	Favorite Sport	Tallies	Number
a	basketball			1
b	football	||||	4
c	tennis	|||	3
d	volleyball	|||	3

3.

Favorite Sport	
soccer	
basketball	
football	
tennis	
volleyball	

Answers

Read and Use Graphs

Page 200 — Your Turn

1. a 5 people b 8 people

Page 201 — Practice

1. a 4 people c 3 people
   b 2 people d 3 people
2. a Omar c Aisha
   b Tyler d 26
3. a 3 chocolate bars
   b gumballs
   c chocolate bars
   d 8 lollipops and chocolate bars
4. a Monday
   b 22 books
   c Wednesday and Friday
   d Tuesday

Data Review — Page 205

1. **Favorite Part of School**

library	★★★★★★☆☆
art	★★☆☆☆☆☆☆
reading	★★★★☆☆☆☆
math	★★★★★★☆☆
lunch	★★★★★★★☆

2. a 25 people
   b library and math
   c art
   d lunch
3. **Favorite Ocean Animal**

	Favorite Ocean Animal	Tallies	Number
a	shark	𝍸	5
b	octopus	||	2
c	dolphin	||	2
d	fish	||||	4

4. a 6 people c chips
   b hamburger d 5 people

12. SPATIAL REASONING

In, On, and Under

Page 208 — Your Turn

1. a  
   b  
   c  

Page 209 — Practice

1. a The cookies are **on** the jar.
   b The cookies are **in** and **on** the jar.
   c The cookies are **under** the jar.
2. a–d Check that drawings are placed appropriately.
3. a in c on
   b under d on
4. a in b on c under

Up and Down

Page 211 — Your Turn

1. a down
   b up
   c down

Page 212 — Practice

1. a up
   b down
   c up

Answers

2. a

3.

4. Check that answers show the specified directions.

Inside and Outside

Page 214 — Your Turn

1. a

b

c

Page 215 — Practice

1. a

b

c

d

2. a outside c inside
   b outside d inside

3. a inside
   b inside
   c outside

4. a The children are **outside** the bus.
   b The children are **inside** the bus.
   c The girl is **outside** the house.
   d The bed is **inside** the room.

Beside and Between

Page 217 — Your Turn

1. a beside c between
   b beside d beside

Page 218 — Practice

1. a The box is **between** the kids.
   b The book is **beside** the lamp.
   c The astronaut is **beside** the alien.
   d The planet is **between** the stars.

2. a

b
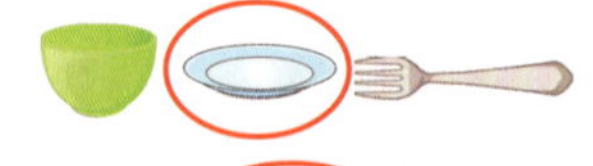

c

d

3. a between c beside
   b beside d beside

4. a between c beside
   b beside d between

In Front and Behind

Page 220 — Your Turn

1. a behind c in front
   b behind d behind

Answers

Page 221 — Practice

1. **a** in front **c** behind
   b behind **d** in front

2. **a**  **c** 
   b **d**

3. **a**  **c**
   b **d** 

4. ● The car is **in front** of the tree.
   a The car is **behind** the dog.
   b The car is **in front** of the gate.
   c The man is **in front** of the car.
   d The car is **in front** of the man.

Spatial Reasoning Review — Page 223

1. **a** behind **c** in front
   b inside **d** beside
2. **a–d** Check that drawings are placed appropriately.
3. **a** below **c** in front of
   b beside **d** above
4. **a** above **c** beside
   b under or below **d** in front of

5. **a** **c** 
   b   **d** 
6. Check that drawings are placed correctly.

13. MONEY

Pennies

Page 226 — Your Turn

1.   

Page 227 — Practice

1. **a** 3¢ **b** 6¢ **c** 7¢
2. **a** Five pennies should be circled.
   b Four pennies should be circled.
   c One penny should be circled.
   d Two pennies should be circled.
3.     

Nickels

Page 228 — Your Turn

1.    

Answers

Page 229 — Practice

1. a Five nickels should be circled.
   b Three nickels should be circled.
   c Four nickels should be circled.
2. a 20¢ b 5¢ c 15¢ d 10¢
3.     

Dimes

Page 230 — Your Turn

1.     

Page 231 — Practice

1. a 50¢ c 30¢
   b 20¢
2. a Two dimes should be circled.
   b Four dimes should be circled.
   c One dime should be circled.
   d Five dimes should be circled.
3.     

Quarters

Page 232 — Your Turn

1.      

Page 233 — Practice

1. a One quarter should be circled.
   b Three quarters should be circled.
   c Four quarters should be circled.
2. a 50¢ c 25¢
   b 100¢
3.      

Money Review — Page 234

1.

	Picture of Coin	Name of Coin	Value
a		penny	1¢
b		nickel	5¢
c		dime	10¢
d		quarter	25¢

2. a 20¢ d 30¢
   b 20¢ e 5¢
   c 50¢
3. a Two nickels should be circled.
   b Four pennies should be circled.
   c Four dimes should be circled.
   d Two quarters should be circled.
4. a 1¢ c 10¢
   b 5¢ d 25¢
5. a  
   b   
   c  
   d  
6. a penny
   b nickel
   c dime
   d quarter

Notes

Notes

Notes

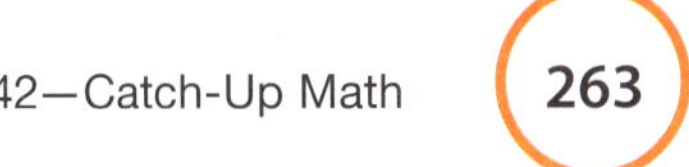

Notes

